TOUCHDOWN! V-I-C-T-O-R-Y!
SCORE! FIGHT! RAH RAH RAH!
HUSTLE! WIN! GOAL! DEFENSE!
WE'RE NUMBER ONE! GO TEAM!
TOUCHDOWN! V-I-C-T-O-R-Y!
SCORE! FIGHT! RAH RAH RAH!
HUSTLE! WIN! GOAL! DEFENSE!
WE'RE NUMBER ONE! GO TEAM!
TOUCHDOWN! V-I-C-T-O-R-Y!
SCORE! FIGHT! RAH RAH RAH!
HUSTLE! WIN! GOAL! DEFENSE!
WE'RE NUMBER ONE! GO TEAM!

Tailgreat

DEDICATION

For my brothers:
Richard Currence, Kelly
English, Tim Hontzas,
Wright Thompson, Stefano
Capomazza, Mac Nichols,
Mac Monteith, Drew Tybus,
and Andy Howorth

Y'all get it. Tailgating is
some *Braveheart* shit.
I'll put on the war paint
with you guys ANY day.

Tailgreat

How to CRUSH IT at TAILGATING

JOHN CURRENCE

photographs by **PETER FRANK EDWARDS**

foreword by **WRIGHT THOMPSON**

TEN SPEED PRESS

California | New York

CONTENTS

RECIPE LIST

FOREWORD

We all love it when John shows up at our tailgate in the fall.

This is because he's a professional chef and an acknowledged Southern master and we are, to use a technical culinary term, slapdicks. We're lucky. He cooks a lot. We'll see him coming across the Grove at Ole Miss on a temperate fall afternoon, mid-October, let's say, with a light breeze riffling through the campus. We'll see him wearing a beat-up dad cap, with his daughter in tow wearing a cheerleader uniform. But as much as we love to see him, we really want to see if there's something in his hand. And, inevitably: *YES! He is carrying something. He is carrying food. The Big Bad Chef is carrying food!*

That's a great moment.

So, first, as the beneficiary of many a meal cooked by John, let me say that this book isn't just a way to stoke your nostalgia, searching for the contrails of your own traditions in the blue sky of someone else's. No, no. This book is a blunt object, a weapon that will dramatically improve your tailgate game. It will make you the star of your tent or your parking lot, whether you're smoking meat or carefully filling stuffed eggs. One day, if you study with devotion, people might see you coming and look at your hands to see if you have brought sweet, delicious salvation. Now that we've established that, we can move on to the truly important and interesting part of sports and of tailgating: existentialism.

Jean-Paul Sarte would know exactly what was going down if he stumbled through the Grove on a Saturday. A tailgate can't be judged by its parts, or even by the sum of them. On its own, as a one-off, a tailgate is practically meaningless.

It can't be judged by concrete details like the mustard tang of the eggs, the crunch of the chicken skin, or the way the chip holds up to the stubborn dip. It doesn't matter if you get your beer ice-cold or even if you bring vermouth to make Manhattans.

The most important part of a tailgate is invisible.

Its value and meaning accrue over time, when repetition evolves into ritual. When a scaffolding of unseen and unspoken things gives it permanence and stability. The more times a group meets, the more meaning is attached to otherwise simple things like whiskey in plastic cups or a plate of cold fried chicken.

Maybe that's why I feel uniquely qualified to write the introduction to this book. I've known John a long time, and we have spent many football games together. We've been in the Grove together and outside the Superdome on many occasions. We've been to college bowl games, Super Bowls, baseball games, the Derby, and more. He understands why people tailgate. Why they break bread together before a shared experience. Maybe this is because he grew up in New Orleans and he lives in Oxford, Mississippi, places where love is often shown on a plate. Maybe it's because he played and adores football; or maybe it's something that rubbed off from growing up Catholic.

No matter the reason, he understands that a tailgate is really a communion. That it's a way to remember the family and friends who once cheered alongside us and are either far away or dead. Because when the company is right, and the laughter, and the birds, and the generator—because, Direct TV, duh, we aren't savages—are humming in concert, these people aren't far away, or even gone. We do this in remembrance of them. They are with us around a table, or in the shade of old oak trees, or a Walmart tent, close enough to touch. Daily bread, indeed.

My job is to cover sports for ESPN, which means that I've been to nearly every type of sporting event imaginable. In the past two months I've been to the CrossFit Games and the Cricket World Cup. That's the range. This has given me some rare insight into what really matters about the games we love. I get the same excitement and rush and thrill that spectators get, but to me it often feels shallow and saccharine, one of those rushes that you can't really remember minutes after it's over. I think that's because sports without community is no different than a sitcom or a reality show. Every game is merely an episode of *The Bachelor* if we strip away our friends and family, our community, our fellow congregants, our fathers and, of course, our mothers.

I wish you could have met John's mother, Becky.

She died in the fall of 2017, and the life of everyone who knew her is less full than it was. John's hosting skills—which have made him a well-known and well-liked man, as well as the person you are now trusting with your pregame festivities—took root when he was a young boy in her kitchen, watching how she did everything. There are so many ways to describe her, but the three words that come to me now are *warm, classy,* and *fun.* So when you are flipping through these pages and deciding which recipe to choose for the next big game, I hope you'll keep that image of her in your mind. I am certain that John does, whether he is feeding his daughter, Mamie, and his wife Bess; hosting a small, intimate dinner at his house; feeding a huge crowd at a food festival; or putting out a spread before a game.

Because that's what we're talking about: hosting, showing that you love people by preparing a feast for them. The point of a tailgate isn't some weird alpha thing. It's not about the smoker, or the speakers, or even the menagerie of meats on the platter. The point is the people. The communion. Tailgates have long served this purpose for me.

I grew up in the Grove at Ole Miss, and when I return there, I also commune with all my past selves, and I get to measure time and where I am now. When John and I started hanging out before games, neither of us had kids. Now we both have daughters who have been to the Grove. I love seeing my girl, Wallace, in her stroller beneath the tent, or seeing Mamie in her little uniform, with her tangle of beautiful curls, as they both take their first steps into a world they'll know long after John and I are gone.

Wallace will never know her grandfather, my late father, who started bringing me to tailgates when I was a baby. But in this communal space, she will come to know him: She will hear stories from his old friends and from his brothers and cousins, and she will also get to just *exist* in this space, where some part of him will always remain. She will carry that part of my dad, and of me, just as Mamie will carry part of John, and Becky, and everyone who ever joined them on those perfect Saturdays, when a group of fans becomes a tribe, and when a tribe's departed elders can return to be briefly among the living.

That's what a tailgate is. Making and transporting food—or even ordering chicken from Popeyes, which both John and I highly recommend—is how we show people that we understand what these gatherings mean. So I'm back where I began. We all love when John cooks for our tailgate in the fall, not because he's a chef, but because it means he thought of us, and we will re-enact the many beautiful days that have come before.

Wright Thompson
Writer, father, tailgater

GIRDING FOR BATTLE

Before moving to Oxford, Mississippi, in 1992, which will be near on thirty years (or more) by the time you read this, I knew jack about tailgating. It's a dirty little secret: While we can find any excuse to throw a party in New Orleans and few cities pull harder for their team, New Orleanians know relatively little about tailgating. This has changed dramatically in the last decade, when the Saints' program became truly competitive, spurring our tailgating game to also level up and go toe-to-toe with great NFL stalwarts in parking lots around the country. But those gatherings were not around when I was growing up.

This may seem curious to folks who don't know New Orleans well, but there is a perfectly good reason. The original Sugar Bowl stadium (Tulane University stadium), where both Tulane and the Saints played until the Superdome was opened in 1975, was located in an affluent neighborhood in uptown New Orleans, adjacent to the Tulane campus. Hundreds of folks within walking distance of the stadium held regular open houses on game days, choosing to stay close to their kitchens, rather than fuss over setting up tailgate spreads. There was also a shortage of parking lots around the stadium, so even if folks had wanted to tailgate, there was not much space for it. That's why when I was a little one, my exposure to tailgating was nothing more than hopping from house party to house party.

In the early 1980s, I trundled off to Hampden-Sydney College, in Virginia (where, some rightfully argue, I did little more than piss away my parents' hard-earned money). H-SC was an amazing place. To step on campus was to step back in time two or three decades. It was safe. It was honest. It was untouched, and tradition ruled supreme.

On cool fall Saturdays, tailgating was one of those well-established traditions. Wagoneers, Country Squires, Eldorados, and the rest filled the tiny oak tree–shaded parking lots next to the football field, their trunks propped open to reveal the bounty of a family's kitchen after days of toil. It was here that I was first brought back to life from a previous night's festivities with a bourbon and Coke, a cold fried chicken thigh, and pimento cheese. The smells of a musty trunk, leaded gasoline, a sun-beaten nylon interior, whiskey, and barbecue are burned on my brain, reminding me of one of the happiest places I can imagine anywhere.

So, after completely fucking away a few years at H-SC, I dropped out. As a result, I found myself under my own financial horsepower and headed off to Chapel Hill, intending to continue my course of study at the University of North Carolina. At UNC, I fell in love with college baseball and stumbled into a group of folks who made sport of cooking out next to the third base line. It was a grittier version of what I had experienced in Virginia, but these guys were bringing out little grills and actually cooking. They brought fish, sausages, wild duck, and lamb. It was a mindblower, but it never dawned on me that this was an experience that had been completely missing from my life. I just knew I was totally sucked in and couldn't get enough of it.

In the spring of 1992, I ended up in Oxford, home of the University of Mississippi and what most folks, who know about such things, consider the mecca of college football tailgating. The Grove, where Ole Miss fans have gathered for decades, is fifteen acres of tree-shaded glory in the middle of the UM campus. The one time I witnessed it prior to moving here was in the early 1980s, when that beautiful meadow was filled with cars, charcoal grills, blankets, silver service, mountains of meticulously prepared food, and perfectly coiffed football fans. It was a cathedral.

In the mid-1980s, the university made the decision to ban cars in the Grove out of concern for the 200-year-old oak trees and the pressure on their root systems. In some folks' eyes, this was a seismic shift, and the Grove was forever changed.

I hardly raised my head for the better part of my first decade in Oxford—I opened City Grocery and started several other ventures, which occupied almost all of my free time. It was not until 2002 that I ventured out on a game day to enjoy myself. The Grove had become an ocean of ten-foot-square tents, which marked off folks' territories. Charcoal was forbidden and the food was of a different stripe than I remembered. It was completely deflating. What was unchanged was the joy. The Grove was still the Grove, and a new generation had moved in as seamlessly as the generation before and the one before that. The conversations and embraces were there, but the spreads were less ambitious.

I continued to spend time there, and that part of the experience continued to slide. The realization I ultimately came to was that our lives have changed significantly since the early years of my adulthood. Most families are no longer single-income, and even if they are, parents now spend a large chunk of time with their children's activities. Gone are the days when the nonworking parent (let's face it: the mom) had three days to stay home, make food for thirty people, get all of the shit together, carefully pack the car, get up at the crack of dawn, set it all up, and entertain in the middle of a field. When you complicate that by separating folks from their cars, so everything has to be unpacked and then the car has to be parked in a remote spot (sometimes two miles away), the whole thing becomes a nightmare.

That scenario has been offset by conveniences like services that will bring tents, TVs, coolers, tables, and almost anything else and set it all up for you. And then there are guys like me who will cater to your every food and bar whim. In addition, every fast-food joint and restaurant in the surrounding county is in on the game of making tailgating life easier.

The downside is that the menus that generally bring joy to the hearts of college students, grown-ups, and youngsters alike are pretty basic and homogeneous. As a result, the offerings from tent to tent look remarkably similar. Let me be very clear here: This is not unique to the Grove. As I have traveled around in the last twenty years and had tailgate experiences at Talladega Raceway, Lambeau Field, Wrigley, several Super Bowls, and more, I've seen this trend everywhere. It's the result of busy lives and a general lack of enthusiasm when it comes to cooking.

Bottom line: Throwing a tailgate is a pain in the ass. It requires so many of the chores we view as drudgery on one of the few days we have for rest. I get it. I tried it. A group of us tried to start hosting a tailgate about five years ago, around the time we were all having our first kids. Let me tell you, the wheels fell off that shit quicker than a knife fight in a phone booth. Our food was usually just as uncreative as everything I have described.

The 2016 Mississippi State–Ole Miss game was the last of that season, and I was in charge of the food. (I had totally phoned in my efforts on the previous times I had to take care of the food. Sorry for that, my friends.) It was going to be my swan song. In the past, I just hadn't been able to find the energy after working six or eight hours on game day to wrap up work and tend to duties at a tailgate. For my last effort though I wanted to do something big, so we pulled out all of the stops. I wrote a menu of things I would want at a perfect tailgate. Then I dragged out a giant Cowboy Cauldron, a fryer, and a slow cooker and went to work. We had

sweet-and-sour collards, Indian-Spiced Shrimp Skewers (page 63), Malaysian BBQ-Glazed Turkey Necks (page 44), Beef and Cheddar Hot Dog Links (page 147), blender drinks, and more. It was glorious. Hundreds of people clamored around the fire, curious about what the hell we were doing. Everyone wanted a piece of it, and all my people had a ball. It was a pile of work, but the joy in everyone's faces totally washed away any of the toil we endured.

On holidays—Fourth of July, Memorial Day, Christmas, Labor Day game days—we completely ignore the perceived drudgery that cooking tasks can imply. American kitchens roar to life. Hundreds of thousands of pounds of charcoal

are ignited in thousands of tiny, glorious pyres as men and women across our great land bring joy to the mouths and stomachs of their friends. The "chores" of shopping and cooking evaporate, if only momentarily, as we celebrate these moments together, by breaking bread. We nosh on bites, snacks, stews, sandwiches, and sweets and sip cocktails. Food knows no political affiliation, race, religion, gender identification, or sexual orientation. It is the one thing that brings us all back together, no matter how far apart we've become. So, this is what I do now: I care more about the joy these moments can bring than I once let myself care.

This is my tailgate. Let's get it on!

TAILGATE ESSENTIALS

1 **KNOW THE RULES.** Everywhere you go will have different rules about when and where you can set up, park, and cook. You want as few surprises as possible when heading into unknown territory. Most universities, arenas, and event organizers have information readily available online, from basic to highly specific.

2 **GIVE YOURSELF PLENTY OF TIME.** The earlier you arrive, the less traffic you'll encounter, and the smaller the crowds in load-in and load-out areas. Setting up a tailgate comes with its own specialized set of stressors. Eliminating time-induced anxiety is entirely within your power. (As much as I tell my wife this, it changes nothing; so I lie to her about departure times. I'd have lost *all* my fucking marbles if I hadn't employed this tactic. Trust me on this.)

3 **TOOLS, TOOLS, TOOLS (THIS COULD NOT BE MORE IMPORTANT).** Always keep a basic set of tools for emergency repairs. All your equipment runs the risk of breaking, so don't let yourself get caught without basic tools to deal with these inconveniences. Build a tool kit with a couple of screwdrivers, pliers, channel locks, a hammer, box cutter, Allen wrenches, and any specialty tools that came along with your equipment when purchased. Light rope, duct tape, zip ties, and trash bags all serve multiple purposes.

4 **TAKE-AWAY GEAR.** Always bring a few extra disposable pans with lids, plastic wrap, aluminum foil, and quart-size containers to neatly pack out when you are done. Several rolls of paper towels are always a good bet.

5   **WATER, WATER (AND ICE!) EVERYWHERE.** Whether you need to wash your hands, douse smoldering coals, do simple clean up, or just take a drink, it's *never* a bad idea to have a couple of extra gallons on hand. While we are at it, extra ice is key as well. Go ahead and double up.

6   **LEARN TO PACK YOUR COOLERS.** For large gatherings, pack some coolers with drinks only and label the coolers to indicate what is inside. Use water bottles and water-filled zip-top bags, which you've frozen the night before, for ice packs for your food (avoid ice cubes except for drinks). Prechill everything to preserve temperature-cooling agents.

7   **MAKE A WARMING BOX OUT OF AN IGLOO COOLER.** Wrap 6 bricks in aluminum foil and heat for 1 hour at 500°F. Place them in the bottom of a cooler and cover with an inverted baking sheet, so your food will not have direct contact. Place items to keep warm on top of the baking sheet.

8   **CHECK YOUR ELECTRONICS.** Make sure your gear is up and running. Nothing is worse when folks show up than going to turn on your big screen and discovering your generator is on the fritz. I've seen it happen time and time again. Keep extra batteries for remotes, flashlights, and other devices.

9   **PUT TOGETHER A NONPERISHABLES KIT.** Bring extra trash bags, disposable plates and cups, napkins, a first-aid kit, pain reliever, sunscreen, and bungee cords. A bottle of cleaning spray never hurt anyone's feelings. Gather a separate container with serving utensils (spoons, forks, a couple of sharp knives, tongs, and spatulas), kitchen towels, oven mitts, and a small cutting board.

10 **PICK YOUR FRIENDS CAREFULLY.** Tailgates are work. If you saddle yourself with friends who aren't prepared to share the load, resentment is sure to follow. Establish ground rules and basic responsibilities. As surely as the August day is long, you will have one person or couple in your group who will take on a lion's share of the responsibilities without complaining, but your group will ultimately fracture if duties aren't shared evenly.

11:00 KICKOFF
FOR BREAKING *the* FAST

I am enormously impatient. At six years old I was busted for getting up in the middle of the night, the night before Christmas, and opening presents—not just my presents, but *everyone's* presents, because I just couldn't wait and I wanted to see what Santa had brought, well, everyone. I was impossible to date as a teenager because I could never be happy to wait and see the person I was infatuated with again after I dropped her off. I called. I snuck out of the house. I left campus when I wasn't supposed to—all because I just couldn't wait. (Decades-late blanket apology.)

Cooking, it turns out, was a perfect career path, as far as immediate gratification is concerned. For all of the psychosis, stress, narcissism, and ego-flexing that goes along with kitchen work, not to mention the enormously uncomfortable conditions that come with commercial kitchens, the one thing that makes it all worthwhile for me is that you can immediately gauge someone's response to something you have prepared for them the very second their mouth closes around the fork. That particular revelation sunk me for life. It completely satisfied my primal impatience.

When I moved to Oxford, Mississippi, to open my first restaurant, City Grocery, at the tender age of twenty-six, I moved into a town whose fall economy was largely driven by crowds of college football fans. Football, in the echelon of things I love, is a very close second to cooking, so living in a town where there was constant SEC (Southeast Conference) football action happening was a dream come true.

Games in the fall kick off at about 11:00 a.m., or 2:30 or 6:00 p.m. As an impatient soul, there is nothing more agonizing than waiting until 6:00 for a big game to start. If 6:00 a.m. were an option, I'd be all for it. So I love when we can jump in on the first kickoff of the day and get the game going.

That said, there is little worse professionally than an early kickoff. We arrive at the catering kitchen at about 2:30 a.m. and are cooking full tilt by 3:00, with first orders going out at 6:00. It makes for brutal mornings, but by 11:00 a.m., our work is done and the game is on!

Our orders on those 11:00 a.m. kickoff days are heavy on breakfast items. Here are a few that travel well and will fuel your folks to scream and holler at an hour they would not likely do so otherwise.

SMOKED HAM BISCUITS
with CULTURED BUTTER

Ham biscuits were a staple at cocktail parties when I was growing up. As mundane as they might sound, they were, first of all, an outstanding little bite, and second, the standard by which the ladies of New Orleans judged one another.

This recipe gets a bump from cultured butter. Once you have tasted it, there is just no way to ever look store-bought butter in the eye again. Making this fermented version of a comparatively bland kitchen staple is both easy and rewarding, and it will make you sound like a supercool, rock-star food geek when you can lecture your friends about the simple rigors and amazing rewards of fermented dairy. Add it to warm buttermilk biscuits and salty ham and blow your friends' minds. You'll need to start the cultured butter 3 days in advance.

Cultured Butter

1 cup heavy cream

2 tablespoons organic live yogurt culture (such as store-bought Greek yogurt)

2 teaspoons salt

Biscuits

2 cups self-rising flour, preferably White Lily (see Notes on page 10)

2 teaspoons sugar

½ teaspoon salt

½ teaspoon MSG (see Notes on page 10)

1 teaspoon freshly ground black pepper

6 tablespoons frozen Cultured Butter or equal amount of store-bought

4 tablespoons unsalted butter, frozen

¾ cup plus 2 tablespoons store-bought full-fat buttermilk (if you have not made your own cultured buttermilk)

2 tablespoons vegetable oil

5 thin slices good-quality country ham

MAKE THE BUTTER Whisk together cream and yogurt in a glass or stainless-steel bowl, cover with cheesecloth, and allow to sit in a warm place for 3 days.

Remove the cheesecloth. The cream should have thickened to a yogurt-like consistency (if it is still slightly runny, don't worry, it will still whip up just fine). Transfer to a stand mixer fitted with a whisk attachment and whisk on medium-low speed as if you were making whipped cream. Continue whisking until the cream seizes up, butter forms, and buttermilk begins to separate out. Remove butter solids from the bowl to a doubled-up piece of cheesecloth and leave the buttermilk in the bowl. Wrap the butter in cheesecloth. Squeeze the butter over the mixing bowl to release as much buttermilk as possible and set aside ¾ cup plus 2 tablespoons for the biscuits. Save the remaining buttermilk for future use. It will keep refrigerated for 8 weeks.

continued

Return the butter to the mixer and put on the paddle attachment. Beat the butter on low speed to release a little more buttermilk and pour it off. Add the salt, raise the mixer speed to medium, and beat the butter until smooth and creamy. Put ¼ cup plus 2 tablespoons of the butter in a small container and freeze until hard (for the biscuits). Refrigerate the remaining butter to spread over the biscuits and for other uses.

MAKE THE BISCUITS Preheat the oven to 400°F. Line a baking sheet with parchment paper.

Whisk together the flour, sugar, salt, MSG, and pepper in a medium mixing bowl and place in the freezer for 1 hour. Remove the flour mix, reserved cultured butter, and unsalted butter from the freezer. Grate the butter with the large holes of a box grater straight into the flour mix. Stir lightly with a fork to combine. Add the reserved cultured buttermilk (or store-bought buttermilk), stirring with the fork until just combined.

Flour your hands and gather up the dough (it will be shaggy and still have wet and dry spots). Working in the bowl, fold it over once or twice, until the dough holds together nicely. Transfer to a floured surface and knead and fold two or three times until smooth, handling it as little as possible. Wrap the dough in plastic wrap and place in freezer for 15 to 30 minutes.

Remove from the freezer and roll out to ¾-inch thickness. Cut with a round cookie cutter (or the mouth of a sturdy champagne flute) into twenty-five 1-inch rounds. Place on the parchment-lined baking sheet and bake for 12 minutes, or until the tops are golden brown.

To assemble the biscuits, heat the oil in a cast-iron skillet over medium heat for 3 minutes. Place 1 or 2 slices of ham in the pan and brown lightly, about 1 minute. Flip over and kiss the second side as well. Remove from the pan and repeat until all the ham slices are warmed. Cut the ham into pieces about the same size as the biscuits.

Split the biscuits. Spoon a little cultured butter on the cut sides. Lay a piece of ham on the bottom half of each biscuit and cover with the top half. Serve immediately or set aside for up to 2 hours before eating.

NOTES

➤ We tested dozens of flours and experimented with various ratios of baking soda to baking powder, but White Lily self-rising flour gave us the best results. Trust me, I have eaten my body weight in biscuits.

➤ Sadly, there is a pathetic misconception about MSG. It doesn't cause anything other than the explosion of deliciousness. It is a naturally occurring amino acid, which makes things taste insane. A limited number of folks may exhibit a sensitivity to MSG, but reactions are not allergic and are not threatening. It's certainly no reason to avoid it, as amazing as it is. We call it "powdered delicious" in our kitchens.

➤ The residual liquid from making your cultured butter is cultured buttermilk. Keep it! Use it! It's amazing. If you insist on buying, please don't even consider "low-fat" buttermilk. It is nothing short of an insult to your final product.

SMOKED SHRIMP BREAKFAST BURRITOS, ROASTED TOMATO SALSA

Holy hell do I love a breakfast burrito! My mom was a high school history teacher, and in spite of her daunting schedule, she made a hot breakfast for my brother and me every day before school. Her dedication to our meals was Herculean. (She also packed lunches and made dinner *every* night, on top of grading papers and creating lesson plans—unthinkable today.) My mom's breakfast ideas came in waves. For a while it was varieties of cheese toast, followed by assorted pancakes. Then sometime during the 1970s, she fell in love with salsa, and our breakfast burrito was born. Literally anything left over from dinner would get warmed, tossed with scrambled eggs, and folded into warmed tortillas, which were topped with her salsa.

These are made for tailgating because they are great both steaming hot and at room temperature. You can build them with whatever you like (for example, last night's meatloaf), but they are elevated with ingredients prepared for the occasion. Make a pile the night before the game, and chill them. Warm them quickly in the morning, and they are good for the day!

This recipe calls for a stove-top smoker. Cameron's makes an excellent and extremely simple one that is the exact size you would need to smoke these shrimp. It is a wonderful piece of equipment that I use to smoke tons of stuff at home. Grilling is a perfectly acceptable alternative for the shrimp, should you not want to spend money on a somewhat frivolous piece of equipment.

Roasted Tomato Salsa

5 tomatoes, cored, halved across the equator, and seeded

6 tablespoons extra-virgin olive oil

Salt and black pepper

5 tablespoons chopped fresh oregano

¼ cup thinly sliced garlic plus 1 tablespoon minced garlic

4 cups seeded and chopped Roma tomatoes

½ bunch cilantro, chopped

1 bunch green onions, greens and white parts, chopped

2 jalapeño peppers, seeded and chopped

5 tablespoons olive oil

Grated zest and juice of 3 limes

2 tablespoons brown sugar

1 tablespoon ground cumin

1 teaspoon ground coriander

Pinch of ground cinnamon

1 to 4 dashes Tabasco sauce (optional)

Filling

1½ pounds extra-large shrimp, peeled and deveined

2½ tablespoons olive oil

Salt and black pepper

2½ teaspoons ground cumin

1 teaspoon chili powder

Grated zest and juice of 2 limes

12 eggs

1 cup whole milk

2 tablespoons clarified butter (see Notes on page 43 and recipe on page 238)

¾ cup diced yellow onion

2 teaspoons minced garlic

1 cup chopped tomato

½ cup chopped fresh cilantro

16 (12-inch) flour tortillas

Lime wedges

Hot sauce, preferably Valentina, for serving

Preheat the oven to 275°F. Cover a baking sheet with aluminum foil.

MAKE THE SALSA Place the tomato halves on the prepared baking sheet, cut-sides up. Drizzle with 4 tablespoons of the extra-virgin oil and sprinkle with salt and black pepper. Distribute the oregano and sliced garlic evenly over the tomato halves and roast for 2½ hours, or until the tomatoes have broken down but not dried out. Remove from the oven, cool, and coarsely chop.

In a large glass bowl, stir together the roasted tomatoes with the chopped Roma tomatoes, cilantro, green onions, minced garlic, jalapeño peppers, the remaining 2 tablespoons extra-virgin olive oil, regular olive oil, lime zest and juice, brown sugar, cumin, coriander, and cinnamon. Allow to sit at room temperature for 30 minutes. Season with salt and black pepper and add Tabasco, if you like. Set aside.

MAKE THE FILLING In a large bowl, toss the shrimp with the olive oil, ¾ teaspoon salt, 1¼ teaspoons black pepper, 1 teaspoon of the cumin, the chili powder, and lime zest and juice. Smoke the shrimp in a stove-top smoker according to manufacturer's directions. (Alternatively, skewer the shrimp and grill them over a hot charcoal fire, 3 minutes per side.) Allow the shrimp to cool, coarsely chop, and set aside.

In a large bowl, whisk together the eggs and milk. Season with salt and black pepper and whisk in the remaining 1½ teaspoons cumin. Set aside.

Heat the clarified butter in a large nonstick skillet over medium heat. Add the onion and garlic and sauté until the onion begins to soften. Stir in the tomato and season lightly with salt and black pepper. Cook briefly until warmed through. Add the egg mix and scramble, stirring often, but allowing the curds to firm up now and then, until the eggs are almost cooked but still moist. Stir in half the cilantro and remove the eggs from the pan. Set aside. Wipe out the pan and warm it over low heat.

One at a time, warm the tortillas on both sides, about 30 to 45 seconds per side, and wrap in a kitchen towel to keep warm. Keep the pan warm over low heat. Working with 2 tortillas at a time (or more if you like), lay out the tortillas on a clean work surface. Spread ¼ cup of the shrimp in the center of each tortilla. Add 1 cup of the egg mix, a pinch of cilantro, and 2 tablespoons of salsa on top of the eggs. Splash with a little hot sauce and pull the edge of the tortilla closest to you up and over the top of the filling, tucking it under the shrimp and eggs tightly. Fold the sides over the top and finish rolling the burrito. Let the assembled burritos rest on their seams. Warm the burritos, two at a time, in the warm pan, searing the seam on the bottom and the top of the burrito to seal it and crisp it up. Serve with extra salsa, lime wedges, and hot sauce. You will never start the day better.

CREOLE BREAKFAST CASSEROLE

Sadly, the casserole has been shamed into culinary nonexistence along with chicken à la king, mayonnaise salads, and TV dinners, which all saw their heyday during what I consider "the period of the great American artistic abominations." It seems from the early '70s through the mid-'80s, everything we did from a design, fashion, and culinary standpoint now resides only in the hallowed halls of the single-wide trailers of our memories.

Fortunately for you, I am here to help blow the lid off of the casserole misconception. A breakfast casserole can save you time and energy. They are cost-efficient, hold their temperature and moisture well, and are universally loved when done right. More importantly, they can be assembled the night before and popped in the oven 30 minutes before you want to serve or transport them, resplendent in their simple beauty.

7 tablespoons butter

8 ounces good-quality andouille sausage, halved lengthwise and sliced into half-moons

10 ounces extra-large shrimp, peeled, deveined, and cut into thirds

8 ounces crawfish tails

Salt and black pepper

¾ cup chopped yellow onion

½ cup diced red bell pepper

½ cup diced green bell pepper

½ cup diced celery

1 tablespoon minced garlic

2½ teaspoons Creole Seasoning (page 236)

12 eggs, well-beaten with a whisk

½ cup heavy cream

½ cup milk

2 tablespoons chopped fresh oregano

½ teaspoon cayenne pepper

¾ cup chopped tomato

Preheat the oven to 350°F. Spray a 9 by 13-inch disposable aluminum pan (or a glass or metal pan) with nonstick cooking spray or wipe it with vegetable oil or melted butter.

Melt 3 tablespoons of the butter in a skillet over medium-high heat. Toss in the andouille and cook, stirring slowly, until the sausage has browned. Remove with a slotted spoon and set aside.

Add the shrimp and crawfish tails to the pan, sprinkle lightly with salt and black pepper, and cook, stirring constantly, until the shrimp begins to turn pink. Immediately remove this from the pan and set aside with the andouille. Stir the onion, both bell peppers, celery, and garlic into the pan. Season lightly with salt, black pepper, and ½ teaspoon of the Creole seasoning (or to taste). Sauté until the onions are transparent. Remove the vegetables from the pan and cool briefly.

Melt the remaining 4 tablespoons butter in the microwave or in a small saucepan and cool slightly. In a large bowl, stir together the eggs, cream, milk, melted butter, oregano, cayenne pepper, the remaining 2 teaspoons Creole seasoning, 2 teaspoons of black pepper, and 1¼ teaspoons salt. Add the reserved sausage, seafood, vegetables, and the tomato, stirring until well combined. Pour into the prepared pan, cover with aluminum foil, and bake for 35 minutes, or until eggs are just set. Serve immediately.

HUEVOS RANCHEROS GRITS CASSEROLE

This recipe puts a Mexican twist on shakshouka, a dish I fell in love with during a trip to Israel in 2015. You can prepare most of it the night before and slam it in the oven 30 minutes before heading out the door, though it is definitely best put together at the last minute. Garnish once you're at the tailgate. It is filling and flavorful, and you can add almost anything to it. Chorizo, roasted chicken, shrimp, roasted mushrooms, sautéed onions and peppers, and bacon all make excellent additions.

Black Beans

2 cups dried black beans

¼ cup unsalted butter

½ cup diced yellow onion

¼ cup diced jalapeño pepper

1 tablespoon minced garlic

2 teaspoons cumin seeds, toasted and crushed

1 teaspoon coriander seeds, toasted and crushed

2 teaspoons dried oregano

4 cups water

¼ cup fresh lime juice

1 bay leaf

¼ cup sherry vinegar

Salt and black pepper

Grits

2 cups milk

2 cups chicken stock or water

1 cup stone-ground grits

6 tablespoons butter, cut into chunks

¼ cup heavy cream

1 cup grated Parmesan cheese

1 teaspoons ground cumin

1½ teaspoons salt

2 teaspoons black pepper

Vegetable oil for frying

3 (8-inch) flour or corn tortillas

For Assembly

8 eggs

Salt and black pepper

¼ cup chopped fresh cilantro

Roasted Tomato Salsa (page 12) or your store-bought favorite, for serving

Sliced avocado

Hot sauce for serving (optional)

MAKE THE BEANS Place the black beans in a medium saucepan and cover with water by 4 inches. Cover the pan with a kitchen towel or cover it loosely with plastic wrap or aluminum foil. Soak the beans for at least 5 hours or up to overnight. Drain the beans, reserving ½ cup of the soaking water, and set aside.

In a large saucepan over medium heat, melt the butter. Sauté the onion, jalapeño, and garlic until tender, stirring constantly, about 3 minutes. Add the cumin, coriander, and oregano and blend well. Add the beans, 4 cups water, lime juice, and bay leaf and cook over low heat until tender, about 1½ hours.

In a small saucepan, cook the sherry over medium heat until reduced by half. Add the reserved soaking water and reduce by a third. Remove ½ cup of the beans and puree them in a food processor or blender. Return the pureed beans to the pot and blend well. Simmer for an additional 5 minutes. Season with salt and black pepper. Cool and set aside.

Preheat oven to 450°F.

MAKE THE GRITS Combine the milk and chicken stock in a large saucepan over medium heat and bring to a boil. Turn down the heat to low and whisk in the grits. Cook, stirring constantly, until the grits are tender, about 20 minutes, depending on the grind (check the package directions; better quality grits will take longer to cook). Blend in the butter, cream, Parmesan, cumin, salt, and black pepper. Stir well to combine and pour the grits into a large cast-iron skillet.

continued

HUEVOS RANCHEROS GRITS CASSEROLE, CONTINUED

Heat 1 inch of vegetable oil in a skillet to 375°F. Roll the tortillas into a cylinder and cut them crosswise into ½-inch-thick slices. Carefully place tortilla strips in the hot oil and stir gently until golden brown. Remove to a paper towel, sprinkle with salt, and drain.

ASSEMBLE THE CASSEROLE Spoon the grits into a large cast iron skillet (14 inches or two smaller skillets) and roughly smooth the top. Spread the beans over the grits and use a large serving spoon to make eight divots in the black beans and grits. Crack an egg into each of the divots

and sprinkle with salt and black pepper. Bake until the whites of the eggs are cooked through, about 15 minutes. Remove from the oven and top with the tortilla strips, cilantro, salsa, avocado, and hot sauce (if you like). Serve hot.

NOTE

► You can also purchase a corn chip you like and crumble roughly instead of frying fresh ones.

DUCK CONFIT *and* HASH BROWN CASSEROLE

This is among the consummate comfort foods. I'm going to take the easy-out and encourage you to buy your confit and duck fat, largely because most folks don't want to undertake the long process, at least 24 hours, to make their own. That said, if you want to try, email me (john@citygroceryonline.com) and I'll be happy to share our recipe.

Now that we have settled that nonsense, make this dish, keep the source of the duck fat a secret, and convince your bedazzled friends that you are a kitchen savant!

3 pounds russet potatoes, washed and peeled

3 cups chopped duck confit, preferably from D'Artagnan (see Note)

2 cups shredded Gruyère cheese

1¼ cups diced yellow onion

1½ cups crème fraîche

¼ cup butter, melted

¼ cup duck fat, preferably from D'Artagnan (see Note)

3 tablespoons minced garlic

3 tablespoons fresh thyme leaves

1 tablespoon black pepper

2 teaspoons salt

1 teaspoon MSG, such as Accent

Preheat the oven to 375°F.

Grease a 9 by 13-inch casserole dish with cold butter and set aside.

Fill a large bowl halfway with cold water and grate the potatoes on the largest holes of a box grater into the bowl. (Alternatively, you can grate them with a food processor and drop them into the water. This is faster and easier, but as a purist chef, I'm required to offer the traditional method.) Stir the potatoes for 15 seconds and pour off the water. Cover with fresh water and allow to sit for 10 minutes. Stir and discard the water again. Place the potatoes in a kitchen towel and squeeze out any excess water.

Transfer the potatoes to a large bowl and add the duck confit, Gruyère, onion, crème fraîche, butter, duck fat, garlic, thyme, pepper, salt, and MSG, stirring until well combined. Pour it into the casserole dish and spread out evenly across. Bake for 45 minutes, or until the top is golden brown.

NOTE

▶ I have been a customer of D'Artagnan (www.dartagnan.com) since the late 1980s. They are wonderful folks. Duck fat is also beginning to make regular appearances in the grocery store in Oxford, Mississippi, which means it is likely in your store, too. Check there first.

BREAKFAST REUBENS

Dan Stein, of Stein's Market and Deli in New Orleans, makes some of the best sandwiches I have ever had. He is crusty, irreverent, and brash, just like his food. For some reason, about a decade ago, he took a shine to me and has always treated me as kindly as, well, he is capable. I love him, his place, and his food.

One of my favorite sandwiches is the Sam, little more than a Reuben with slaw instead of kraut. And one of my favorite moments in life is splitting one with my brother Richard at a picnic table out front with a couple of cold beers.

Sweet Slaw

3 cups shredded green cabbage

½ cup finely diced yellow onion

¼ cup shredded carrot

½ cup mayonnaise, preferably Duke's

3 tablespoons sugar

¼ cup sweet pickle relish, plus 2 tablespoons of the juice

1½ tablespoons white vinegar

1 tablespoon vegetable oil

1 tablespoon hot sauce, preferably Texas Pete

1 teaspoon salt

1 teaspoon black pepper

Russian Dressing

1 cup mayonnaise, preferably Duke's

½ cup chili sauce, preferably Heinz

2 teaspoons Sriracha

1½ tablespoons prepared horseradish

2 tablespoons grated yellow onion

2 teaspoons Worcestershire

¼ teaspoon paprika

½ teaspoon salt

½ teaspoon MSG, such as Accent

Sandwiches

12 English muffins

12 eggs

Salt and black pepper

¾ cup mayonnaise, preferably Duke's

1½ pounds sliced pastrami

12 slices Swiss cheese

¼ teaspoon celery seeds

MAKE THE SLAW Place the cabbage, onion, and carrot in a large bowl and set aside. Whisk together the mayonnaise, sugar, pickle relish and juice, vinegar, oil, hot sauce, salt, and pepper in a 2-cup glass measuring cup or something similar. Pour the dressing over the slaw and stir to blend well. Refrigerate for at least 2 hours. Set aside 2¼ cups for the sandwiches and save the rest for another use.

MAKE THE RUSSIAN DRESSING In a small glass bowl, whisk together the mayonnaise, chili sauce, Sriracha, horseradish, onion, Worcestershire, paprika, salt, and MSG and refrigerate for at least 2 hours.

MAKE THE SANDWICHES Position a rack in the top of the oven and preheat it to 350°F. Grease a twelve-muffin tin with melted butter. Split the English muffins, place the halves on baking sheets, and toast in the oven until crispy and golden brown. Remove from the oven and set aside.

Crack an egg into each muffin cup and sprinkle with salt and pepper. Place in the oven on the top rack and cook for 12 minutes, or until the eggs are fully set.

Meanwhile, on each of the English muffin bottoms, spread 1 tablespoon mayonnaise. Layer each with 2 ounces pastrami, 3 tablespoons sweet slaw, and 1 Swiss cheese slice. Return the baking sheet to the oven until the cheese has melted. Remove and set aside.

On each of the English muffin tops, spread 1 tablespoon Russian dressing. Remove the eggs from the muffin tin and place one on the cheese for each sandwich. Cover with the muffin tops and serve hot. These will benefit by some warmth, though they are perfectly good at room temperature. The Igloo warming box described on page 5 is perfect for holding these.

DAY-OLD CROISSANT *and* SAUSAGE "BREAD PUDDING"

Let's be honest with each other from the outset: There is no reason on God's green earth that there should ever be leftover croissants, unless they were shitty to begin with. But let's just say that you find yourself at La Boulangerie, on Magazine Street in New Orleans, around closing time. The pastry chef has had an enormous brain fart and made too many croissants, and Donald Link, the owner, marches in, fresh off a giant crawfish boil lunch and cannot imagine eating another thing. So he gifts you with a pile of them, because he overheard your conversation about a spicy sausage and croissant bread pudding. He is intrigued and expects that, in return for his generosity, you will bring him a scoop of this deliciousness when he is feeling a little peckish again the next morning. You take the bag and sprint out of the door before you wake up from this Carrollian dream (that's Lewis Carroll—I'm a quasi-intellectual, I freely admit) and scurry home to prepare the following recipe. Please bring Donald his sample. He was awfully kind in the dream.

Bullshit aside, you can frequently barter a deal at the end of the day at local bakeries to keep them from tossing out their goodies. (This strategy rarely works with cookies, but give it a shot; maybe it's just chubby bald guys they don't cotton to.)

8 cups torn or cubed 1- or 2-day-old croissants

2 tablespoons olive oil

12 ounces spicy breakfast sausage, crumbled, or smoked link sausage, thinly sliced

1½ cups finely diced yellow onion

¾ cup diced celery

1 tablespoon minced garlic

10 eggs

2½ cups milk

1 cup heavy cream

½ cup butter, melted

½ cup chopped fresh chives

½ cup chopped fresh parley

1 teaspoon salt

2 teaspoons black pepper

½ cup grated Parmesan

½ cup grated cheddar

Preheat the oven to 350°F. Spray a 9 by 13-inch disposable aluminum pan (or a glass or metal pan) with nonstick cooking spray or wipe it with vegetable oil or melted butter.

Put the croissants in a large bowl and set aside. Heat the oil in a large skillet over medium heat until it begins to shimmer. Add the sausage and brown until almost fully cooked. Remove from the pan and set aside. Add the onion, celery, and garlic and sauté until the onion is transparent. Remove from the pan and cool slightly. Pour off and reserve the oil and sausage fat as well.

Whisk together the eggs, milk, cream, butter, chives, parsley, salt, and pepper in a large bowl. Pour over the croissant pieces and blend well. Stir in the sausage, vegetables, and reserved oil. Pour into the prepared dish, cover with aluminum foil, and bake for 30 minutes, or until the pudding is set up in the middle.

Turn the oven to broil.

Uncover, sprinkle with the Parmesan and cheddar, and place under the broiler until the cheese is browned. Serve hot.

SHRIMP *and* CHEESE GRIT SOUFFLÉ

One of my favorite Christmas dishes, which appeared on the buffet every year, almost magically, was my mom's cheese grits soufflé. It was sublimely airy, but rich, and deeply flavorful, though it only had a handful of ingredients. It was beautiful and perfect.

Adding shrimp and bacon seemed only logical. This has become the go-to dish for my family's Christmas breakfast. It holds temperature well, and although it will collapse during the trip to a tailgate, it will still be amazing. It is delicious and filling and a perfectly acceptable version of shrimp and grits.

2½ cups chopped raw shrimp (Gulf brown shrimp are my favorite)

Salt and black pepper

1½ cups grated Parmesan cheese

4 cups milk

2 cups chicken stock

1½ cups stone-ground grits

1 cup cold butter, cubed

8 eggs, separated

¾ cup grated sharp cheddar cheese, preferably white

¾ cup chopped green onion, white and green parts

½ cup chopped crispy cooked bacon

¼ cup chopped fresh parsley

1 tablespoon minced garlic

2 tablespoons fresh lemon juice

½ teaspoon cayenne pepper

Preheat the oven to 400°F.

Place the shrimp in a bowl and sprinkle with salt and black pepper. Set aside.

Thoroughly brush the inside of a soufflé dish 10 inches in diameter and 4 inches high with melted butter. Sprinkle with ¼ cup of the Parmesan, coating the dish well. Set aside.

In a large saucepan, bring the milk, chicken stock, and 2 teaspoons salt to a boil over medium heat. Turn down the heat to low and whisk in the grits. Cook, stirring constantly, until the grits are tender, about 20 minutes, depending on the grind (check the package directions).

Remove from the heat and add the cold butter, stirring until fully melted and incorporated. Add the reserved shrimp, the egg yolks, cheddar, the remaining 1¼ cups Parmesan, the green onion, bacon, parsley, garlic, lemon juice, and cayenne, stirring until well combined.

In a stand mixer fitted with a whisk, whip the egg whites on high speed until they form stiff peaks. Fold one-third of the whites gently into the grits to loosen them, then gently fold in the remainder, stirring until fully and evenly combined. Pour into prepared soufflé dish. Bake for 20 minutes, or until the top is golden brown and rises 2 inches above the rim of the dish. Serve hot.

LAMB KHEEMA PUFFS, SPICY INDIAN KETCHUP

Have I told you how insanely talented, considerate, and generous my friend Vishwesh Bhatt is? We have been cooking together for over a quarter century, and it took twenty years of him inviting me to visit his home in Ahmedabad, India, before I made it.

We finally went together for the first time in 2016. In the two weeks I was there, I ate some of the most amazing food I have ever had. And in those two weeks, we never even considered eating at the same place twice, because each meal was seemingly better than the last. That was until we went to Kyani and Company, an Irani-Indian bakery and tea shop in Mumbai. It was there that I had my first taste of kheema. I could not stop thinking about the flavors and texture, and I pestered Vish until he agreed we could go a second time. It was the only place in the entire trip where we duplicated meals . . . amazing.

Go we did, and this dish haunts my fucking dreams now. Make. Eat. Enjoy. It is also killer with Parker House rolls and scrambled eggs.

2 (18-ounce) boxes frozen puff pastry

¼ cup olive oil

2 cups finely diced yellow onion

1 tablespoon ground coriander

2½ teaspoons red pepper flakes

1½ teaspoons turmeric

1½ teaspoons ground fennel

¾ teaspoon cayenne pepper

2½ tablespoons minced ginger

3 tablespoons minced garlic

1½ pounds ground lamb

Salt

1 tablespoon black pepper

¾ cup canned crushed San Marzano tomatoes

1 cup chicken stock

2 cups green peas

¾ cup chopped fresh cilantro

2 eggs, lightly beaten

Thaw the puff pastry according to the directions on the package.

In a medium Dutch oven, heat the oil over medium heat until it begins to shimmer. Add the onion and sauté until transparent. Stir in the coriander, red pepper flakes, turmeric, fennel, and cayenne pepper and continue sautéing until the spices become aromatic. Add the ginger and garlic and stir to blend well. Sauté for 1 minute more. Add the lamb, 1½ teaspoons salt, and the black pepper and stir to combine well. Cook, stirring constantly, until the lamb has browned and all the moisture has evaporated from the pot. Add the tomatoes and stir to combine well.

Bring to a simmer and continue simmering until the sauce has thickened, 7 to 10 minutes. Stir in the chicken stock. Return to a simmer, cover, and simmer over low heat for about 15 minutes. Remove the lid and stir in the peas. Simmer until the kheema has thickened. Stir in the cilantro and season with salt. Remove from the heat and set aside to cool.

Preheat the oven to 375°F.

Cut each puff pastry sheet into four equal rectangles. Scoop a heaping ¼ cup of kheema onto each of the rectangles. Blend the eggs with 2 tablespoons water and brush the edges of the pastries. Fold the dough in half, lengthwise, and seal the edges with a fork. Brush the tops of the pastries with the egg wash and bake until golden brown and flaky, about 20 minutes.

GRILLED VEGETABLE QUICHE, RED BELL PEPPER COULIS

We have traveled light-years from the time when consuming quiche defined your sexual orientation. In the politically correct twenty-first century, "real men" can eat quiche confidently. They can sip rosé, guzzle brightly colored things they mistakenly call martinis, consume bowls *full* of quinoa, and eat all the goddamn avocado toast the nation's restaurants can produce. I guess, in retrospect, quiche is arguably one of the more masculine "healthy" menu items out there.

Kidding aside, quiche is an awesome breakfast crowd-pleaser. Like an omelet or breakfast casserole, you can fill it with whatever you fancy. Make it the night before (with a store-bought crust, if you must), put a kitchen towel over it, leave it on the countertop, and slice and serve in the morning at room temperature.

2 cups all-purpose flour	Kosher salt
½ teaspoon sugar	Black pepper
1¼ teaspoons kosher salt	5 eggs
Black pepper	½ cup whole milk
1 cup plus 2 tablespoons butter, cubed	½ cup crème fraîche
¼ cup ice water	1½ tablespoons chopped mixed fresh herbs (parsley, basil, thyme, rosemary, tarragon, oregano, chives, or whatever you like)
½ medium tomato, cored and seeded	
½ cup sliced zucchini	
½ cup sliced asparagus	Red Bell Pepper Coulis (recipe follows) for serving
½ cup sliced yellow onion	
2 tablespoons extra-virgin olive oil	

Preheat the oven to 350°F.

Stir together the flour, sugar, kosher salt, and ¾ teaspoon pepper in a bowl and place in the freezer for 20 minutes. Place the butter in the freezer for 20 minutes as well. Remove both from the freezer. Working quickly, use your fingertips to break up the butter pieces in the flour until the mix looks like coarse meal. Stir in the ice water with a fork and blend until the dough begins to come together. Working quickly, use your hands to continue bringing dough together. Turn out onto a floured surface and knead until the dough is uniform and relatively smooth. Wrap in plastic wrap and refrigerate.

Prepare a hot wood or charcoal fire.

In a large bowl, toss the tomato, zucchini, asparagus, and onion with the olive oil and sprinkle with a little salt and pepper. Place on the grill and toss and turn until vegetables are cooked all the way through. They should be tender, with nice color, without falling apart. The time will differ by the density of the vegetable. Squash cooks quickly, in a matter of a few minutes. Onion will take longer—7 to 10 minutes for thick slices. Bottom line is you really can't do it wrong unless you completely incinerate them. (Alternatively, you can roast the vegetables on a baking sheet in a 425°F oven, if you like. You'll need to remove softer vegetables as the others finish cooking). Remove, allow to cool, and chop them all together.

continued

Remove the dough from the refrigerator, unwrap, and pat it out to a round disk. Dust with flour and roll out into a circle 12 inches in diameter and ¼ inch thick. Lay the dough in a deep 9-inch pie pan and pierce all over with the tines of a fork. Crimp the edges as you would a dessert pie. Line with parchment paper and weight it down with pie weights or dried beans. Bake for 15 minutes. The piecrust will be lightly golden. Remove from the oven, take out the parchment paper and pie weights, and allow to cool.

In a blender, blend together the eggs, milk, crème fraîche, fresh herbs, ¾ teaspoon salt, and 1 teaspoon pepper for 15 seconds. Spread the chopped grilled vegetables across the bottom of the crust. Pour the egg mix over the top and bake for 25 minutes, or until the eggs are set in the center of quiche. Remove from the oven and allow to cool. Slice, drizzle with the coulis, and serve.

MAKES 2 CUPS

RED BELL PEPPER COULIS

3 medium red bell peppers

1 tablespoon olive oil

2 tablespoons sherry vinegar

1 tablespoon fresh thyme leaves

½ teaspoon salt

½ teaspoon sugar

Brush the peppers with the oil and char the skin of each over the open flame of a gas stove burner or wood fire, turning constantly, until charred all over. Place the warm peppers in a bowl and cover tightly with plastic wrap. Allow to sit for 20 minutes. Remove the peppers and, under cool running water, remove the stems, skin, seeds, and interior membrane. Place the pepper flesh in a blender, add the vinegar, thyme, salt, and sugar and blend, covered, on high speed until smooth, about 5 minutes. This will keep for 3 weeks in the refrigerator.

POTATO PANCAKES, HOMEMADE YOGURT, SMOKED TROUT, PICKLED RED ONIONS

These pancakes are silky and divine. Ideally, I would make these little bites of deliciousness and eat them as soon as they came out of the pan. They are the perfect vehicle for smoked trout. The yogurt cuts through the smoke on the fish, and the pickled red onions add brightness.

This is a great dish for the pocketbook. A pound of smoked trout is enough for fifty to sixty pancakes, and you already have most of the other ingredients in your pantry. This is also the perfect way to use up leftover mashed potatoes.

MAKE THE PICKLED ONION Place the sliced onions in a stainless-steel or glass bowl and set aside.

In a medium nonreactive saucepan, stir together the garlic, vinegar, wine, sugar, salt, bay leaves, mustard seeds, peppercorns, and cloves and bring to a simmer over medium heat. Immediately pour the mix over the onions and allow to sit until completely cool. Cover the bowl and chill. The onions will keep for up to 6 weeks in the refrigerator.

MAKE THE PANCAKES In a medium bowl, mix together the potatoes, milk, eggs and egg yolk, and the melted butter. Set aside. In a large bowl, whisk together the flour, baking soda, baking powder, salt, and pepper. Whisk the wet ingredients into the dry and blend well. Add the green onion and stir until well blended.

Heat 1½ tablespoons of the butter in a medium sauté pan over medium heat until the butter melts and begins to foam. Add 1½ tablespoons of the batter for each pancake and cook until the batter begins to bubble, about 1½ minutes. Flip the pancakes and brown for 1 minute on the second side. Remove from the pan and repeat until all of the batter is used up.

To assemble the pancakes, top each one with a teaspoon of yogurt, a flaked piece of smoked trout, a pickled onion ring, and a pinch of chives. Serve hot.

continued

Pickled Red Onions

2 red onions, very thinly sliced and separated into rings

1½ tablespoons minced garlic

1 cup apple cider vinegar

⅓ cup white wine

½ cup sugar

1½ tablespoons salt

2 bay leaves

1½ tablespoons mustard seeds

2 teaspoons black peppercorns

2 whole cloves

Pancakes

2 cups cold mashed potatoes (see page 172)

½ cup milk

3 whole eggs plus 1 yolk, lightly beaten

4½ tablespoons butter, melted, plus 1 cup for cooking

1¾ cups all-purpose flour

½ teaspoon baking soda

½ teaspoon baking powder

¾ teaspoon salt

1½ teaspoons black pepper

½ cup minced green onion, green part only

Homemade Yogurt for serving (recipe follows)

1½ pounds smoked trout (see Note)

½ cup chopped fresh chives

NOTE

► Smoked trout is available at specialty stores or from Sunburst Trout Farms (www.sunbursttrout.com/online-store/).

MAKES 3 CUPS

HOMEMADE YOGURT

You can certainly take a shortcut and use store-bought yogurt for the pancakes, but then you won't be able to say something pretentious to your friends like "You know I make my _own_ yogurt, right?"

3 cups organic whole milk

2 tablespoons organic live yogurt (like store-bought Greek yogurt)

Heat ¾ gallon of water in a large saucepan until boiling. Place two pint jars in the water on their sides, completely submerged, and allow them to boil for 10 minutes. Remove the jars from the water and drain them on a clean kitchen towel, open-side down. Do not touch until ready to fill.

Heat the milk in a small saucepan until it reaches 180°F. Remove from the heat and allow to cool to 110°F. Stir in the yogurt. Divide between the two sterilized pint jars and screw down the lids loosely. Set the jars in a deep ovenproof pot and fill with water just to the bottom of the ring. Place on the middle shelf in either a gas oven with just the pilot light on or an electric oven set as low as it will go. Allow to sit in the oven for 12 hours, checking the water temperature regularly; it should stay between 110° and 120°F. Remove from the oven and refrigerate. The yogurt will keep for up to 2 weeks in the refrigerator. If the whey separates, simply stir it back in.

CHALK TALK

PRE-PREGAME PICKUP SNACKS

Tony Reginelli, my high school football coach, used to give brilliant chalk talks after practice and before games. To say that Coach "Reg" had a way with words is a major understatement. He was master of malapropisms, once telling us to "simonize" our watches so we would arrive at the locker room on time. He was one of most inspiring people in my young life, and in spite of the occasional grammatical gaff, there was nothing I would not do to win his approval. Preparedness was a huge part of his discipline routine. Thinking ahead was key to victory. His chalk talks were about little else. Mental and physical preparedness were his alpha and omega.

Successful tailgating is a masterful blend of satisfying dishes and ones that are simple to consume. For the latter, think about things that are easy to graze on, pickup items that require nothing more than a cocktail napkin to wipe your hands with. Table space is at a premium at most tailgate gatherings, and one hand is usually busy, at least at the tailgates I attend, with a drink or a beer. So the less hassle, the better. In this chapter you'll find items that are super easy to put out and guaranteed to start the fueling process for a big game.

2

INDIAN-SPICED OYSTER CRACKER CHAAT

One of the widely believed origins of the word *chaat* is a Prakrit (an ancient Indian dialect derived from Sanskrit) word meaning "to consume with joy." Chaat is a snack, which is usually tangy, spicy, and crunchy. For this one, I have drawn inspiration from the very first bite of food I had in India, early on the morning I arrived on my first trip. I went to Gandhi's ashram in Ahmedabad, where an elderly gentleman was making a chickpea snack called *chana jor garam*. It was absolutely spectacular and remains one of best bites of food I have ever had. In this version, I substitute oyster crackers for the smashed, fried chickpeas I had in India. Serve it in a bowl and let folks grab some by the handful.

2 (9-ounce) bags oyster crackers

3 cups roasted and salted peanuts

3 cups roasted and salted cashew pieces

2 tablespoons chaat masala (see Note)

1 tablespoon garlic powder

½ teaspoon cayenne pepper

Salt and black pepper

¾ cup butter, melted

2½ cups finely diced red onion

2 cups finely diced Roma tomatoes

1½ cups chopped fresh cilantro

¾ cup thinly sliced serrano pepper

Grated zest and juice of 3 limes

1½ teaspoons garam masala

Preheat the oven to 300°F.

In a 2-gallon zip-top freezer bag, combine the oyster crackers, peanuts, cashews, chaat masala, garlic powder, cayenne, 2 teaspoons salt, 1 tablespoon black pepper, and the butter. Close the top of the bag and combine gently but thoroughly. Remove the mix from the bag and spread it out evenly and thinly on baking sheets. Bake for 20 minutes, stirring every 5 minutes. Remove from the oven and allow to cool on the sheets to room temperature. Set aside.

When ready to serve, transfer the cracker mix to a large bowl. Add the onion, tomatoes, cilantro, serrano pepper, lime zest and juice, and garam masala. Stir to blend well. Season with salt and black pepper. Serve immediately (the oyster crackers will lose their crunch!).

NOTE

► Chaat masala is available at any Indian specialty stores. *Masala* is the Indian word for "spice blend" (not a literal translation, but close enough). There are dozens of different blends for different applications, and each differs from cook to cook. Chaat masala typically has cumin, coriander, fennel, dried mint, chile pepper, salt, and powdered green mango or ginger as the base. Garam masala (available at most grocery stores) can be substituted, though I recommend the addition of mango powder or a touch of lime juice to give it a slightly more authentic chaat flavor.

PIMENTO CHEESE SAUSAGE BALLS

Blair Hobbs, doyenne of the Dutch oven, poet extraordinaire, and the yin to John T. Edge's yang, is entirely responsible for the popular resurgence of the lowly sausage ball. For twenty-five years she has appeared at almost every party we attended together with a brown paper bag filled with these, warm from the oven.

A decade or so ago, in search of relief from the deliciously agonizing nostalgia that Blair awakened in me, I developed this recipe for our tailgate take-out service in Oxford. Clearly they have had the exact same effect on all of our clients, as we make *thousands* of these little buggers for every home game weekend in the fall.

I personally recommend eating them with yellow mustard. They are like sausage-and-cheese biscuit bites. Friggin' perfect.

4¼ cups store-bought biscuit mix (like Bisquick, but I prefer Jim 'N Nick's Cheese Biscuit Mix, if you can find it), plus more as needed

1¼ pounds uncooked breakfast sausage

2 cups pimento cheese

¾ cup buttermilk, plus more as needed

3 tablespoons butter, melted

½ teaspoon cayenne pepper

1½ teaspoons salt

1 tablespoon black pepper

Yellow mustard for serving

Preheat the oven to 400°F. Line a baking sheet with parchment paper.

Combine the biscuit mix, sausage, pimento cheese, buttermilk, butter, cayenne, salt, and black pepper in the bowl of a stand mixer fitted with the paddle attachment and mix on low speed until well combined. The mix should be like a tacky biscuit dough. If it is dry, add a spot more buttermilk; if too wet, add more biscuit mix, a tablespoon at a time.

Scoop out the dough onto the prepared baking sheet with a 1-ounce ice cream scoop and bake for 20 minutes, or until golden brown. Serve hot with yellow mustard. Place these in a brown paper bag or disposable aluminum foil baking tray and transport them in an Igloo hot box (see page 5).

CUCUMBER "QUICK" PICKLES

My buddy Josh Quick, the chef at Odette in Florence, Alabama (stellar food and maybe the best whisky selection in the state), makes the most addictive pickles I have ever tasted. Josh will serve you a bowl with about three pounds of pickles in it, and four folks can mow through those fucking things in no time. They are ridiculous.

Josh is so generous that he has even shared his recipe with me. I have tinkered with it, tweaked it, pulled it all the way apart, reassembled it dozens of times, and concluded that his original recipe is the best. I can sit and eat a mess of these pickles; they're awfully damn good. This is my version of what Josh does perfectly, but I'll never be as happy as when I'm sitting on North Court Street eating his.

2 tablespoons crumbled bay leaves

1 tablespoon plus 1 teaspoon black peppercorns

1 tablespoon plus 1 teaspoon mustard seeds

2 teaspoons fennel seeds

¾ teaspoon cumin seeds

2 tablespoons red pepper flakes

1¼ tablespoons dried dill

¼ teaspoon celery seeds

1¼ tablespoons MSG, such as Accent

3½ cups white vinegar

1½ cups water

½ cup sugar

¼ cup plus 1 tablespoon salt

¼ cup minced garlic

5 pounds seedless English cucumbers, cut into spears or halves, if you like (this should yield the equivalent of 6 quarts of spears)

Combine the bay leaves, peppercorns, mustard seeds, fennel seeds, cumin seeds, red pepper flakes, dried dill, celery seeds, MSG, vinegar, water, sugar, salt, and garlic in a nonreactive saucepan and bring to a simmer over medium heat. Remove from the heat and allow to cool for 10 minutes. Place the cucumbers in a large plastic container and pour the warm pickling liquid over them. Allow to cool to room temperature. Divide the pickles, pickling liquid, and spices among three quart-size glass jars or cover and store them in the plastic container. They will be ready to eat in a couple of hours but need about 72 hours before they really shine. Store in the refrigerator for up to 3 months.

BAKED VEGETABLE SAMOSAS, SPICY RED BELL PEPPER AIOLI

The café in the Dekalb Farmers Market in Decatur, Georgia, is where I had my first samosa—and it's still maybe the best I have ever had. That market was the perfect place for a young, aspiring cook. It was the size of a Sam's Club. A full third of the floor space was given to fresh produce, 60 percent of which I could not begin to identify. Several thousand square feet were devoted to dried goods, canned goods, and noodles. One bakery continually put out fresh flatbreads from India, Mexico, Italy, and Ethiopia. There was a space where they ground coffee beans from every corner of the planet, and a wine and spirits section that occupied a full 30 percent of the floor space. But the real gem was the little café in the corner of the market, where they prepared dishes from all over the world. And those samosas, busting at the seams with potatoes, peas, turmeric, and cumin seeds, still haunt my dreams.

These require some dedication and zeal, but they are totally worth it. They were also the first thing I ever tasted with Sriracha. I recommend the combination highly.

Dough

1½ cups all-purpose flour

½ cup whole-wheat flour

½ teaspoon salt

½ cup yogurt

1½ teaspoons whole ajwain (also spelled ajowan) seeds, or ½ teaspoon ground cumin + ½ teaspoon ground thyme (see Notes on page 38)

¼ cup butter, melted

¼ cup water, plus more if needed

Filling

2 large yellow waxy potatoes

3 tablespoons canola oil

2 teaspoons mustard seeds

1½ teaspoons cumin seeds

3 curry leaves (see Notes, page 38)

1½ tablespoons minced garlic

1½ tablespoons minced fresh ginger

1 serrano pepper, sliced

¾ cup chopped red onion

1¼ cups green peas

½ teaspoon turmeric

¼ teaspoon cayenne pepper

2 teaspoons salt

2 teaspoons black pepper

Spicy Red Pepper Aioli

2 cups mayonnaise, preferably Duke's

1 tablespoon minced garlic

⅓ cup Harissa (page 103)

½ teaspoon salt

3 cups oil for frying

MAKE THE DOUGH In a medium bowl, blend the flours and salt together with a fork. Add the yogurt and ajwain seeds, stirring with the fork to blend. Add the butter, stirring until the dough begins to come together. Add water a tablespoon at a time until the dough comes together fully. Turn out onto a floured work surface and knead until the dough is smooth and elastic, about 4 to 5 minutes. Wrap in plastic and allow to rest at room temperature for 30 minutes.

continued

MAKE THE FILLING Place the potatoes in a small pot and cover with water. Bring to a boil, then turn down the heat to low. Simmer until the point of a knife pierces them easily, about 25 minutes. Drain and place the potatoes in a bowl of cold water to cool. Drain, pat dry, and peel the potatoes. Transfer to a bowl, mash briefly, and set aside. You want some lumps in your filling, so don't mash the potatoes until smooth.

In a large sauté pan, heat the canola oil over medium heat for 1 minute and add the mustard seeds, cumin seeds, and curry leaves. Sauté for 30 seconds. Stir in the garlic, ginger, and serrano pepper and cook for 2 minutes, stirring constantly. Stir in the red onion, peas, turmeric, and cayenne and sauté until the onion is transparent, about 5 minutes. Add the reserved potatoes, salt, and black pepper and continue to cook until the mix is warmed through. Remove from the heat and set aside.

MAKE THE AIOLI Stir together the mayonnaise, garlic, harissa, and salt in a glass bowl until well combined. Store aioli in a covered container in the refrigerator for up to 1 week.

Divide the dough into ten balls. Roll each one into a thin 6-inch disk and cut it in half. Pick up a half round of dough by the two corners of the cut side and, with your hands, shape the dough into a cone and seal the edge with a touch of water. Hold the cone in your hand like an ice cream cone and fill with some of the filling. Fold the top over and seal the top of the samosa with a touch of water. Repeat with the remaining dough and filling.

Heat 1½ inches of oil in a large skillet (cast iron, preferably) to 350°F. Fry the samosas in batches for 2 minutes per side, turning regularly, until golden brown all over. Serve hot with the aioli.

NOTES

► Ajwain seeds, also known as "bishop's weed," has an aroma and flavor of thyme and a hint of anisette. It can be found easily online and frequently at Whole Foods or any local health foods store.

► Curry leaves are kryptonite for mere mortals. They are the best-kept secret in the culinary world, and employing them in your cooking moves you a solid step closer to creating Indian food you can hang your hat on. Fresh is the only way to really use curry leaves. They can be found at Indian specialty stores. A little goes a long way, so if you procure a package, store the remainder in your freezer, where they keep perfectly. Dried are available and certainly serve a purpose, but dry leaves do not produce the same result as fresh when seasoning an oil.

OIL-POACHED TUNA, CAPER *and* ANCHOVY AIOLI

Canned tuna gets a bad rap, and for a good reason. We have no idea of its origin or quality, and it's boiled with no seasoning and packed in a low-grade oil or in water. That said, generations of moms and grandmoms have blended it with enough mayonnaise, boiled egg, and sweet pickle relish that the cat-food-for-human-consumption variety continues to thrive.

Here we are taking classic tuna salad and substituting quality ingredients and a slightly different process for making it. And while this recipe suggests simply flaking the tuna and serving it on crusty bread with a touch of mayo, you can certainly grab your mom's recipe, sub in this for canned tuna, and make the best freaking tuna sandwich you've ever dreamed of.

Tuna

3 pounds good-quality tuna (see Note)

1½ teaspoons salt

2 teaspoons black pepper

4 cups extra-virgin olive oil

10 bay leaves

3 shallots, thinly sliced

1½ tablespoons minced garlic

1 tablespoon red pepper flakes

12 sprigs fresh thyme

12 sprigs fresh tarragon

1 lemon, thinly sliced

Anchovy Aioli

2 cups mayonnaise, preferably Duke's

1½ tablespoons minced anchovy fillets

1 tablespoon minced garlic

4 tablespoons capers, chopped

Zest of 1 lemon, plus 2 teaspoons fresh lemon juice

2 teaspoons chopped fresh thyme leaves

Salt and black pepper

MAKE THE TUNA Cut the tuna into 2-inch cubes. Season with the salt and black pepper and refrigerate for at least 2 hours or, preferably, overnight.

Preheat the oven to 175°F.

In a Dutch oven, heat ¼ cup of the oil over high heat and, working in batches, sear tuna pieces on all sides. Remove the tuna from the pan and allow the pan to cool for 10 minutes. Place half of the bay leaves in the bottom of the pan and layer the tuna over them. Cover with the remaining oil and scatter the shallots, garlic, red pepper flakes, thyme, tarragon, lemon, and the remaining 2 bay leaves over the top of the tuna. Cover and place in the oven for 1½ hours. Remove and allow to cool for 20 minutes. Spoon the tuna into three clean quart-size mason jars. Top with the cooked vegetables and bay leaves and fill the jars with poaching oil. Cover with the lids and store refrigerated for up to 2 weeks.

MAKE THE AIOLI Stir together the mayonnaise, anchovies, garlic, capers, lemon zest and juice, and thyme in a medium bowl and allow to stand at room temperature for 30 minutes. Season to taste with salt, black pepper, and more lemon juice, as needed.

NOTE

▶ When buying tuna, choose deep red, clear meat trimmed of the grayish-black blood line. It should look like casino dice.

BEEF EMPANADAS, TRADITIONAL CHIMICHURRI

The Rio Grande Valley was once the Valhalla of dove shooting. I say "shooting" and not "hunting" for a reason, and that is because it was just *that* . . . plain old shooting. I refuse to misrepresent it by calling it "hunting," because it would have really only been challenging if you had to use a tennis racquet instead of a shotgun. By the late 1980s, however, the area had been over-hunted. The local authorities had gotten so bad about shaking down the outfitters, and rides had gotten so long from the lodges to fields where there were allegedly birds, that the destination lost its appeal.

Argentina became the next go-to for slaughtering doves. The facilities are nicer, the people are friendlier, and the food is insane! I have been going down there to shoot for over twenty-five years now, and I go as much for the food as anything else.

The first time beef empanadas with chimichurri crossed my lips, I was weak-kneed in love. These little packages of beefy goodness deliver an unimaginable punch of sweet-spicy-savory in the mouth. I could only eat these faster if I had a third arm. If you're looking for a shortcut, you can substitute frozen pie dough, thawed, for the pastry dough and still get a very nice end empanada.

Filling

2 tablespoons extra-virgin olive oil

1½ cups diced yellow onion

2 tablespoons minced garlic

1½ cups diced green bell pepper

2 pounds ground beef

2 teaspoons ground cumin

½ teaspoon cayenne pepper

2 teaspoons kosher salt

1 tablespoon black pepper

1 cup pitted green olives, chopped

¾ cup chopped raisins

½ cup chopped pimento

1 tablespoon honey

2 teaspoons hot sauce, preferably Crystal (Texas Pete or Frank's will be fine substitutes)

4 egg whites

Pastry Dough

1 cup unsalted butter, at room temperature

8 ounces cream cheese, at room temperature

½ cup heavy cream

3 cups plus 2 tablespoons all-purpose flour

1 teaspoon salt

Chimichurri

2 cups finely chopped fresh cilantro

1½ cups finely chopped fresh parsley

4½ tablespoons minced fresh oregano

½ cup minced shallot

3 tablespoons minced garlic

2 tablespoons red pepper flakes

1¾ cups extra-virgin olive oil

¾ cup red wine vinegar

Salt and black pepper

4 egg yolks

1 tablespoon milk

MAKE THE FILLING Heat the olive oil in a large sauté pan over medium heat until it begins to shimmer. Stir in onion, garlic, and bell pepper and sauté until the onion is transparent. Raise the heat to high and add the ground beef.

continued

Season with the cumin, cayenne, salt, and black pepper and cook, stirring constantly to break up the clumps of meat, until fully cooked.

Stir in the olives, raisins, pimento, honey, and hot sauce. Cook until the liquid has evaporated and the flavors have blended, about 5 to 7 minutes. Remove from the heat, cool to room temperature, and refrigerate. When completely cold, remove from the fridge and stir in the egg whites.

MAKE THE PASTRY DOUGH In a stand mixer fitted with the paddle attachment, beat the butter, cream cheese, and cream at low speed until thoroughly combined. Add the flour and salt and blend until just combined and the dough holds together. Turn out the dough onto a floured work surface and knead for 3 to 4 minutes, or until the dough is smooth and elastic. Divide into two pieces. Flatten into disks and wrap each in plastic wrap. Refrigerate for at least 30 minutes or, ideally, overnight. (If you refrigerate overnight, take the dough out 15 minutes before rolling to allow it to warm up slightly.)

Place one of the disks on a floured work surface. Roll out gently from the center of the dough to the top and bottom edges. Rotate the disk and roll to the top and bottom edges again. Reflour the work surface and the dough lightly, turn over the dough, and continue to roll from the center out to the edges. Turn over and roll out again, rotating the disk to ensure even rolling, until the dough is about ¼ inch thick. Using a large circular cutter or an overturned bowl, cut out 4-inch circles. Gather the dough scraps and continue rolling out and cutting. Repeat with the second disk of dough and set aside the rounds. This should make about 16 to 20 rounds total.

MAKE THE CHIMICHURRI Combine the cilantro, parsley, oregano, shallot, garlic, red pepper flakes, olive oil, and vinegar in a food processor and pulse until well blended. Season with salt and black pepper. Refrigerate, covered, in a plastic or glass container.

Preheat the oven to 375°F. Line a baking sheet with parchment paper.

Spread out all the dough circles on a floured work surface. In a small bowl, beat the egg yolks with the milk to make an egg wash. Place ¼ cup of filling on one side of a dough round. Brush the edges of the dough with the egg wash. Fold the dough over the filling to form a half-moon. Crimp the edges with a fork. Repeat until all of the dough rounds and filling have been used.

Place the empanadas on the prepared baking sheet and refrigerate for about 10 minutes. Prick each empanada on top twice with a fork. Brush some egg wash over each empanada. Bake for 20 to 25 minutes, until golden brown.

Serve the empanadas warm, drizzled with chimichurri. The empanadas can be frozen after they are formed; freeze on a baking sheet and remove to a zip-top bag for longer storage. To cook from frozen, preheat the oven to 275°F, remove them from the freezer, and place on a baking sheet lined with parchment paper. Place the empanadas in the oven for 20 minutes. Turn the heat up to 375°F and allow empanadas to cook about 20 more minutes, or until golden brown.

SPICY FRIED CHICKEN BUTTERED POPCORN

I often forget how satisfying popcorn can be. It's one of those foods that occupies a very specific place in my sensory memory, which I rarely visit unless I'm in a movie theater or a bank lobby on casual Friday. Popcorn seems to have an almost universal effect on people when they walk into a room and smell it, so it occurred to me that playing with some nontraditional versions would make for interesting tailgate offerings. With all the spice blends out there, the possibilities are endless. This spicy fried chicken version is crazy fun and surprising.

This is a stove-top method. The ratio of fat to popcorn kernels is going to seem insane, but trust me on this. I am a professional. You *do* need to be careful popping the corn this way as the fat can spatter and burn. Follow the instructions and you will be fine—and make the best popcorn ever.

NOTES

► Chicken base (or boullion) is available in grocery stores, but it is typically higher in sodium than chicken flavor. In a pinch, it will work, but it delivers a very salty product. Low-sodium powdered chicken base is available widely on the interwebs.

► When butter is clarified, its water and milk solids have been removed. Clarified butter has a much higher smoke point than whole butter, but it still needs to be treated with care so it doesn't burn. It is available at Indian markets, where it is called ghee, and at well-stocked supermarkets in the baking aisle. It is excellent for cooking fish, beef, and vegetables. See recipe on page 238.

1½ tablespoon low-salt powdered chicken base (see Notes)

1½ teaspoons MSG, such as Accent

1½ teaspoons nutritional yeast

1 teaspoon garlic powder

⅛ teaspoon cayenne pepper

1 tablespoon lard

½ cup plus 3 tablespoons clarified butter (see Notes)

½ cup popping corn

In a small bowl, use a fork to stir together the chicken base, MSG, nutritional yeast, garlic powder, and cayenne and set aside.

Combine the lard and clarified butter in a large saucepan with a lid. Pour in the popcorn kernels and turn the heat to medium-high. Cover the pot and heat the popcorn and fat for 2 minutes. Begin slowly swirling the pot, and as soon as you hear the first kernel pop, turn down the heat to low and start agitating the pot more aggressively. The corn will begin popping rapidly.

Crack the lid slightly to allow steam to escape, re-cover the pot, and continue shaking to keep the kernels and popped corn moving. The corn will pop quickly for about 30 to 45 seconds and then immediately slow down. Once the popping slows to one pop every 4 to 5 seconds, remove the pan from the heat. Crack open the top again to allow steam to escape and then dump the hot popcorn into a large bowl. Sprinkle with the dry seasonings and toss to coat evenly.

Serve immediately or cool completely, transfer to zip-top bags, seal, and store in the refrigerator. Popcorn will keep for 3 to 5 days.

MALAYSIAN BBQ-GLAZED TURKEY NECKS

Chefs are constantly on the hunt for the next inexpensive ingredient they can get the public hooked on. The cauliflower craze that has been sweeping the nation for the last five years is a testament. In 2012, we couldn't give it away. In 2019, we can't prepare it quickly enough.

The lowly turkey neck is one of those things that sits at the crossroads of Cheap Avenue and Potentially Delicious Boulevard. There is a surprising amount of meat on the neck, and when handled properly, it's nothing like your dad's overcooked, dry-ass, tough-as-shoe-leather Thanksgiving turkey, which likely haunts your holiday dreams.

These are a total crowd-pleaser and wonderfully surprising. I've seen homecoming queens and perfectly coiffed Junior League moms cover themselves in barbecue sauce eating these things. They really are that damn good.

Turkey Necks

12 turkey necks, each halved crosswise into 2 (4-inch) pieces

Salt and black pepper

2 cups all-purpose flour

½ teaspoon cayenne pepper

¾ teaspoon garlic powder

½ teaspoon onion powder

1 cup extra-virgin olive oil

1 medium yellow onion, quartered

6 garlic cloves, smashed

2 celery stalks, chopped

2 carrots, peeled and chopped

3 bay leaves

1 (2-inch) piece fresh ginger, peeled and chopped

1 tablespoon black peppercorns

½ tablespoon red pepper flakes

1 tablespoon fish sauce

¾ cup soy sauce

Malaysian Barbecue Sauce

1 cup apple cider vinegar

½ cup plus 1 tablespoon brown sugar

½ cup plus 1 tablespoon tomato paste

½ cup plus 1 tablespoon molasses

¼ cup minced ginger

3 tablespoons minced garlic

1 jalapeño pepper, minced

1 teaspoon salt

1 tablespoon black pepper

2 tablespoons red pepper flakes

3 tablespoons soy sauce

Grated zest and juice of 2 limes

½ cup minced shallots

1 teaspoon cayenne pepper

2 teaspoons finely ground coffee

½ cup orange juice

1½ teaspoons ground star anise

¾ teaspoon ground cinnamon

½ cup extra-virgin olive oil

1 tablespoon sesame oil

Salt

¼ cup toasted sesame seeds

¼ cup chopped fresh cilantro

MAKE THE TURKEY NECKS Season the turkey necks with salt and black pepper and refrigerate for 2 hours or overnight.

Preheat the oven to 325°F.

Remove the turkey necks from the refrigerator and pat dry. In a small bowl, use a fork to mix together the flour, cayenne, garlic powder, onion powder, 1 teaspoon salt, and 1½ teaspoons black pepper. Dust the necks with the flour mixture.

Heat ½ cup of the olive oil in a large Dutch oven over medium heat the until it begins to shimmer. In batches, brown the necks on both sides, transferring them to a plate when done. Set aside. In the same pot, heat the remaining ½ cup olive oil over medium heat until it begins to shimmer and stir in the onion, garlic, celery, and carrots and sauté until the onion begins to turn transparent. Return the turkey necks to the pan and cover with water and add the bay leaves, ginger, peppercorns, red pepper flakes, fish sauce, and soy sauce. Cover the Dutch oven and cook the necks in the oven for 3 hours, or until tender. Remove from the oven and allow the necks to cool in the pot to room temperature. Remove the necks and refrigerate until completely chilled. (If you like, strain the stock and skim the fat for a nice base for a soup. Or just eat the broth, as is.)

MAKE THE BARBECUE SAUCE Blend the vinegar, brown sugar, tomato paste, molasses, ginger, garlic, jalapeño, salt, black pepper, red pepper flakes, soy sauce, lime zest and juice, shallots, cayenne, coffee, orange juice, star anise, and cinnamon together in a nonreactive saucepan and bring to a simmer over medium heat. Cook, stirring, for 5 minutes. Remove from the heat and cool to room temperature. Store, covered, in a glass or plastic container in the refrigerator for up to 4 weeks.

Make a hot charcoal or wood fire.

In a large shallow bowl, stir together the extra-virgin olive oil and sesame oil. Toss the turkey necks in the oil, coating them well. Sprinkle with salt. Cook over a hot spot on the grill until the necks color nicely. Transfer to a large bowl, add 1 cup of the barbecue sauce, and toss. Put the necks on a tray or platter, sprinkle with sesame seeds and cilantro, and dig in!

CRAB-BOIL BOILED PEANUTS

Boiled peanuts are a religion. Just ask Matt and Ted Lee, aka the Lee Brothers; they've made a Low Country fortune in their ground nut missionary work over the last twenty years. The boiled peanut is, oddly, at the center of a hotly contested debate. They are considered sublime and iconic by some, while others revile them as slimy, disgusting nonsense. I contend those who identify with the latter group have either never eaten them or had unfortunate experiences at a gas station crock pot. A peanut boiled and seasoned properly is one of the most wonderful bites there is. For the record, once you dive in, if you don't have the salty brine running down your chin *and* forearms, you are doing it wrong.

2 pounds raw or green peanuts, preferably colossal size (see Notes)

½ cup salt

1 (3-ounce) bag Zatarain's crab boil

2 tablespoons Zatarain's liquid crab boil

2 tablespoons Tabasco sauce

1 lemon, thinly sliced

1 (2-inch) piece fresh ginger, peeled and chopped

Place the peanuts in a pressure cooker or Instant Pot and cover with water. Stir in the salt, dry and liquid crab boils, Tabasco, lemon, and ginger. Lock the lid in place. Cook in the pressure cooker over medium heat, or set the Instant Pot to Pressure Cook for 1½ hours and then allow the pressure to release naturally. Serve hot or drain the peanuts and store them in a large zip-top bag in the refrigerator for up to 10 days.

NOTES

▶ Green peanuts are freshly picked and, usually, slightly immature. They are still a little moist and cook more quickly than raw ones. The raw variety (usually easier to find) are picked later, and there is never any telling how long they have been around. They take significantly longer to cook but are still delicious.

▶ These can be cooked on the stove top, traditionally, but they usually take north of 3 to 4 hours to fully cook. If you do so, cook covered, simmering over low-medium heat. Keep your eye on the pot and add water as needed.

BECKY'S CHEESE PUFFS

These were a staple at Mom and Dad's cocktail parties when I was a kid. They are as simple as they come, but they make the house smell unbelievably good while they cook. It sounds like hyperbole, but I could eat these as fast as my mom and her friends would bake them. And, yes, I once ate enough of them to make myself sick.

For years I tried to re-create the recipe. In typical fashion, I overthought every single aspect of the process. I made spreads full of egg whites, herbs, mustards—nothing came out right. It wasn't until my mother passed and I became the keeper of four generations of my extended family's recipe card files that I stumbled on Mom's recipe for these and received a profound slap in the face. The recipe and ingredients could not be any simpler. My dad and I made these together on a cool night the spring after she passed. I followed her directions precisely. The smell that filled our house brought a swelling to my chest, and the first taste sent tears streaming down my cheeks, and my dad's, too.

One of the great things about these is that they can be assembled and frozen, then cooked later. I recommend making huge batches and always keeping these on hand.

Preheat oven to 300°F.

With a biscuit or cookie cutter, cut the bread into four 2-inch circles per slice. Or cut off the crusts and cut into squares, eliminating any waste. Brush the bread circles with melted butter and toast them in the oven until lightly crisped on the outside, but still soft on the inside, about 5 minutes. Remove from the oven and set aside.

Preheat the broiler.

In a medium bowl, use a hand mixer to beat the cream cheese until creamy. Add the mayonnaise, beating until well combined. With a wooden spoon, stir in the onion, garlic, Parmesan, cayenne, pepper, mustard powder, and chives and continue stirring until well combined. Spread the mix evenly across the tops of the toasts, covering them completely. Sprinkle with additional Parmesan and broil until puffy and lightly browned, about 3 to 4 minutes. You need to keep a vigilant eye on things in the broiler. Each broiler is different, and cooking time will depend both on temperature and how close to the heat source the cheese puffs are.

2 loaves white sandwich bread, preferably Wonder Bread

½ cup melted butter

8 ounces cream cheese, at room temperature

1 cup mayonnaise, preferably Blue Plate

2 tablespoons grated onion (see Note)

1 teaspoon minced garlic, mashed into a paste

½ cup grated Parmesan cheese, plus more as needed

⅛ teaspoon cayenne pepper

1 teaspoon mustard powder

2 tablespoons chopped fresh chives

NOTE

▶ Just trust me and grate your onion for this recipe on a box grater. My mom, grandmother, and great grandmother all grated onion for multiple recipes. Grating breaks down the onion fiber and releases the onion juice (which also used to be a prolific ingredient).

KOREAN BBQ WINGS

There is little better in this world than a late-night run out Buford Highway, on the outskirts of Atlanta, for Korean barbecue. About a twelve-mile stretch of this somewhat desolate highway boasts a litany of mom-and-pop ethnic restaurants. Though heavily Vietnamese and Thai, there is everything from Bangladeshi to Ethiopian to Mexican. It is amazing. And though I am certain that there are bad meals to be had, I have never experienced one.

The following recipe is one I wrote as a tribute to those late evening runs and the explosive flavors that are their reward. This is what I call a cheater's version of barbecue wings because they are cooked twice, once in the oven so they are nice and tender, and then again over a hot fire for color and caramelization. After you make this once, you can apply almost any sauce to the wings and you'll be just as happy.

5 pounds chicken wings, whole or wingettes and drumettes, rinsed and drained

Marinade

¼ cup plus 2 tablespoons gochujang (see Note)

3 tablespoons brown sugar

2 teaspoons good-quality fish sauce

¼ cup soy sauce

2 tablespoons sesame oil

2 tablespoons rice wine vinegar

3 tablespoons minced garlic

2 tablespoons minced ginger

2 tablespoons minced shallot

2 serrano peppers, seeded and chopped

2 teaspoons black pepper

2 tablespoons lime juice

¼ cup white wine

¼ cup honey

¼ cup water

2 tablespoons soy sauce

¼ cup mirin

½ teaspoon red pepper flakes

1 teaspoon cornstarch

¼ cup chopped cilantro or green onion for garnish

2 tablespoons toasted sesame seeds for garnish

MAKE THE MARINADE Combine the gochujang, brown sugar, fish sauce, soy sauce, sesame oil, vinegar, garlic, ginger, shallot, serrano peppers, black pepper, lime juice, and wine in a 2-gallon zipper-top freezer bag and massage to blend well. Add the wings, press out the air, and seal. Marinate in the refrigerator for at least 4 hours or preferably overnight.

Preheat the oven to 325°F. Line a baking sheet with parchment paper.

Remove the wings from the marinade, set aside the liquid, and reserve. Place the wings on the prepared baking sheet in a single layer. Roast for 35 minutes. Remove from the oven and set aside until ready to serve. If, by any chance the wings have not cooked fully at this point (there is very little chance they will not have, unless you purchased some sort of pterodactyl-size chicken wings), they will definitely finish cooking on the grill in the next step.

Prepare a hot charcoal or wood fire.

Pour the reserved marinade into a small sauce-pan and stir in the honey, water, soy sauce, mirin, red pepper flakes, and cornstarch. Bring to a boil, turn down the heat, and simmer until reduced by half. Remove from the heat and set aside.

Place the wings on the grill and cook, turning constantly, until hot and the edges are colored nicely, about 7 to 10 minutes, brushing the wings with sauce on each turn. Transfer to a large bowl and toss with the remaining sauce. Garnish with cilantro and sesame seeds and serve hot.

NOTE

▶ Gochujang is a Korean chile paste, thickened with cooked rice and soybean paste that is available in the Asian section of most grocery stores.

SWEET-SPICY ROSEMARY PECANS

We first made these for a tailgating client as a little lagniappe. They had been extremely good to us, and we wanted to shoot them a little something to say thank-you. They loved them so much that they started ordering about ten pounds every weekend. The pecans quickly made it into the rotation on our tailgate menu, where they are a favorite. We make hundreds of pounds of them for our Christmas baskets.

The key is adding the rosemary after the pecans come out of the oven for the second time, so the rosemary releases its oil but isn't cooked. These can be blamed for the significant "shrinkage" of most of the clothing in my closet.

3 pounds pecan halves

½ cup butter, melted

2 tablespoons sugar

2 teaspoons salt

½ teaspoon cayenne pepper

1 tablespoon Worcestershire sauce

¼ cup chopped fresh rosemary

Preheat the oven to 350°F. Line a baking sheet with parchment pepper.

Spread out the pecans on the baking sheet and toast for 7 minutes, or until fragrant. Remove from the oven but do not turn it off. Pour the pecans into a large bowl, add the butter, sugar, salt, cayenne, and Worcestershire and toss to blend thoroughly. Return the nuts to the baking sheet, spreading them out evenly. Toast for an additional 7 minutes. Remove from the oven, return to the bowl, and toss with the chopped rosemary. These are never better than when straight out of the oven but are perfectly acceptable, if not insanely delicious, at room temperature.

GREEN ONION *and* COUNTRY HAM HUSH PUPPIES, PINEAPPLE-RUM BARBECUE SAUCE

Hush puppies are oft glossed over as a simple and unappreciated member of the "sides" collection. In reality, a good hush puppy is frequently very hard to find. The right balance of flour and cornmeal is critical so the crumb is right and it is more a "hush puppy" than a "fritter." A fritter is eggier and more chewy than a hush puppy; hush puppies are crispy on the outside and cakey on the inside. And they can be transcendent with chopped ham, green onions, smoked shrimp, or crawfish tails added. While they transport nicely, they are never better than eaten as soon as they have cooled enough to pop right into your mouth.

Pineapple-Rum Barbecue Sauce

1½ cups ketchup

½ cup tomato paste

2 cups chopped fresh pineapple

¼ cup plus 2 tablespoons brown sugar

½ cup water

¼ cup plus 2 tablespoons apple cider vinegar

¼ cup dark rum

¼ cup strong brewed coffee

¼ cup minced yellow onion

2 tablespoons minced garlic

1½ tablespoons Worcestershire sauce

2 teaspoons liquid smoke

⅛ teaspoon cayenne pepper

1 tablespoon black pepper

½ teaspoon salt

1 tablespoon cornstarch

Hush Puppies

1½ quarts vegetable oil, peanut oil, or lard (or a blend of any or all of these)

⅓ cup self-rising flour, preferably White Lily

3½ cups yellow cornmeal

2 tablespoons baking powder

1½ teaspoons salt

2 teaspoons sugar

½ teaspoon baking soda

2 eggs

1½ cups buttermilk

¾ cup green onion, chopped

1¼ cups cheddar cheese

1 cup minced country ham

2 teaspoons black pepper

MAKE THE BARBECUE SAUCE Combine the ketchup, tomato paste, pineapple, brown sugar, water, vinegar, rum, coffee, onion, garlic, Worcestershire, liquid smoke, cayenne, black pepper, salt, and cornstarch in a medium saucepan and bring to a simmer over medium heat. Cook, stirring constantly, for 20 minutes. Transfer the sauce to a blender and puree on high speed until extremely smooth. Add a touch more water if the sauce is too thick.

MAKE THE HUSH PUPPIES In a large Dutch oven, heat the oil to 350°F.

With a whisk or fork, blend together the flour, cornmeal, baking powder, salt, sugar, and baking soda in a large bowl. Set aside. In a second bowl, whisk together the eggs and buttermilk. Blend the buttermilk mix into the cornmeal mix, stirring until well combined. Stir in the green onion, cheddar, ham, and black pepper. The batter should be like a very thick pancake batter.

Using a 1-ounce ice cream scoop, drop the batter into the oil and fry until golden and crispy, about 3 to 4 minutes. Serve piping hot with the pineapple-rum barbecue sauce. These can be fried at the last minute, transported in an Igloo hot box, and held warm for 30 to 45 minutes (see page 5). Fortunately, hush puppies are one of the very few fried things still good after they have cooled.

CHILE-ROASTED MIXED NUT CHEX "MEX"

Like so many other things in my life, Chex Mix was a love-at-first-bite experience. The familiarity of that crunchy corn flavor colliding with the explosive tanginess of concentrated Worcestershire was epic for my four-year-old taste buds. I have totally chased that combination of acid, fat, sweet, and sour since that moment and have never quite arrived.

I have used Wheat Chex as a delivery vehicle for loads of different flavors. This is one of my favorites. If you have lots of beer you need to get rid of, I recommend making a batch of this and inviting the crew over. You can use whatever combination of your favorite Chex cereals you like. Start munching, and that beer will be gone in no time.

1 cup pecan halves

1 cup roasted and salted peanuts

1 cup roasted and salted cashews

½ cup plus 5 tablespoons butter, melted

2 teaspoons sugar

Salt

1½ teaspoons black pepper

1½ teaspoons paprika

¾ teaspoon chili powder

½ teaspoon cayenne pepper

4 cups Corn Chex

3 cups Rice Chex

2 cups Wheat Chex

1½ cups oyster crackers

2½ tablespoons Worcestershire sauce

1 teaspoon Tabasco sauce

1 teaspoon garlic powder

1 tablespoon dried parsley

Preheat the oven to 300°F.

Spread out the nuts on a baking sheet in one layer. Toast for 15 minutes, stirring once. Remove from the oven and pour into a medium bowl. Toss with 6 tablespoons of the butter, the sugar, 1 teaspoon salt, the black pepper, paprika, chili powder, and cayenne until well combined. Spread out the nuts on the baking sheet again and toast for 5 another minutes. Remove from the oven and set aside. Leave the oven on.

Combine the Chex cereals in a large freezer bag and add the oyster crackers. In a medium bowl, stir together the remaining 7 tablespoons of butter, the Worcestershire, Tabasco, garlic powder, parsley, and 1 teaspoon salt. Pour over the Chex Mix, seal the bag, and toss gently until well combined. Spread out the mix on another baking sheet and toast in the oven for 40 minutes, stirring every 10 minutes, until the mix is dry and toasty. Remove from the oven and cool briefly.

In a large bowl, stir together the Chex mix and nuts and serve. Store the leftovers in zip-top bags at room temperature for up to 10 days.

VIETNAMESE VEGGIE SPRING ROLLS, SWEET DIPPING SAUCE

Rice paper rolls exploding with fresh, raw vegetables are arguably the best item there is for a hot-weather tailgate (other than something out of an ice chest and full of booze—let's be straight with one another). These are light and fresh and do not load you down. The filling, spiked playfully with mint and cilantro, tastes great with the flavorful, acidic dipping sauce.

The rolls are stable, with nothing other than fresh vegetables and a little dressing rolled inside. The skins can get a little tacky, so leave space between them and layer with plastic wrap.

I can eat these until my stomach explodes.

Rolls

1½ cups thinly sliced green cabbage

1½ cups thinly sliced red cabbage

1½ cups julienned carrot

1½ cups julienned green onion

1½ cups julienned yellow bell pepper

1½ cups julienned cucumber

¾ cup julienned radishes

¾ cup fresh mint leaves

¾ cup fresh cilantro leaves

2 teaspoons sesame oil

Grated zest and juice of 1 lime

1 tablespoon rice wine vinegar

1½ teaspoons sugar

1 teaspoon salt

1½ teaspoons fish sauce

20 rice paper spring roll wraps

Dipping Sauce (Nuoc Cham)

½ cup warm water

¼ cup sugar

Grated zest and juice of 5 limes

2½ tablespoons rice wine vinegar

2 tablespoons fish sauce

2 serrano peppers, thinly sliced

1 shallot, minced

1 tablespoon minced garlic

2 teaspoons red pepper flakes

MAKE THE ROLLS In a large bowl, stir together both cabbages, the carrot, green onion, bell pepper, cucumber, radishes, mint, and cilantro. Set aside. In a small bowl, whisk together the sesame oil, lime zest and juice, rice wine vinegar, sugar, salt, and fish sauce. Pour over the vegetables and blend well.

Pour 1 to 2 inches of room-temperature water into a wide shallow bowl or a baking pan. Soak a rice paper wrap in the water for 10 to 12 seconds, or until it is completely pliable. (If they are over-soaked they become a challenge to work with and tear very easily.) Remove and lay it out flat on a work surface. Lay ½ cup of the dressed vegetable mix across the center of the wrap. Bring the bottom up and over the vegetable mix and pull back to make a tight cylinder. Fold the sides over toward the center and roll up the spring roll. Place it on a tray or platter and cover with plastic wrap. Repeat with the remaining wraps and filling, separating the layers of spring rolls on the tray with plastic wrap. Cover with plastic and refrigerate.

MAKE THE DIPPING SAUCE In a medium bowl, whisk together the warm water and sugar, stirring until the sugar is completely dissolved. Add the lime zest and juice, rice wine vinegar, fish sauce, serrano peppers, shallot, garlic, and red pepper flakes, stirring to blend completely. Taste and make any adjustments to balance the sweet, salty, and spicy flavors to your personal taste.

To serve, cut the rolls in half crosswise and serve with the sauce (in a separate bowl) on the side.

ALABAMA FIRECRACKERS *and* FRIED CHICKEN SALAD

It only makes sense that chicken salad made with fried chicken would be better than chicken salad made with boiled, baked, grilled, or roasted chicken. Because fried chicken kicks the crap out of any other kind of chicken, right? If you don't agree, well, I don't give a damn, because I happen to be right, and this is one of those instances that is entirely unequivocal, so that is that. Let's move on. . . .

If you've never had Alabama firecrackers, and, having made these, you want to erect a statue of me as a token of thanks, I completely understand. These are one of the best little snack items there is, and you will likely keep them around the house forever, like I do. Tip: You will need 2-gallon freezer bags to make these.

Alabama Firecrackers

¼ cup olive oil

¼ cup extra-virgin olive oil (see Note)

1½ teaspoons garlic powder

1 teaspoon onion powder

1 teaspoon MSG, such as Accent

1 teaspoon cayenne pepper

2 tablespoons red pepper flakes

1 tablespoon lemon pepper

2 (1-ounce) packages buttermilk ranch dressing powder

1 (1-pound) box saltine-like (aka soda) crackers

Fried Chicken Salad

1½ cups mayonnaise, preferably Blue Plate

½ cup buttermilk

2 tablespoons hot sauce, preferably Crystal

1 cup minced celery

¾ cup grated sweet yellow onion

1 tablespoon red pepper flakes

2½ teaspoons salt

1½ tablespoons black pepper

7 cups finely diced leftover fried chicken, including the skin and fried bits

MAKE THE FIRECRACKERS In a 2-gallon freezer bag, combine the olive oils, garlic powder, onion powder, MSG, cayenne, red pepper flakes, lemon pepper, and ranch dressing powder. Seal the top and shake gently but thoroughly to combine well. Add the crackers and mix until the crackers are evenly dressed. Allow the bag to sit in the refrigerator overnight before finishing the crackers.

Preheat oven to 275°F. Line 2 baking sheets with parchment paper.

Remove the crackers from the bag and lay them out in a single layer on the prepared sheets. Bake for 20 minutes, or until golden and fragrant. Store, refrigerated, in zip-top bags for up to 3 weeks.

MAKE THE CHICKEN SALAD In a large bowl, combine the mayonnaise, buttermilk, hot sauce, celery, onion, red pepper flakes, salt, and black pepper, stirring to blend well. Add the in chicken and stir until fully coated. Refrigerate overnight. Serve cold with the Alabama firecrackers.

NOTES

▶ If you have chile oil, substitute 1 or 2 tablespoons for the extra-virgin olive oil for more spice.

▶ Vish totally stole this recipe and put it to work on the Snackbar menu. So if you had them there and are still talking about them, now you know the provenance. Screw you, Vish!

CHARGRILLED OYSTERS, NEW ORLEANS—STYLE REMOULADE

I love that it is my Hawaiian buddy, Billy Thompson (ex–line cook extraordinaire and one of the funniest sons of a bitch to ever walk the planet), who took my dumb ass out to Drago's in Fat City (the '70s disco district in New Orleans) for the very first time, twenty-some years ago. Until that day, I was blithely unaware that the Cvitanovich family had taken up some kind of oyster voodoo and started doing the original charbroiled oyster. I don't know anyone in the '90s who had their first one out on Severn Avenue that was not just as kicked in the nuts as I was.

We spent a long time overthinking how to re-create these before we finally pulled the throttle back and went simple. And it worked. The product is not a Drago's oyster, but a very decent facsimile. The key here is to make a superhot fire and cook the oysters close to it. You want the cheese to melt, but not at the expense of the oyster's integrity. They should be nice and warm, but not cooked until shriveled.

Thanks, Tommy. Love your work.

Remoulade

1½ cups mayonnaise

¼ cup fresh lemon juice

¾ cup chopped yellow onion

½ cup chopped green onions

½ cup chopped celery

3 tablespoons chopped garlic

¼ cup plus 3 tablespoons ketchup

¼ cup plus 2 tablespoons yellow mustard

¼ cup Creole mustard

¼ cup prepared horseradish

¼ cup plus 2 tablespoons chopped fresh parsley

2 teaspoons salt

1½ teaspoons Creole Seasoning (page 236)

1½ teaspoons black pepper

Oysters

2½ cups butter

¼ cup plus 2 tablespoons chopped fresh garlic

1 tablespoon lemon pepper

1½ teaspoons freshly ground black pepper

2 teaspoons salt

1½ cups freshly grated Parmesan cheese

1½ cups grated Pecorino Romano cheese

½ cup chopped fresh parsley

3 tablespoons fresh thyme leaves

30 freshly shucked oysters (muscle severed from shell)

MAKE THE REMOULADE Combine the mayonnaise, lemon juice, both onions, celery, garlic, ketchup, both mustards, horseradish, parsley, salt, Creole seasoning, and black pepper in the bowl of a food processor and process for 30 seconds. It should be well combined but slightly chunky. Transfer to a bowl and set aside.

MAKE THE OYSTERS In a medium saucepan over low heat, melt the butter with the garlic, lemon pepper, black pepper, and salt. Remove from the heat as soon as the butter melts.

In a medium bowl, combine both cheeses, the parsley, and thyme and set aside. Spoon the butter mix over the oysters, stirring the mix each time so you get some garlic and pepper in each spoonful. Place the oysters in the cooler for at least 15 minutes so the butter congeals.

Prepare a hot charcoal or wood fire.

Sprinkle the oysters liberally with the cheese mix and place on the grill. Cook until the butter melts and begins to bubble around the edges. Sprinkle with some cheese again and pull off the fire as soon as the cheese melts. Serve with a touch of remoulade.

WRAPPIN' IT UP *and* MOVIN' *the* STICKS

WRAPS *and* STICKS, GET IT?

Ben Stiller, one of the contemporary masters of theater and screen, famously declared in *There's Something About Mary*, "I say they should put more meats on a stick, you know? They got a lot of sweets on sticks—Popsicles, Fudgsicles, lollipops—but hardly any meat." Few truer or more profound things have ever been uttered. Everyone (at least everyone I want to spend any time with) loves meat on a stick. And while we are at it, most folks love a wrap. Lettuce, pita, tortilla, lavash, nori. There is something empowering about managing to put an entire meal in a package and hold it one hand.

One of the most shocking food moments I had on a trip to Israel was stopping at a roadside falafel stand, thinking that there was no choice except falafel, but when I entered the shop there were actually two choices: falafel and pita, and schnitzel and pita. I have nothing against schnitzel, mind you. It was just that I could think of nothing more German, and that juxtaposition confused the shit out of me. I was even more perplexed to learn from my buddy Michael Solomonov that, in Israel, schnitzel in pita is not an anomaly and, in fact, is about as common as it gets. That said, I dove headfirst into a pita wrap stuffed with fried chicken, hummus, onion, lettuce, cucumber, and carrots. I was hooked.

A year later, at a late-night market in Penang, Malaysia, some super-spicy grilled chicken was stripped off a skewer and into a freshly cooked roti, wrapped up with lentils and yellow onion, and placed in my hand. And it dawned on me that it didn't make sense to eat anything else but these foods ever again. I adore being "in touch" with my food. There is something holistic, organic, honest, and fun about eating with your hands, something I have always embraced but was raised to believe was wrong. What you will find in the next few pages is validation and celebration for those of you who appreciate things compact, simple, and direct.

So, Stiller was right: they should put more meats on sticks. But what they really need to do is, yes, make more of them, and then take them off that stick and roll them up into something delicious. That's all I have to say about that.

INDIAN-SPICED SHRIMP SKEWERS, HARISSA

Weaving through the pitch black and deadly silent streets of the old city in Ahmedabad, India, I found it hard to imagine that I was in one of the larger cities in the country, at around six million people. The blistering heat and bustle of the day had given in to a cool evening and empty streets. A sudden turn down an impossibly tight alley and a second turn onto another shop-lined street revealed a market lit only by the fires of street vendors and naan ovens, and the occasional string bulb. A cacophony of smells assaulted me, and I tumbled deliriously into an orgy of meats, vegetables, and flatbreads pouring forth from the forty or so stalls that make up this little market. That moment is burned into my brain, and this dish is the expression of that experience, rolled up into a ball.

These shrimp are just dy-no-mite! If you like spice, turn up the cayenne or add some of your favorite hot sauce. For God's sake, please don't overcook the shrimp, and don't hold back on the lime wedges when you serve.

In a large bowl, stir together the yogurt, ½ cup of the cilantro, the lime zest and juice, shallots, ginger, garlic, cumin, turmeric, garam masala, cayenne, and black pepper. Add the shrimp, stirring to coat well. Marinate in the refrigerator for 2 to 4 hours.

Prepare a hot wood or charcoal fire. Remove the shrimp from the marinade and divide and thread them evenly onto twelve bamboo skewers.

Once the fire has burned down, cook the shrimp until they just begin to color on one side. Flip the skewers and cook for an additional 4 to 5 minutes, or until the shrimp are firm to the touch and opaque. Serve hot, straight off the grill, garnished with the remaining ¼ cup chopped cilantro and with the lime wedges and harissa.

NOTE

Stonefire brand (widely available in stores across the country) is an excellent substitute for fresh or homemade naan.

1½ cups Greek yogurt

¾ cup chopped cilantro

Grated zest and juice of 2 limes, plus 3 limes, cut into wedges for serving

¼ cup minced shallots

¼ cup minced ginger

2 tablespoons minced garlic

1 tablespoon ground cumin

2 teaspoons turmeric

2 teaspoons garam masala

1 teaspoon cayenne pepper

1 tablespoon black pepper

4 pounds extra-jumbo fresh shrimp, peeled, with tails on

Butterhead lettuce leaves or toasted naan (see Note) for serving

Harissa (page 103)

THAI-SPICED CHICKEN SKEWERS, PEANUT DIPPING SAUCE

Complete transparency here: I have never been to Thailand. This is a shameless appropriation based on American versions of Thai food I have had and food by friends of Thai ancestry. If I admit I am an asshole, may I please avoid further criticism?

I first had this dish about thirty years ago and developed a recipe for it soon after we opened City Grocery. Chicken dries out easily, so try to flash grill these right before serving. They only take a few minutes to cook and are best straight off the fire.

MAKE THE SAUCE Heat the olive oil in a medium saucepan over medium heat and sauté the garlic and shallots until the shallots are transparent. Whisk in the veal stock, peanut butter, hoisin, eel sauce, tomato paste, Sriracha, and sesame oil. Bring to a boil, turn down the heat to low, and simmer for 5 minutes. Remove from the heat and allow to cool to room temperature. Season to taste with salt and white pepper. Reserve.

PREPARE THE CHICKEN Skewer the tenders, 2 per bamboo skewer, season with salt and pepper, and place in a baking dish. Blend the olive oil, sesame oil, garlic, green onion, ginger, lemongrass, fish sauce, lime zest and juice, soy sauce, rice wine vinegar, brown sugar, turmeric, red pepper flakes, and 1 teaspoon salt in a medium bowl and pour over the chicken. Allow the chicken to marinate for at least 2 hours or overnight. Turn the skewers from time to time so they all spend some time soaking in the marinade.

Prepare a hot charcoal or wood fire. When the fire burns down, place the chicken skewers on the hot grill and cook for 4 minutes, then flip and cook for an additional 3 to 4 minutes, or until the tenders are firm to the touch. Serve hot off the grill with peanut sauce for dipping.

Peanut Sauce

2 tablespoons olive oil

3 tablespoons minced garlic

2 shallots, diced

2 cups veal stock

1¼ cups smooth natural peanut butter

½ cup hoisin sauce (see page 65)

¼ cup eel sauce (see Note)

3 tablespoons tomato paste

2 tablespoons Sriracha

1 tablespoon sesame oil

Salt and white pepper

Chicken

3 pounds boneless, skinless chicken breast tenders, preferably organic and hormone-free

Salt and black pepper

½ cup olive oil

2 tablespoons sesame oil

2 tablespoons minced garlic

¼ cup minced green onion, white and light green parts only

3 tablespoons minced ginger

¾ cup minced lemongrass, tender white part of the stalk only

3 tablespoons fish sauce

Zest and juice of 3 limes

3 tablespoons soy sauce

¼ cup rice wine vinegar

½ cup brown sugar

1½ teaspoons turmeric

½ teaspoon red pepper flakes

NOTES

► Eel sauce, which is called unagi sauce in Japan, is a thickened, sweetened soy sauce. It is wonderful on all kinds of grilled meats and fish. It is available in Asian markets and specialty food stores.

► These are also nice as lettuce wraps.

ASIAN DUCK MEATBALL LETTUCE WRAPS, TANGY HOISIN

In 2011, my mom, my wife, and my publicist, all extraordinarily persuasive women, equally capable of applying different varieties of the same Pacific Ocean–floor pressure, ganged up on me and coerced me into accepting an invitation to participate in what would be the final season of *Top Chef Masters*. (As an aside, I am not convinced that my performance had anything to do with that.)

I get extraordinarily anxious before events, so rolling out onto the set for a surprise challenge against twelve chefs who were all, to a person, better than I'll ever dream of being, had me doubled over a trash can immediately before set call. When we hit the set, we were met by Kelis, of "My Milkshake Brings All the Boys to the Yard" fame, who challenged us to make meatballs with a hand grinder. I was assigned chicken and made a concoction similar to this recipe. I took home the prize for the day, and while I remained anxious for the rest of my time on the show, I did manage to retain my "cookies," much to the delight of whoever had to handle the trash on set, I am sure.

Hoisin sauce has been one of my favorite flavor vehicles since the first time I tasted it on Peking duck at the Edinburgh Rendezvous in the city of the same name in the early 1970s. Store-bought versions are mostly pathetic attempts, so I recommend taking the few minutes to throw this together. You'll be glad you did.

Meatballs

4 (1-pound) duck breasts, with skin, or 2 breasts plus 2 leg quarters

2 teaspoons brown sugar

2½ teaspoons salt

1 cup chopped green onion, green and white parts

¼ cup minced ginger

3 tablespoons minced garlic

2 whole eggs, plus 2 egg yolks

1 tablespoon sesame oil

2½ cups panko bread crumbs or unseasoned regular bread crumbs

Hoisin Sauce

½ cup soy sauce

¼ cup eel sauce (see Note on page 64)

½ cup smooth natural peanut butter

½ cup honey

7 tablespoons brown sugar

3 tablespoons rice wine vinegar

2½ tablespoons garlic paste

1 tablespoon Sriracha

1½ teaspoons red miso paste

½ teaspoon five spice powder

Butter lettuce cups

Chopped green onions or cilantro

Sliced serrano peppers

Toasted sesame seeds

MAKE THE MEATBALLS Cut the duck breasts, with the skin still on, into 1-inch cubes and refrigerate. Grind through a countertop meat grinder, on the largest die holes you have, into the bowl of a stand mixer and chill again for 30 minutes. Place the bowl in the mixer, fitted with the paddle attachment, and beat for 1 minute on medium speed, until it begins to look smooth. Do not beat too much. Add the brown sugar, salt, green onion, ginger, and garlic, beating to combine well. Add the eggs and egg yolks, sesame oil, and panko and beat again until well

continued

blended. Refrigerate the mix for 30 minutes. Remove and divide into 3-ounce portions and form each into a cylinder, the diameter of a hot dog, but only two-thirds as long. Thread onto skewers, if you are going to cook over an open fire, and refrigerate until ready to cook.

MAKE THE HOISIN SAUCE Combine the soy sauce, eel sauce, peanut butter, honey, brown sugar, rice wine vinegar, garlic paste, Sriracha, miso, and five-spice powder in a high-sided container and stir together until blended. Blend with an immersion blender until uniform and smooth. (Store leftover hoisin sauce, covered, in the refrigerator for up to 2 weeks.)

Prepare a hot charcoal or wood fire. When the coals have burned down and you are ready to cook, place the meat on the hottest part of the fire and cook on three sides, 3 to 4 minutes per side, until the meatballs are firm to the touch. Remove from fire. Serve warm with the hoisin sauce, butter lettuce cups, green onion, serrano peppers, and toasted sesame seeds.

CARAMELIZED ONIONS *and* SOY-BRAISED PORK LETTUCE WRAPS

Fifteen years later, I still cannot find the words to describe the degree or range of emotions I felt in the tumult of watching my hometown engulfed in the floodwaters that resulted from levee failure following Hurricane Katrina. The aftermath brought little in the way of joy for most of us from New Orleans. We struggled. We drank. We tried to imagine what New Orleans would look like if we ever made it back. Our victories were tiny, and hope flickered from time-to-time, mostly in good deeds done. For me, however, those sad, dark weeks accidently brought me together with the amazing woman who would ultimately become my wife and the mother of our beautiful daughter. She, Bess, was living in New York at the time. A chance email, sent on the day the storm slammed into New Orleans and changed everyone's life in an instant, started a conversation that begat a relationship. Our commuter courtship resulted in both my first trips to the newly opened Momofuku Noodle Bar and, later, Ssäm Bar, and a new friendship with a young David Chang.

The now legendary dish bo ssäm, a mammoth, crusty, soy-roasted pork butt served with various Korean accoutrements, was still but a glimmer in Dave's eyes when we first met, but I remember everything about my first bite when he finally got around to it and opened Momofuku. It was explosive, wild, and wonderful and struck so close to home for me. It was the essence of comfort food. It was playful while being entirely thoughtful, and it told a significant story about where Chang had come from.

This version is a cross between Dave's bo ssäm, which we have cooked together a couple of times, and a dish my dear friend Lolis Elie, columnist for the New Orleans *Times-Picayune* and writer on the HBO series *Treme*, shared with me in those months after Katrina. It is a total crowd-pleaser, ringing the chords of umami perfectly. It is sweet, sour, tart, and tasty simultaneously. What's more, it's super simple to throw together.

1 (3½- to 4-pound) boneless pork butt, cut into 4 equal chunks

¾ cup plus 2 tablespoons granulated sugar

¾ cup brown sugar

Salt

½ cup olive oil

⅓ cup butter

3 medium yellow onions, thinly sliced root to stem

3 cups pineapple juice

1 cup orange juice

1 cup beef stock

½ cup soy sauce

6 serrano peppers, thinly sliced (optional)

½ cup chopped fresh ginger

1 tablespoon cumin seeds

36 to 40 butter lettuce leaves

1 cup sambal (see Note)

3 shallots, thinly sliced

¼ cup toasted sesame seeds

5 limes, cut into wedges

Place the pork in a 1-gallon zip-top freezer bag with ¾ cup of the granulated sugar, ½ cup of the brown sugar, and ½ cup salt. Toss to coat well and refrigerate for 4 hours or, preferably, overnight.

Heat the oil in a large pressure cooker over high heat until the oil shimmers. Remove the pork from freezer bag, brush off any sugar/salt still on the surface of the butt, and pat it dry with paper towels. Sear on all sides, one or two chunks at a time. Remove the meat from the pot and set aside. Turn down the heat to medium.

Melt the butter in the pressure cooker and stir in the onions and the remaining 2 tablespoons granulated sugar. Cook, stirring, until the onions begin to wilt. Continue cooking and stirring for 10 to 12 minutes, or until the onions begin to change color. As the bottom of the pot begins to dry out, add 1 to 2 tablespoons water and cook, stirring. When the pan dries out again, add a little more water. Continue in this way until the onions turn amber, but not dark brown.

Return the pork to the pot and add the pineapple juice, orange juice, stock, soy sauce, serrano peppers, ginger, and cumin seeds. Lock the lid in place and cook over medium heat. When the pot begins to hiss, turn down the heat to low and cook for 1 hour. Remove from the heat and allow the pressure to release naturally. Shred the pork with a fork and set aside.

Strain the cooking liquid into a small saucepan and stir in the remaining ¼ cup brown sugar. Bring to a simmer and cook over low heat until reduced by half. Skim off the fat and season with salt.

Serve the pork in a bowl with the sauce, butter lettuce, sambal, shallots, sesame seeds, and lime wedges alongside.

NOTE

► Sambal is an Indonesian chile paste that is available in many well-stocked local grocery stores across the United States (including in Oxford, Mississippi). It is a great base for sauces, vinaigrettes, and some pasta dishes. It *is* spicy, let there be no doubt. Taste a little and gauge your tolerance.

TURKEY *and* HAM "COBB" WRAP

I love that there has been a resurgence of interest in Cobb salad. It was such a part of my childhood landscape (much like the wedge), and it is so deliciously appealing and satisfying. It's also simple, a dish that is truly no better than the sum of its parts. If anything in the salad is not spot on, it stands out, almost freakishly so.

These make great and superlight pickup items. The vinaigrette adds a nice acidic layer to the flavors, and the aioli brings a slight richness.

Basil Aioli

1½ cups mayonnaise, preferably Duke's

¾ cup chopped fresh basil

Grated zest and juice of 1 lemon

2 teaspoons minced garlic

Salt (optional)

Red Wine Vinaigrette

¼ cup olive oil

¼ cup extra-virgin olive oil

¼ cup plus 2 tablespoons red wine vinegar

1½ teaspoons Dijon mustard

1 teaspoon minced shallot

½ teaspoon minced garlic

4 cups arugula

4 cups thinly sliced romaine lettuce

¼ teaspoon salt

¾ teaspoon freshly ground black pepper

2 ripe avocados

2 tablespoons fresh lime juice

10 (10-inch) flour tortillas

1¼ pounds sliced smoked turkey, cut into thin strips

1¼ pounds sliced honey smoked ham, cut into thin strips

2 ripe medium tomatoes, thinly sliced

6 hard-boiled eggs, coarsely chopped

2 cups chopped crispy cooked bacon (10 to 12 strips)

½ cup chopped fresh chives

2 cups crumbled blue cheese

MAKE THE AIOLI Combine the mayonnaise, basil, lemon zest and juice, and garlic in a deep bowl and blend with an immersion blender until smooth and uniformly green. Allow to sit for 30 minutes. Taste and season lightly with salt, if needed.

MAKE THE VINAIGRETTE Whisk together both oils, the vinegar, mustard, shallot, and garlic in a small bowl until well combined.

Place the arugula and romaine lettuce in a large salad bowl and drizzle with 3 to 4 tablespoon of the vinaigrette. Toss until the greens are just coated, add the salt and black pepper, and toss again. Set aside. Pit, peel, and slice the avocados. In a medium bowl, toss well with the lime juice and set aside.

Heat a large nonstick skillet over medium heat. One at a time, warm the tortillas for 10 to 15 seconds on each side. Transfer to a work surface and again, working one at a time, spoon out and spread about 1½ tablespoons of basil aioli evenly across the center of a tortilla. Lay out 2 ounces each of turkey and ham across the center of the tortilla. Layer the avocados, tomatoes, eggs, bacon, chives, and blue cheese in thin lines next to each other across the center of the tortilla. Cover with ½ cup of the dressed greens. Bring the bottom of the tortilla up and over the filling, tucking it under to make a tight cylinder. Fold the sides over toward the center, and then finish rolling up the wrap. Secure it with toothpicks. Repeat until all of the wraps are made. Store in the refrigerator for up to 8 hours.

GRILLED SHRIMP *and* CRUNCHY VEGETABLE WRAPS, SWEET AND SPICY DIP

Cook the shrimp right, keep those vegetables cool and crispy, and I swear this is the food of the gods. Delicious and light, these are impossible to beat for food that you can feel good about piling into your mouth hole, especially on a hot day. Another great thing about these is they are shelf-stable and can sit out on a table for a while. Plus, they are beautiful.

Shrimp

2 pounds large shrimp, peeled and deveined

1½ teaspoons salt

2 teaspoons black pepper

⅓ cup olive oil

Zest and juice of 3 limes

2 tablespoons minced garlic

2 tablespoons minced fresh ginger

Wraps

1½ cups thinly sliced green or Napa cabbage

1½ cups thinly sliced red cabbage

1½ cups julienned carrot

1½ cups julienned green onion

1½ cups julienned yellow bell pepper

1½ cups julienned cucumber

¾ cup fresh cilantro leaves

¾ cup chiffonade of fresh basil leaves (see Note)

¾ cup julienned radishes

2 teaspoons sesame oil

1 tablespoon olive oil

Zest and juice of 2 limes

1 tablespoon rice wine vinegar

1½ teaspoons sugar

1 teaspoon salt

24 rice paper spring roll wraps

Sweet and Spicy Dip

1 cup sugar

½ teaspoon cornstarch

½ cup warm water

¾ cup white vinegar

3 tablespoons rice wine vinegar

2 teaspoons soy sauce

1 serrano pepper, seeded and minced

2 teaspoons minced garlic

1 teaspoon red pepper flakes

1 teaspoon salt

½ teaspoon MSG, such as Accent

MAKE THE SHRIMP Thread 6 to 8 shrimp on each skewer. Sprinkle with the salt and pepper and place in a large shallow bowl or baking dish. Whisk together olive oil, lime zest and juice, garlic, and ginger in a small bowl. Pour over the shrimp skewers and marinate in the refrigerator for 2 to 4 hours.

Prepare a hot charcoal or wood fire. Grill the shrimp skewers on the hottest part of the fire for 3 to 4 minutes, or until they begin to color on the first side. Flip and cook for an additional 2 to 3 minutes, or until the shrimp are just cooked through. Remove from the fire and cool.

Pull the shrimp off the skewers and halve them lengthwise. Set aside.

MAKE THE WRAPS In a large bowl, stir together the cabbages, carrot, green onion, bell pepper, cucumber, cilantro, basil, and radishes. Set aside. Whisk together the sesame oil, olive oil, lime zest and juice, rice wine vinegar, sugar, and salt. Pour over the vegetables and blend well.

Pour 1 to 2 inches of room-temperature water into a wide, shallow bowl or a baking pan. Soak a rice paper wrap in the water for 10 to 12 seconds, or until completely pliable. Remove and lay it out flat on a work surface. Lay 4 of the shrimp halves across the center of the wrap. Heap ½ cup of the dressed vegetable mix across the center of the wrap, covering the shrimp. Bring the bottom of the wrap up and over the vegetable mix, tucking it under to make a tight cylinder. Fold the sides toward the center and roll up the wrap. Repeat with the remaining wraps and filling and place the finished wraps on a baking sheet covered with plastic wrap.

Separate the layers of wraps with plastic wrap, cover with still more plastic, and refrigerate.

MAKE THE DIP In a small bowl, whisk the sugar and cornstarch with the warm water until smooth and the sugar has dissolved. In a non-reactive saucepan whisk together the vinegars, soy sauce, serrano pepper, garlic, red pepper flakes, salt, and MSG. Add the sugar and water mix and bring to a boil over medium heat. Turn down the heat to low and simmer for 10 minutes. Remove from heat and cool.

Slice the chilled wraps in half and serve with dipping sauce.

NOTE

▶ The "chiffonade" is a traditional French cut for fresh herbs or leafy vegetables. Stack 10 to 12 basil leaves on top of each other and roll into a tight cylinder. Slice the cylinder crosswise into thin ribbons, and there you have your chiffonade.

GRILLED TUNA TOSTADAS, SPICY AVOCADO, PICKLED ONION PICO

In 2005, I had one of the greatest trips of my entire life. One of my best friends and I took our bikes on a weeklong trip through the Baja Peninsula. We would ride all day, find somewhere to stop and gas up, eat street food, drink tequila, rinse, and repeat the next day. We started in Los Angeles, crossed the Calexico-Mexicali border, rode down to San Felipe, across the Baja mountains to Ensenada, down to Guerrero Negro, back up through the Guadalupe Valley and crossed back into the States at Tecate. We burned a lot of rubber and brain cells. The entire trip cost about $24, and I'd pay $240,000 to do it again.

One long day after we went from sweltering heat in the eastern desert, through freezing rain in the Baja mountains, and then back into the balmy breeze of Ensenada, we stopped for much-needed food and libation at a little taco stand overlooking the Pacific. Rather than the fried fish that you normally get in fish tacos, they were serving grilled mahi. In that moment, it was one of the most divine bites of food I have ever had. The memory haunts me to this day. Make these as soon after the fish comes off the grill as you can, while it's still moist and warm. And do not spare ice-cold beer.

Pico de Gallo

3 cups chopped Roma tomatoes

¾ cup chopped Pickled Red Onions (page 27)

1 cup diced red onion

¾ cup chopped fresh cilantro

1 jalapeño pepper, seeded and minced

½ teaspoon salt

1½ teaspoons black pepper

Grated zest and juice of 2 limes

Avocado Puree

½ cup sour cream

½ cup mayonnaise, preferably Duke's

3 ripe avocados, pitted and peeled

¾ cup chopped fresh cilantro

Grated zest and juice of 3 limes

1 jalapeño pepper, seeded and chopped

2 teaspoons minced garlic

½ teaspoon ground cumin

Salt

Tabasco sauce

Tuna

3 pounds tuna, cut into ¾-inch-thick steaks

Salt and black pepper

½ cup olive oil

¼ cup fresh lime juice

3 tablespoons minced garlic

1 tablespoon dried oregano

1 tablespoon ground cumin

2 teaspoons paprika

1 teaspoon ancho chile powder

½ teaspoon cayenne pepper

2 cups vegetable or peanut oil

12 (6-inch) flour tortillas, quartered

Salt

Cilantro leaves for garnish

MAKE THE PICO DE GALLO In a glass bowl, combine the tomatoes, pickled and fresh onions, cilantro, and jalapeño and allow to sit for 30 minutes at room temperature. Add the salt, black pepper, and lime zest and juice gradually to suit your taste.

MAKE THE AVOCADO PUREE Place the sour cream, mayonnaise, avocados, cilantro, lime zest and juice, jalapeño, garlic, and cumin in a blender and blend until perfectly smooth. Season with salt and add as much Tabasco as you like.

MARINATE THE TUNA Cut the tuna into ¾-inch cubes and place them in a 1-gallon zip-top freezer bag with 1 teaspoon salt and 2 teaspoons black pepper. Turn the bag over and over, massaging to distribute the salt and pepper evenly. Add the olive oil, lime juice, garlic, oregano, cumin, paprika, ancho, and cayenne and toss until the tuna is coated evenly. Refrigerate for 2 hours.

Prepare a hot charcoal or wood fire.

Place a cooling rack on a baking sheet. Heat the vegetable oil in a large cast-iron skillet to 350°F. Working in batches, fry the tortillas until golden and crispy, about 3 minutes, stirring and turning constantly. Remove from the oil with a slotted spoon and transfer to the prepared baking sheet. Sprinkle lightly with salt and set aside.

Thread the tuna on the skewers and season lightly with salt. Clean and oil the grill rack well. Place skewers over the hottest part of the fire, 3 or 4 at a time. Grill for 2 minutes, or until nicely marked, and then flip. Grill for an additional 2 minutes and remove from the heat. Continue grilling the rest as close "to order" as needed.

Spread out the fried tortillas on a platter and spread each with ½ teaspoon of the avocado puree. Place a tuna cube on each and top with the pico and a cilantro leaf.

GRILLED WEDGE SALAD _on a_ STICK, BLACK PEPPER RANCH DRESSING

In the last 30 years at City Grocery, we have from time to time found ourselves on the leading edge of a trend in food. A decade ago, bored with the '80s-style Caesar salad in a glass bowl we had been serving, we decided to change it. We reimagined our Caesar as a wedge, seasoned, oiled, and lightly grilled, with a lighter dressing—more in line with the original—an olive tapenade with a touch of anchovy aioli. A dangerously calculated move that, for the most part, worked out. Guests loved it.

This is a basic wedge given the same treatment. The skewer holds the iceberg together and gives it a kebab look. Folks will marvel at your creativity.

Black Pepper Ranch Dressing

1½ cups mayonnaise, preferably Duke's

1 cup buttermilk

¼ cup chopped fresh parsley

1 teaspoon celery salt

Grated zest and juice of 1 lemon

1½ tablespoons red wine vinegar

¾ tablespoon onion powder

¾ tablespoon garlic powder

2 tablespoons freshly ground black pepper

Salt (optional)

Salad

2 heads iceberg lettuce, quartered root to tip, each held intact at the core

4 medium tomatoes, cored and cut into 6 wedges each

2 sweet onions, cut into 8 wedges each

2 ears sweet corn, shucked

½ cup extra-virgin olive oil

Salt and black pepper

2 cups sliced cucumber (cut lengthwise first and then slice into half-moons)

1½ cups salted roasted pecan halves

½ cup fresh dill fronds

MAKE THE DRESSING Whisk together the mayonnaise, buttermilk, parsley, celery salt, lemon zest and juice, vinegar, onion powder, garlic powder, and pepper in a medium bowl and refrigerate for 30 minutes. Season lightly with salt, if needed. Store for up to 10 days in the refrigerator.

MAKE THE SALAD Prepare a hot charcoal or wood fire. Preheat the oven to 375°F.

Thread the lettuce quarters lengthwise on skewers to hold the leaves together. Add 2 tomato wedges and 2 onion wedges to each skewer. Drizzle the skewers and the corn with the olive oil and season lightly with salt and pepper.

When fire has burned down to coals, place the corn on the grill and cook, turning to mark it all around with grill marks. Transfer to the oven and roast for 15 minutes. Remove from the oven, slice the kernels off the cob, and set aside.

Place the skewers on the hottest part of the fire and sear the lettuce wedges on each side until marked. The point is not to "cook" any of the ingredients, but just to put some char marks on them and flavor them with a little smoke. Transfer to a platter and drizzle liberally with the dressing. Top with the corn, cucumber, pecans, and dill. Serve immediately.

INDIAN-SPICED LAMB KEBABS, RAITA, NAAN

Discovering these kebabs, cooked on medieval swordlike skewers in Delhi, was such a memorable moment. The meat mixture was formed around the thick blades of the skewers and suspended over the fire to cook. The outside was crispy due to the occasional direct kiss of the flame and the heat of the coals, while the inside was moist and delicious, benefitting from the heat of the metal skewer running through it. It was divine.

Take the time to make them and bring a grill out to the tailgate, and I guarantee your friends will hoist you upon their shoulders and built a monument with your likeness upon it.

Kebabs

1 tablespoon ground cumin

1 tablespoon ground coriander

1 tablespoon garam masala

2¼ teaspoons turmeric

3 pounds ground lamb

¾ cup grated onion

¼ cup plus 1 tablespoon minced garlic

3 tablespoons minced serrano peppers

2 tablespoons minced ginger

¼ cup chopped fresh cilantro

2½ teaspoons salt

1½ tablespoons black pepper

3 eggs

2 cups bread crumbs

Raita

1½ cups Greek yogurt

1 cup finely diced cucumber

¼ cup plus 1 tablespoon chopped fresh cilantro

Zest and juice of 1 lime

1½ tablespoons minced ginger

2¼ teaspoons minced serrano pepper

2 teaspoons chaat masala (see Note on page 32)

¾ teaspoon salt

½ teaspoon white pepper

6 rounds of naan

Salt

FORM THE KEBABS Blend together cumin, coriander, garam masala, and turmeric in a small bowl or cup. Place the lamb in the bowl of a stand mixer fitted with the paddle attachment. On low speed, add the spices and beat with the lamb to combine. Beat in the onion, garlic, serrano peppers, ginger, cilantro, salt, black pepper, eggs, and bread crumbs. Take a tablespoon of mix and cook it in a small sauté pan over medium heat until firm. Taste and adjust the seasonings.

Shape ⅓ cup of the lamb into a hot dog–shaped log and repeat with the remaining lamb. Thread each kebab onto a skewer and refrigerate, covered, until you're ready to cook.

MAKE THE RAITA In a medium bowl, stir together the yogurt, cucumber, cilantro, lime zest and juice, ginger, serrano pepper, and chaat masala. Allow to sit in the refrigerator for 30 minutes while the flavors develop. Season with the salt and white pepper.

Prepare a hot charcoal or wood fire.

Wipe the grill grate with a rag moistened with vegetable oil. Place lamb skewers on the hottest part of the grill and cook, turning several times, for 4 to 5 minutes. Transfer to the cool side of the grill and keep warm. Warm the naan over the fire, sprinkle lightly with salt, and cool briefly. Tear or cut each round into quarters. Serve the lamb immediately with the naan and raita.

BBQ CHICKEN *and* APPLE KEBABS

My dad was a master of the grill and a giant in my eyes when I was a kid. He didn't mess around getting his charcoal grill lit. He would carefully build a perfect pyramid of briquettes, splash them with a little gasoline from the can he filled the lawnmower with, and, with the subtlest of flourishes, strike a wooden match and casually toss it in the grill, sparking a *whoosh*, a fireball, and a very quick start to his fire. His most exciting performance was the night he and a couple buddies took a long swim in the Johnnie Walker bottle before starting the fire. When he finally got around to his duty, he may have gotten a little heavy-handed with the gasoline, and the "flourish" of the flames blew most of his eyebrows and part of his comb-over clean off.

My folks regularly had a pile of neighbors over in the late '60s and early '70s for dinner and/or cookouts. As skilled as dad was over the grill, it was my mom who prepped for him so he could practice his craft. They went through phases together. During one period, they cooked whole fish; during another, whole muscle (like lamb legs, whole beef tenders, pork butts). Usually, though, it was steaks and/or burgers, but they had a brief fascination for kebabs, when they skewered any and every combination of meat, vegetable, and fruit you might imagine. This was not one of their creations, but it's inspired by my memories of their antics and a marriage of flavors I love off the grill.

Kebabs

12 boneless, skinless chicken breasts, each cut crosswise into 4 pieces

6 Granny Smith apples, each cored and cut into 8 wedges

6 Vidalia onions, each cut into 8 wedges

¾ cup extra-virgin olive oil

Grated zest and juice of 3 lemons

2 tablespoons minced garlic

3 tablespoons chopped fresh oregano

1 tablespoon fresh thyme leaves

2 teaspoons salt

1½ tablespoons black pepper

BBQ Sauce

1½ cups ketchup

¼ cup bourbon

3 tablespoons brown sugar

2 tablespoons molasses

2 tablespoons strong brewed coffee

¼ cup apple cider vinegar

2 tablespoons Worcestershire sauce

1 tablespoon soy sauce

1 tablespoon yellow mustard

2 teaspoons liquid smoke

2 tablespoons grated onion

1 tablespoon minced garlic

2 teaspoons smoked paprika

⅛ teaspoon ground cinnamon

1 teaspoon red pepper flakes

½ teaspoon salt

1 teaspoon black pepper

24 bamboo skewers, soaked in water for 2 hours

MARINATE THE KEBABS On each skewer, thread a chicken strip, apple wedge, and onion wedge, in that order, twice. Place skewers in a baking dish.

In a blender, combine the olive oil, lemon zest and juice, garlic, oregano, thyme, salt, and black pepper and puree for 15 seconds. Pour over the chicken skewers and make sure all are well covered. Marinate in the refrigerator for 2 to 4 hours.

Prepare a hot charcoal or wood fire.

MAKE THE BBQ SAUCE In a medium saucepan, whisk together the ketchup, bourbon, brown sugar, molasses, coffee, vinegar, Worcestershire, soy sauce, mustard, liquid smoke, onion, garlic, smoked paprika, cinnamon, red pepper flakes, salt, and black pepper and bring to a simmer over medium heat. Turn down the heat to low and simmer, stirring constantly, for 10 minutes.

Remove the chicken from the marinade and grill over the hottest part of the grill, turning every several minutes, until the chicken is firm (should be 10 to 12 minutes, depending on how hot your fire is). Brush liberally with the sauce, flip, and brush again. Serve immediately with the remaining sauce on the side.

THE "OLE CHILI DIPPER"

WHEN *a* SCOOP WILL DO *the* TRICK

Fifteen or so years ago, one of my chefs got carried away with dips. When he sent me a menu to edit, the appetizer section had *five* different dips on it. My immediate reaction was to dial him up to find out what the hell was going on. "Five fucking dips, dude? This is a seated service restaurant, not a goddamn tailgate party!"

My boy had hit a low, and dips were something he could produce en masse and quickly, cutting his workload tremendously. At this particular restaurant, we served way more student guests than at our other ones, so it wasn't entirely wide of the mark: that menu did look a little like one for a tailgate party.

Dips have universal appeal: delicious, cheesy, gooey nonsense you can scoop with corn chips or potato chips, toasted bread, grilled pita, or raw vegetables, all without putting your drink down or really interrupting the conversation! That said, there are a few rules: (1) Do *not* double dip, and (2) retrieve all broken bits of your extraction tool, should it break. Sadly, most folks tend to ignore the second rule these days (I suspect these are the same assholes who spit chewing gum in urinals).

These dips are the best we have produced for our tailgate menus. There is almost nothing healthy about most of them, which is why they are excellent prebattle *Braveheart* foods. Added bonus: They (for the most part) are just as good after the game. Trust me, when you spend enough time drinking away the agony of defeat, as I do (I am a lifelong Saints fan and three-decade Ole Miss fan), it pays to have leftover dip to dive into when the final whistle blows.

SPINACH *and* ROASTED MUSHROOM DIP

In 1972 I started a lifelong love affair after my first bite of my grandmother's Spinach Madeline. It ratcheted into a full-blown passion on my first trip to a Houston's in 1982. A decade later, when we opened City Grocery, I began chasing the spinach dragon for the restaurant. It's only in the last few years that I finally found my groove, and I blame Hidden Valley ranch dressing powder entirely for my grand success. The roasted shiitakes add an earthy richness, which sends this dip over the top. Corn chip scoops are the perfect vehicle for this delicious insanity.

4 cups shiitake mushroom caps

¼ cup extra-virgin olive oil

Salt and black pepper

3 (10-ounce) boxes frozen chopped spinach, thawed

¼ cup butter

2 large sweet onions, finely diced

2 tablespoons minced garlic

2 tablespoons fresh thyme leaves

1 pound cream cheese, at room temperature

1 cup sour cream

1 cup mayonnaise, preferably Duke's

1 (¼-ounce) package Hidden Valley buttermilk ranch dressing powder

2½ cups grated Parmesan cheese

2½ cups grated pepper Jack cheese

3 tablespoons hot sauce, preferably Crystal

Corn chips for serving

Preheat the oven to 375°F. Line a baking sheet with parchment paper.

In a medium bowl, toss the mushroom caps with the olive oil and sprinkle with salt and pepper. Place the caps, gills-side up, on the prepared baking sheet. Bake for 2 minutes, or until the edges begin to turn golden and crispy. Remove from the oven. When cool, julienne and set aside.

Place the spinach in the center of large kitchen towels and squeeze as much of the moisture out as possible.

In a large Dutch oven, melt the butter over medium heat. Stir in the onions and garlic and warm through but do not cook. Stir in the spinach and thyme and stir until the spinach is warmed through. Remove from the heat and stir in the cream cheese, sour cream, mayonnaise, ranch dressing powder, 2 cups of the Parmesan, 2 cups of the pepper Jack, and the hot sauce. Mix well and stir in the mushrooms.

Pour the mix into a large soufflé dish or a Dutch oven and sprinkle with the remaining ½ cup Parmesan and ½ cup pepper Jack. Bake for 30 minutes, or until golden brown and bubbly. Serve immediately with whatever you want. This stuff is bananas!

WARM CARAMELIZED ONION
and BLUE CHEESE DIP

This is literally the very first recipe we wrote for a tailgating menu, twenty-five years ago. It has always been one of our most requested items. This is best hot, but it's still exceptional warm or at room temperature. Serve with toasted pita, celery sticks, or buttered French bread croutons.

2 pounds cream cheese, at room temperature

2 cups crumbled blue cheese

1 cup mayonnaise

½ cup heavy cream

½ cup crumbled crispy cooked bacon

1 tablespoon plus 1 teaspoon minced garlic

1 tablespoon Worcestershire sauce

¼ teaspoon cayenne pepper

1½ teaspoons black pepper

3 medium yellow onions, caramelized (see page 68)

Toasted pita bread, celery sticks, or buttered French bread croutons (see Note), for serving

Preheat the oven to 375°F. Butter a 2½-quart soufflé dish well and set aside.

Place the cream cheese in a stand mixer fitted with paddle attachment and beat on medium speed until creamy. Slowly add the blue cheese, mayonnaise, cream, bacon, garlic, Worcestershire, cayenne, and black pepper and beat until well combined. Remove the bowl from the mixer and stir in the onions by hand. Pour the mix into the prepared soufflé dish. Bake for 30 minutes, or until golden brown and bubbly.

NOTE

► For French bread croutons, preheat the oven to 350°F. Slice a 10- to 12-inch baguette into 40 to 50 (¼-inch-thick) slices. Brush one side with melted butter and sprinkle with kosher salt and black pepper. Place them, buttered-side up on a baking sheet and bake for 10 to 12 minutes, or until croutons are golden brown.

GRILLED CORN GUACAMOLE

You know how you see guacamole everywhere in the summer and it's never, ever flavored with anything else? It's just plain delicious guacamole, right? Do you know why that is? Well, I'll tell you: Guacamole is perfect when it is done right. Ripe avocado, smashed with a little lime, some onion, a touch of oil, hint of cumin, a sprinkle of salt—that's all that guac needs to achieve wonderfully sublime perfection. It's that simple.

Then comes me. Big, dumb white guy with his chef coat and goddamn Beard medal, stomping around in the bucolic tranquility of guac-land and putting other shit in it. I just can't leave well enough alone. Fortunately for you, I happen to be a little bit of a genius, because sweet corn at the height of the season makes a killer addition. We'll just agree to leave it alone after this. The gods might not forgive us twice.

3 ears sweet corn, shucked

2 tablespoons vegetable oil

Salt and black pepper

6 fully ripe avocados, pitted, peeled, and diced

3 Roma tomatoes, seeded and diced

1¼ cups finely diced yellow onion

1 jalapeño pepper, minced

Grated zest and juice of 4 limes

¾ cup chopped fresh cilantro

1½ tablespoons minced garlic

3 tablespoons extra-virgin olive oil

¼ teaspoon cayenne pepper

2½ teaspoons ground cumin

2 to 4 dashes Tabasco sauce (optional)

Good-quality corn chips for serving

Hot sauce for serving, preferably Valentina

Prepare a hot charcoal or wood fire.

Rub the corn with the vegetable oil and sprinkle with salt and black pepper. Place over the hottest part of the grill and cook, turning every 4 minutes, for 15 minutes, or until well colored all over. Remove from the heat and allow to cool. Slice the kernels off the cob and discard the cobs.

Transfer the grilled corn to a large bowl and add the avocados, tomatoes, onion, jalapeño, lime zest and juice, cilantro, garlic, olive oil, cayenne, and cumin, stirring until well blended. Season lightly with salt and black pepper. Allow to sit in the cooler for 20 minutes and taste again for seasoning. Add several splashes of Tabasco, if desired, and a touch of salt and black pepper, if needed.

Serve with good-quality corn chips and a dash of Valentina hot sauce.

CHILI *and* CHEESE FRITO PIE

My grandfather ran the Lion's Club concession stand at the local minor league baseball stadium in Lenior, North Carolina, during the summers when I was a kid. At six or seven, I am sure I was entirely underfoot all the time, but my grand-dad took me along on these outings anyway. Frito chili pie was one of their concession items, and the most likely reason an open bag full of chili with onions and mustard was shoved in my hand was to keep me occupied for a few minutes while he tried to do his work. Still, this is the most glorious payoff anyone ever got for being a pain-in-the-ass kid.

To be frank, little will ever be better (or messier) than eating this sloppy concoction from the bag. (If you don't feel that way, you should just agree to disagree, walk away, and find a new snack.) This version provides a slightly more civilized delivery method for the same experience. The upside is that you can eat it without feeling like you need to be hosed down once you are done. You are big boys and girls, and you can decide for yourselves.

While technically this isn't a dip, I threw it together late one night with a couple of friends and we devoured it with a bag of scoops (scoop-shaped chips) and finished the crust like savages.

Crust

12 cups corn chips, crushed lightly by hand

1½ cups all-purpose flour

1 cup butter, melted

1½ cups grated Parmesan cheese

1 teaspoon ground cumin

1½ teaspoons cayenne pepper

Chili

¼ cup plus 2 tablespoons lard

3½ cups diced yellow onion

3 tablespoons minced garlic

2 teaspoons minced jalapeño pepper

1½ pounds ground beef

1½ pounds ground pork

Salt and black pepper

3½ tablespoons chili powder

3 tablespoons ground cumin

1½ tablespoons smoked paprika

1 tablespoon red pepper flakes

⅛ teaspoon ground cinnamon

5 cups canned crushed tomatoes

1 cup tomato paste

3 cups chicken stock

3 tablespoons masa harina

Spiced Sour Cream

1½ cups sour cream

Grated zest and juice of 1 lime

½ teaspoon cayenne pepper

½ teaspoon ground cumin

1 teaspoon paprika

1 teaspoon salt

2 cups grated sharp cheddar cheese

¾ cup slivered green onion, green part only

¾ cup chopped fresh cilantro

Corn chips

continued

MAKE THE CRUST Preheat the oven to 350°F. Lightly butter two 9-inch pie pans.

Place the corn chips in a food processor and process until they reach the consistency of a meal. Add the flour, melted butter, Parmesan, cumin, and cayenne and process until well blended. The mix should resemble wet sand and hold together when mashed with your fingers. Split the mix in half and press into the pie pans, across the bottom and up the sides. Bake for 30 minutes, or until the crust is golden brown. Remove from the oven and allow to cool. Leave the oven on.

MAKE THE CHILI Melt the lard in a medium-large Dutch oven over medium heat. As soon as the lard begins to shimmer, add the onion and garlic and sauté, stirring constantly, until the onion is transparent. Stir in the jalapeño and sauté for 1 minute. Add the beef and pork and cook, breaking up the large chunks with a spoon, and season with salt and black pepper. Stir in the chili powder, cumin, paprika, red pepper flakes, and cinnamon. Cook, stirring and breaking up the meat, until it is completely cooked through and crumbly. Add the tomatoes and tomato paste and blend thoroughly. Stir in the chicken stock and bring to a simmer. In a cup, stir together some of the hot cooking liquid with the masa harina and then stir it into the chili, cover, and simmer for 20 to 30 minutes. Season with salt and black pepper. When the chili has thickened and is no longer runny, remove from the heat and allow to cool briefly.

MAKE THE SPICED SOUR CREAM Combine the sour cream, lime zest and juice, cayenne, cumin, paprika, and salt. Set aside.

Divide the chili between the two pie shells and cover the tops evenly with the shredded cheddar. (At this point, you can refrigerate the chili for up 48 hours or freeze for up to 3 months; see Note.) Bake for 15 minutes, or until bubbly and lightly browned. Remove from the oven, garnish with the green onions and cilantro, and serve hot with more corn chips and the spiced sour cream. The first slice will probably be a little difficult to get out, but for the record, this isn't supposed to be pretty, just tasty.

NOTE

▶ If cooking from chilled, bake, covered, for 20 minutes, then remove the foil and cook for an additional 12 minutes. Internal temperature should be 175°F. If cooking from frozen, place the covered pie in the oven and set it to 250°F, and bake for 1 hour. Turn the oven up to 350°F, remove foil, and cook for an additional 20 minutes.

CUMIN-SCENTED PINTO BEAN DIP, SOUR CREAM *and* LIME

When I was a kid, Frito-Lay made a canned bean dip that very regularly appeared at my parents' gatherings. I found it altogether fine straight out of the can, but, as with many prepared foods, my mom could transform the simple into the sublime with the flip of her wrist. She would take the canned bean dip, scoop it into a bowl, splash in a few ingredients, pop it in the oven, and, invariably, mystify guests with her black magic. Sadly, her recipe went to the grave with her, so this is my interpretation of what she did. I like to think she would approve. You can be the judge.

2 (16-ounce) cans spicy refried beans, preferably Rosarita

8 ounces cream cheese, at room temperature

1 cup sour cream

1½ tablespoons lard, melted

¾ cup diced yellow onion

1¾ tablespoons minced garlic

½ cup minced pickled jalapeño peppers

1½ teaspoons hot sauce, preferably Frank's

1 teaspoon chili powder

1 teaspoon ground cumin

¼ teaspoon cayenne pepper

1½ cups grated cheddar cheese

1½ cups grated pepper Jack cheese

6 tablespoons Spiced Sour Cream (page 89)

½ cup thinly sliced green onions

¼ cup chopped fresh cilantro

Preheat the oven to 375°F.

In a large bowl, stir together the beans, cream cheese, sour cream, lard, onion, garlic, jalapeños, hot sauce, chili powder, cumin, cayenne, and 1½ cups of each of the cheeses. Pour the mix into a large casserole dish and bake for 25 minutes. Remove from the oven and sprinkle with the remaining ½ cup of each cheese and return to oven for an additional 10 minutes, or until the cheese has melted thoroughly. Remove from oven and cool briefly. Drizzle with the spiced sour cream, green onions, and cilantro.

GOD'S OWN BUFFALO CHICKEN DIP

There is no better chicken to make this with than Popeyes spicy, dark meat fried chicken. I have tried. Trust me. Nothing else measures up.

This is one of the most popular dishes on our current tailgate menu. I freely admit we cannot get enough Popeyes to make the twenty or so gallons of this we put out every home game, but it is decidedly better with the gold standard of fried chicken. If you can't get Popeyes, another brand or homemade will do (tenders are an easy way to go, but boneless thighs crush it). I am secretly researching a project to genetically engineer a chicken that is nothing but eight thighs. To date it appears to be an enormously ugly but delicious bird. (Do I smell Nobel attention? I think so. You read it here first.)

8 cups finely chopped leftover commercially fried chicken, preferably Popeyes (see Note)

1½ pounds cream cheese, at room temperature

2 cups mayonnaise, preferably Duke's

1 cup buttermilk

1 tablespoon plus 2 teaspoons chopped fresh dill

1 tablespoon chopped fresh parsley

1½ tablespoons chopped fresh chives

2½ teaspoons garlic powder

2 teaspoons onion powder

½ teaspoon cayenne pepper

2 teaspoons salt

1 tablespoon black pepper

½ cup hot sauce, preferably Texas Pete

Grated zest and juice of 2 lemons

1½ cups crumbled blue cheese

½ cup sliced green onion, for garnish

Celery sticks, crackers, or chips for serving

Preheat the oven to 350°F. Butter a 4-quart soufflé dish.

Place the chicken in a large bowl and set aside.

In the bowl of a stand mixer fitted with the paddle attachment, beat the cream cheese on medium speed until smooth. Turn down the mixer to low and add the mayonnaise and buttermilk, beating until smooth. Add the dill, parsley, chives, garlic powder, onion powder, cayenne, salt, and black pepper, beating until well combined. Slowly add the hot sauce and lemon zest and juice. Pour the mix over the chicken, stirring to blend. Stir in the blue cheese. Pour into the prepared soufflé dish and bake for 25 minutes, or until bubbly and slightly browned on top.

Garnish with the green onion and serve hot with celery, crackers, chips, or a combination.

NOTE

For those of you who still stick to health-consciousness when it comes to your tailgate affairs, you can substitute rotisserie chicken, but you will never know the glory of excess and we can never be friends.

SMOKED TROUT DIP, HOMEMADE SESAME CRACKERS

Fish dip is a relatively well-kept secret of the western end of the Florida Panhandle, where the protein of choice is fresh mullet. Like all oily fish, mullet is unbelievably good fresh out of the water, but it turns sour very quickly. I have had mackerel in my station cooler that was perfectly fine at the beginning of service but had to be tossed out by the end because it had turned.

Fresh-caught mullet that has been cleaned and smoked immediately is as delicious a bite of fish as you are likely to have. But it's hard to get if you can't walk to a source. If you can find it, by all means, sub it in here. Otherwise, fresh-smoked trout is beautiful in its own right. This is a wonderful surprise dish for most folks, and despite appearances, it holds well for a period at room temperature.

Crackers

1⅔ cups warm water (around 95°F)

2 teaspoons active dry yeast

1 tablespoon plus 2 teaspoons sugar

5 cups plus 5 tablespoons all-purpose flour

Salt

¼ cup toasted sesame seeds

3 tablespoons brown butter (see Note)

2 eggs, lightly beaten

Melted butter for brushing the crackers

Trout Dip

12 ounces cream cheese, at room temperature

1½ cups mayonnaise

Grated zest and juice of 2 lemons

½ cup minced shallot

½ cup minced celery

¼ cup minced green onion, green part only

3 tablespoons capers, drained and chopped

1 tablespoon hot sauce, preferably Crystal

1½ teaspoons Creole Seasoning (page 236)

¾ teaspoon salt

2 pounds smoked trout fillets (see Note on page 27), flaked

3 tablespoons chopped fresh parsley

MAKE THE CRACKERS Preheat the oven to 350°F.

Pour the water into a small bowl and whisk in the yeast and sugar. Allow to sit for 10 minutes. Meanwhile, in a large bowl, whisk together the flour, 2½ teaspoons salt, and the sesame seeds.

Transfer the yeast mix to the bowl of a stand mixer fitted with the dough hook and beat the brown butter and eggs into the yeast mix at medium speed. Add the flour mix, 1 cup at a time, beating after each addition until well combined. When the dough is kneaded and smooth, transfer to an oiled bowl, cover, and allow to rise until doubled in size, about an hour. Punch down the dough, remove from the bowl, and cut into eight balls.

One at a time, roll out the balls of dough on a lightly floured work surface as thinly as possible (⅛ inch in diameter is ideal) . Brush with melted butter and sprinkle with salt. You can cut the dough into shapes or leave it whole and break it apart by hand after it's baked and cooled. Bake for 12 to 15 minutes, until golden brown. The crackers will keep in a sealed container at room temperature for 1 week.

MAKE THE DIP Place the cream cheese in the clean bowl of the stand mixer fitted with the paddle attachment and beat on medium speed until smooth and creamy. Add the mayonnaise, lemon zest and juice, shallots, celery, green onion, capers, hot sauce, Creole seasoning, and salt, beating until well combined. Beat in the smoked just until combined. Garnish with the parsley and serve with the crackers.

NOTE

▶ You can substitute plain melted butter here, but the brown butter really shines in this recipe, and it's great to use for cooking if you have any left over. To make brown butter, place however much butter you would like to brown in a small, light-colored saucepan over low heat, swirling the pan constantly. Once the butter melts, it will begin to foam. Continue swirling and, as the foam subsides, milk solids will sink to the bottom of the pan and the butter's water content will slowly boil off. Swirl for 10 to 12 minutes; the milk solids on the bottom of the pan will begin to brown slightly. Continue cooking for an additional 3 to 4 minutes and the butter should begin to give off a distinctly rich, nutty aroma. Once golden brown–looking and nutty-smelling, pour the melted butter into a small container, so cooking will stop immediately (carryover heat from the pan can burn your butter otherwise).

TRADITIONAL CRUDITÉS *with* HERBED FROMAGE BLANC

For a decade and a half, I hosted a gathering of chefs at my house on Sunday afternoon following the Southern Foodways Alliance Fall Symposium. We would gather together exhausted, frequently hungover, and always desperately in need of raw vegetables. The symposium often provided a meat-heavy experience, leaving most normal people jonesing for a vegetable fix. So, on those Sundays, a regular cast of characters, peppered with a few rookies here and there, would find their way to our house, where we would assemble the ingredients to help us "re-veg" our bodies. There would be a couple of giant salads, a variety of velvety hummuses, and a pot of spicy red beans. Crudités frequently made an appearance, almost always delivered by the deft hand of my dear, sweet friend and virtuoso of the vegetable, Chef Ashley Christensen of the Raleigh, North Carolina, AC Restaurant Empire.

This is perfect for a tailgate spread, as the vegetables hold up well even in the hottest conditions but are also filling even in cold weather. Go on, get your veg on; you'll feel better for it.

Fromage Blanc Dip

1 pound fresh goat cheese, crumbled

½ cup finely grated Parmesan cheese

1 cup crème fraîche or sour cream

Grated zest and juice of 1 lemon

3 tablespoons finely minced fresh chives

2 tablespoons chopped fresh tarragon leaves

1½ tablespoons chopped fresh thyme

2 tablespoons minced shallot

1½ tablespoons minced garlic

1 teaspoon MSG, such as Accent

Salt and black pepper

Crudités

1 pint grape tomatoes

1 bunch asparagus, trimmed of woody ends and peeled

1 pound young carrots, peeled

1 pound celery, cut into 4-inch lengths

1½ pounds cucumber, cut into 4-inch wedges

1 pound green beans, stemmed and strings pulled

1 pint radishes, quartered

MAKE THE FROMAGE BLANC Place the cheeses, the crème fraîche, lemon zest and juice, fresh herbs, shallot, garlic, and MSG in a food processor and process until smooth. Season lightly with salt and pepper. Refrigerate for 1 hour or overnight.

Serve cold with the crudités.

THE SIXTH MAN

ADDING STRENGTH *to the* TEAM

"You're only as good as your bench is deep," said somebody, somewhere, sometime—or at least they should have. You see, in basketball, the sixth man is the player on the bench who is not quite solid enough to make the starting five but, when needed, can provide the sudden burst of offense to change the pace of a game. Without your bench, you have a few stars who eventually get worn out and become forgettable. Your support players keep the team fresh, energetic, and vibrant. Frequently, bench players become stars in their own right, and the cast is always growing and changing. These recipes are great supporting players to center-plate "stars" and are frequently interchangeable. They are also a whole load of fun.

ELOTE SALAD (ESQUITES)

I remember exactly where I was standing in San Felipe, Mexico, the night I had my first bite of elote in February 2005. It was astounding. A high school girlfriend's sister turned me onto the magic of yellow mustard with corn in the early '80s, and I was convinced then that I had rocketed straight to the end of corn's amazing possibilities. But then I had my first bite of elote; wood fire–grilled corn, hot off the grill; a liberal slather of sweet Mexican mayonnaise; a squirt of lime; a sublime coating of finely ground cotija; and the kick of paprika and cayenne. I was an ant under a magnifying glass and exploded in a blaze of culinary glory in that moment. I am only sad that I never get to taste that for the first time again.

I came home dreaming of a million things I wanted to do with my new favorite food, and created this version for the wedding of my buddy Joe York, my crazy-cool documentary filmmaker buddy. It was a smash hit, and I have never looked back. This is, of course, best in the summertime, when corn is fresh and sweet, but you can pull it off any time of year with halfway decent corn. It's just that good.

8 ears sweet corn, shucked

3 tablespoons vegetable oil or lard

Salt

¼ cup plus 1 tablespoon mayonnaise, preferably Kewpie (see Note)

¾ cup cotija cheese

1 cup chopped fresh cilantro

1 cup minced red onion

¾ cup minced green onion, green part only

2 jalapeño peppers, seeded and minced

1½ tablespoons minced garlic

Grated zest and juice of 3 limes

1 tablespoon hot sauce, preferably Valentina

1½ teaspoons chili powder

½ teaspoon cayenne pepper

1½ teaspoons MSG, such as Accent

Black pepper

Prepare a hot charcoal or wood fire.

Rub the corn with vegetable oil and sprinkle with 2 teaspoons salt. Place on the hottest part of the fire and cook, turning every couple minutes, until the corn is charred all over. Remove from the grill and allow to cool.

Slice the kernels off the cobs into a large bowl. Add the mayonnaise, cotija, cilantro, red onion, green onion, jalapeños, garlic, lime zest and juice, hot sauce, chili powder, cayenne, and MSG and stir to blend well. Season with salt and black pepper.

NOTE

► Kewpie is a Japanese brand of mayonnaise available at Asian specialty stores. It is supersweet and comes in a crazy-cool dispenser. It is very easy to fall in love with. If you have ever eaten sushi rolls, you have had Kewpie.

THE SIXTH MAN

MOROCCAN-SPICED DEVILED EGGS

Once you have made this harissa, you are going to want to put it all over everything: grilled beef, roasted pork, vegetables, ice cream, your neighbor's cat. Okay, I am kidding about the ice cream, but you get the point.

Deviled eggs saw a resurgence in popularity with the renaissance of Southern food starting in the early years of the twenty-first century. There were dozens upon dozens of "updates" on the curry powder–paprika original—even more than there were for shrimp and grits—and the failure rate was catastrophic. I'm not kidding. I have tasted more inedible, overthought versions of deviled eggs than you could ever dream of. So many so, that those nasty mouthfuls actually pushed me off deviled eggs completely for almost a decade. As I have grown more and more obsessed with minimalism, I have returned to a number of things I have witnessed the ruination of, and I have been revisioning. This version, while not entirely "stripped down," is a nod to traditional flavors with a subtle twist. Totally worth it.

Bonus: There will be harissa seasoning left for putting on grilled meats, sprinkling on salads, and flavoring mashed potatoes or grits.

18 eggs

2 tablespoons white vinegar

1½ cups mayonnaise, preferably Duke's

2 tablespoons Harissa (recipe follows)

2 teaspoons fresh lemon juice

Salt and white pepper

Chopped, toasted sliced almonds for garnish

Chopped fresh cilantro for garnish

Chopped fresh chives for garnish

Aleppo pepper or sweet paprika (*not* smoked) for garnish

Place the eggs in a large saucepan and cover with water by 1 inch. Add the vinegar. Bring the eggs to a boil over high heat. Turn down the heat to low and cook for exactly 8 minutes. Remove from the heat and allow the eggs to cool in the pan for 5 additional minutes. Remove from pan and set aside.

Peel the eggs and cut them in half lengthwise. Remove and place the yolks in a medium mixing bowl. With a hand mixer, beat in the mayonnaise, harissa, and lemon juice, mixing until smooth and creamy. Season with salt and pepper. Put the mix into a freezer bag (or, better, a piping bag, if you have one) and slice off the tip. Pipe some of the yolk mix into each egg half. Garnish with almonds, cilantro, chives, and Aleppo pepper.

HARISSA

2 red bell peppers

1 teaspoon cumin seeds

1½ teaspoons
coriander seeds

1 teaspoon
caraway seeds

½ teaspoon red
pepper flakes

1½ teaspoons black
peppercorns

4 tablespoons
extra-virgin olive oil

2½ cups diced
yellow onion

2 tablespoons
minced garlic

2 dried ancho chiles,
soaked in boiling water
for 30 minutes

2½ teaspoons sumac

1 tablespoon
tomato paste

Grated zest and juice
of 2 lemons

Salt

Roast the peppers over the open flame of a gas stove burner or wood fire, turning constantly, until charred all over. Place the warm peppers in a bowl and cover tightly with plastic wrap. Allow to sit for 20 minutes. Remove the peppers and, under cool running water, remove the stems, skin, seeds, and interior membrane. Place the pepper flesh in a blender and set aside.

Toast the cumin, coriander, and caraway seeds, the red pepper flakes, and the peppercorns in a sauté pan over medium heat until fragrant. Remove from the heat, cool, and either grind in a spice grinder or crush with a mortar and pestle. Transfer the crushed spices to the blender.

In the same pan in which you toasted the spices, warm 2 tablespoons of the oil over medium heat and sauté the onion and garlic until the onion begins to brown slightly. Transfer to the blender.

Seed the ancho chiles and transfer to the blender. Add the remaining 2 tablespoons oil, sumac, the tomato paste, and lemon zest and juice and blend until very smooth. Season with salt.

Harissa keeps for 1 week in the refrigerator.

NOTES

► Sumac is a spice used primarily in Middle Eastern foods. It has a tart, citrusy flavor and is available in specialty markets and widely on the internet.

ROASTED POTATO *and* BLUE CHEESE POT SAL

Ubiquity can be a sad place to dwell. Consider potato salad for a moment—totally taken for granted when it can be altogether divine, given the proper attention. More often than not, though, it is just glossed over in conversation and consideration. Well, I, for one, have always held potato salad in the highest regard. I know this sounds personal, and that's because it is. I've had endless varieties of potato salad—my mother's, of course, being the best—everything from simple American with cubed boiled potato, mayonnaise, boiled egg, and celery; to potato salad where the potatoes are fully mashed; to German potato salad, rich with mustard; to pure vinegar and spice potato salad. And I love all of them. This one combines my favorite ingredients in a loaded baked potato and the crispy texture of a roasted new potato skin. Trust me on this. I didn't get to be as round as I am by *not* tasting all the potato salads.

3 pounds new potatoes (about the same size)

½ cup extra-virgin olive oil

Salt and black pepper

1½ cups crumbled blue cheese

1 cup chopped hard-boiled eggs

1 cup mayonnaise

¾ cup sour cream

1 cup chopped celery

½ cup thinly sliced green onions

⅓ cup crumbled crispy cooked bacon

2 tablespoons grainy mustard

3 tablespoons white wine vinegar

2 teaspoons sugar

Preheat the oven to 375°F.

Toss the whole potatoes with the olive oil and sprinkle with salt and pepper. Spread out on baking sheets in a single layer and roast for 30 minutes, or until a knife plunges easily through the largest potato. Remove from the oven and cool the potatoes for 20 minutes.

Meanwhile, in large bowl, combine the blue cheese, hard-boiled eggs, mayonnaise, sour cream, chopped celery, green onions, bacon, mustard, vinegar, sugar, 1½ tablespoons of pepper and 1½ teaspoons of salt.

Halve the potatoes and then quarter the halves, to make eight chunks from each potato. Place them in a large mixing bowl, pour the dressing over the potatoes, and stir gently until well combined. Store chilled in plastic or glass for up to 1 week.

SMOKED SHRIMP SALAD

I am fascinated by how people will gush over crabmeat ravigote (a variation on remoulade) yet are equally dismissive of crab salad. Same-ish thing, haters.

Mayonnaise largely went out of vogue in the '80s, eschewed as unhealthy and passé. For chefs, recipes with mayo were viewed as dinosaurs of the '50s and '60s, which had no place on modern American menus. To the media, mayo was grossly unhealthy and one-dimensional. To this guy, mayo recipes are what I'll be bringing to my visit with St. Peter in order to distract him from my past transgressions.

Through the last two decades, I have explored these culinary gems, endeavoring to add nuance and complexity. And while I recognize that there are mayonnaise haters out there, most of those same people don't hate Caesar dressing or ranch. So just give this shrimp salad a shot. You'll be a better human for admitting you are wrong. Start the bay oil at least a day in advance.

In a 2-gallon zip-top freezer bag, toss the shrimp with the olive oil, 2 teaspoons salt, 1½ tablespoons pepper, and the lemon juice. Squeeze out the air, seal, and allow to marinate in the refrigerator for 2 hours.

When you're ready to make the salad, preheat the oven to 400°F. Line two baking sheets with parchment paper.

Remove the shrimp from the bag and spread them out on the prepared baking sheets. Roast for 10 to 12 minutes, or until the shrimp are just cooked through. Remove from the oven, transfer to a large bowl, and cool.

In the bowl of a stand mixer fitted with the paddle attachment, beat the cream cheese on medium until creamy. Add the mayonnaise, mustard, onion, celery, fresh herbs, lemon zest and juice, horseradish, bay oil, and Tabasco and beat until well combined. Pour over the shrimp and stir until well coated. Season with salt and pepper. Store chilled for up to 4 days.

5 pounds large shrimp, peeled and deveined

⅓ cup extra-virgin olive oil

Salt and black pepper

2 tablespoons fresh lemon juice

2 ounces cream cheese, at room temperature

1 cup mayonnaise, preferably Blue Plate

⅓ cup Creole mustard

1 cup diced yellow onion

1 cup diced celery

½ cup chopped mixed herbs, such as tarragon, basil, and thyme

Grated zest and juice of 2 lemons

2½ tablespoons prepared horseradish

2 teaspoons Bay Oil (page 238)

2 teaspoons Tabasco sauce

HOPPIN' JOHN SALAD, CRISPY BACON, SHERRY VINAIGRETTE

Bill Neal of Crook's Corner, in Chapel Hill, North Carolina, introduced me to the subtle beauty of this largely unknown Low Country staple in the early '80s; Sean Brock illustrated the intergalactic possibilities it held twenty years later. I am certain my obsession with Hoppin' John is directly linked to my boundless, lifelong love of red beans and rice. But unlike red beans, Hoppin' John can be elegant and nuanced. (Red beans and rice is, more often than not, a lumbering hulk of a dish . . . a straight punch to the mouth, and that's okay.)

Almost always eaten hot, Hoppin' John lends itself extremely nicely to a chilled "salad" interpretation. (I am certain there is a Charlestonian octogenarian or two who would slap the shit out of me for such blasphemy, but so be it.) This is perfect for a hot game-day tailgate setup, as it is light and bright but filling. Apologies to my friends in South Carolina.

Black-Eyed Peas

4 cups dried black-eyed peas, soaked overnight in water

2 tablespoons olive oil

½ pound bacon, chopped

1 cups diced yellow onions

2 tablespoons minced garlic

¾ cup diced celery

1½ tablespoons fresh thyme leaves

2 bay leaves

2 teaspoons red pepper flakes

4 cups chicken stock

Sherry Vinaigrette

½ cup olive oil

¼ cup extra-virgin olive oil

½ cup sherry vinegar

2 tablespoons Dijon mustard

Grated zest and juice of 1 lemon

2 tablespoons minced shallots

1½ teaspoons minced garlic

1 tablespoon chopped fresh oregano

Salt and black pepper

6 cups hot cooked white rice

2 cups diced yellow onions

2 cups chopped tomatoes

1 red bell pepper, finely diced

1 green bell pepper, finely diced

1 cup diced celery

1 garlic clove, minced

2 tablespoons chopped fresh basil

2 tablespoons fresh thyme leaves

3 tablespoons chopped fresh parsley

1½ teaspoons smoked paprika

Salt and black pepper

¾ cup chopped green onions

MAKE THE BLACK-EYED PEAS Heat the oil in a large saucepan over medium heat. Cook the chopped bacon until crispy, then remove it from the pan. Stir in the onions and garlic and sauté until the onions are transparent. Stir in the celery and sauté for 3 minutes. Drain the peas and add to pot. Add the thyme, bay leaves, red pepper flakes, and chicken stock, stirring to blend. Add enough water to cover the beans. Bring to a simmer, turn down the heat to low, and simmer until the peas are tender, about 30 minutes. Remove from the heat, drain the peas, remove the solids, and set aside to cool.

MAKE THE VINAIGRETTE Whisk together the olive oils, vinegar, mustard, lemon zest and juice, shallot, garlic, and oregano in a small nonreactive bowl and season with salt and pepper.

To serve, place the cooked peas a large bowl and add the rice, 1¼ cups vinaigrette, onions, tomatoes, bell peppers, celery, garlic, basil, thyme, parsley, and paprika. Season with salt and black pepper, and garnish with the chopped green onions. Refrigerate for at least 2 hours, but preferably overnight, so flavors can mingle. Serve cold.

GRANDMOTHER'S CREAM CORN

It's staggering how terrible most processed food tastes these days, but I notice it especially with creamed corn. Canned creamed corn was so good forty years ago that I would gladly eat it instead of my grandmother's, which was spectacular. But a couple of years ago, after having a can of fucking cat vomit labeled "creamed corn," I started trying to re-create my grandmother's. Sadly, I could not come close. When my mother passed away in late 2017, I inherited her pile of recipe boxes (which no one in the family knew existed). In one of them I found my grandmother's recipe for creamed corn and discovered the secret ingredient that made it sing—cream cheese. So this is my gift to you. Your life should be a rich, ripe oyster now.

¼ cup butter

1 tablespoon bacon fat

1½ cups diced sweet onion

1 tablespoon minced garlic

6 cups sweet corn (preferably fresh, but I will look the other way if you must use frozen— no judgment, I swear)

6 ounces cream cheese

1 cup whole milk

1½ tablespoons sugar

2 teaspoon black pepper

1 teaspoon salt

½ teaspoon cayenne pepper

3 tablespoons finely chopped green onion

Melt the butter and bacon fat in a large saucepan over medium heat. Stir in the onion and garlic and sauté until the onion is transparent. Stir in the corn and sauté for an additional 5 minutes. Stir in the cream cheese, milk, sugar, salt, black pepper, and cayenne and turn the heat to low. Simmer, stirring constantly, until the milk has mostly evaporated. Right before serving, stir in the green onion.

MISSISSIPPI DELTA CUCUMBER *and* WHITE ONION SALAD

This is one of my favorite summer sides. My very first bite came thirty years ago at a country fish shack outside of Oxford. A small melamine bowlful of this monument to minimalism was slid in front of me as soon as we sat down (it was their "bread service" offering). One bite of its acidic, sweet, crunchy magic was all it took to convince me this little dish deserved its own religion.

As usual, in my attempts to reproduce it, I used my ignorant "more-is-more approach," and I kept hitting wide of the mark for years. It wasn't until I took a completely different approach and simplified everything that this recipe began to take shape. On top of being crazy delicious, cuke and onion salad is wonderfully healthy.

4 cucumbers, halved lengthwise and sliced into half-moons

2 sweet onions, thinly sliced into rings

1½ tablespoons minced garlic

1 cup white vinegar or white wine vinegar

¼ cup water

¼ cup extra-virgin olive oil

1 tablespoon sugar

3 tablespoons chopped mixed fresh herbs (basil, thyme, oregano, chives, or whatever you like)

2 teaspoons salt

1 tablespoon black pepper

Place the cucumbers and onions in a large bowl and set aside.

In a medium bowl, whisk together the garlic, vinegar, water, olive oil, sugar, and fresh herbs. Pour the dressing over the cucumbers and onions and allow the salad to sit in the refrigerator, stirring every 10 minutes, for 1 hour. Season with the salt and pepper.

CHILI *and* LIME PASTA SALAD

When it comes to tailgating, I can't think of anything more versatile than pasta salad, and this version can safely sit out for a long period. Even better, you can add roasted chicken, shrimp, carnitas, or crawfish (among other things) to give it another layer of flavor and nourishment. Make no mistake, there is a *lot* of bad pasta salad out there. We have all fallen victim to a scoop of it on occasion, thinking it was the "healthy" alternative on the food table. This recipe is meant to be the antidote to the dull, flat versions we have all dug into in the past. For best results, throw this together at the very last moment. Otherwise, the acid will cause the pasta to break down if it sits for more than 12 hours.

MAKE THE VINAIGRETTE In a blender, combine the olive oils, vinegars, lime zest and juice, shallot, jalapeño, garlic, chili powder, cumin, paprika, and cilantro and puree on high until well combined and creamy looking. Season with salt and black pepper and measure out 1¾ cups for this recipe. Set aside.

MAKE THE PASTA SALAD In a large bowl, toss together the pasta, onion, jalapeño (if using), asparagus, tomatoes, bell pepper, corn, and black beans. Stir in the reserved vinaigrette. Season well with salt and black pepper. When you're ready to serve, stir in avocado and sprinkle with the cilantro.

Chili-Lime Vinaigrette

1 cup olive oil

2 tablespoons extra-virgin olive oil

½ cup sherry vinegar

3 tablespoons apple cider vinegar

Grated zest and juice of 1 lime

3 tablespoons minced shallot

2 teaspoons minced jalapeño pepper

1 teaspoon minced garlic

1½ teaspoons chili powder

¾ teaspoon ground cumin

½ teaspoon smoked paprika

2 tablespoons chopped fresh cilantro

Salt and black pepper

Pasta Salad

8 cups cooked penne, elbow macaroni, farfalle, or fusilli

1 cup thinly sliced red onion (root to stem)

¼ cup sliced jalapeño pepper (optional)

1½ cups asparagus tips

1½ cups halved cherry tomatoes

1 cup diced yellow bell pepper

1 cup roasted corn kernels (see Notes)

¾ cup cooked black beans, or 1 (12-ounce) can black beans, rinsed

Salt and black pepper

1 cup diced avocado

½ cup chopped cilantro

NOTES

▶ Pasta salad can frequently be one-dimensional, which is largely due to the fact that pasta tends to neutralize flavor when it sits for too long. Refresh this right before serving with a little more vinaigrette, so it is bright with acid from the vinegar. Alternatively, spritz it with a little lime juice.

▶ To roast corn, preheat oven to 375°F. Shuck 2 ears of corn and rub the kernels with 2 tablespoons of extra-virgin olive oil, sprinkle with salt and pepper, and place in the oven for 15 minutes. Remove from the oven, allow to cool, and carefully slice the roasted kernels from the cobs.

▶ Wanna take corn off the cob without covering the entire floor of your kitchen with runaway kernels? Place a 2-cup plastic container (like a hummus container) upside down in the bottom of a medium-size mixing bowl. Place the bottom of the cob on the upturned bottom of the plastic container and slice the kernels off. They will all be contained in the bowl. No mess!

STEEN'S ROASTED CARROTS, CHÈVRE, HELL FIRE—SPICED PECANS, MICROGREENS

Carrots were one of the first vegetables I learned to love as a kid. My brother and I would sit in our family's little kitchen on Prytania Street in New Orleans and do homework while Mom cooked supper. She would slice carrot coins and celery sticks for us to snack on while she cooked, and at some point, I discovered the wonderful voodoo of dunking sweet raw carrot in the horseradish-y spiciness of Zatarain's Creole mustard. A lifelong obsession was born, and a world of possibilities would ensue once I dove into cooking.

Carrots are loaded with natural sugars, and roasting them adds a delicious layer of caramelization. They are hearty enough to stand up to a relatively hard roast, but if they overcook, they release their water and collapse into a leathery shell. Check them as they cook and test them with a knife from time to time. Once the knife plunges through the carrot easily and the outside has a little color, pull them out of the oven and serve them.

Pecans

2 cups pecan halves

6 tablespoons butter, melted

2 teaspoons cayenne pepper

2½ teaspoons sugar

1 teaspoon salt

2 teaspoons black pepper

Chèvre Spread

1¼ pounds fresh goat cheese

½ cup buttermilk

Grated zest and juice of 1 lime

1 tablespoon honey

2 teaspoons chopped fresh rosemary

⅛ teaspoon cayenne pepper

Pinch of ground cinnamon

Salt and black pepper

Carrots

3 pounds market-fresh baby carrots, with their greens

4 tablespoons extra-virgin olive oil

Salt and black pepper

¼ teaspoon cayenne pepper

¼ cup cane syrup, preferably Steen's, or your favorite sorghum molasses

1 cup micro mustard greens, radish sprouts, or arugula

Apple cider vinegar for misting the salad

MAKE THE PECANS Preheat the oven to 350°F.

Spread out the pecans on a baking sheet and toast for 5 to 7 minutes, or until fragrant. Remove from the oven and immediately dump into a medium-size mixing bowl. Add the butter, cayenne, sugar, salt, and black pepper, stirring until well blended. Spread out evenly on the baking sheet and bake for an additional 5 minutes, or until nicely fragrant. Remove from the oven and stir them occasionally on the baking sheet until the pecans have cooled completely. Set aside. These will keep nicely for 1 week in an airtight container at room temperature.

Turn the oven up to 400°F.

continued

MAKE THE CHÈVRE SPREAD In the bowl of a stand mixer fitted with the paddle attachment, beat the chèvre on medium until smooth. Add the buttermilk and mix until well combined. Beat in the lime zest and juice, honey, rosemary, cayenne, and cinnamon. Season with salt and black pepper. Store, covered, in the refrigerator for up to 2 weeks.

MAKE THE CARROTS Cut the greens off of the carrots, leaving ½ inch of the stem intact. Wash the greens. Wash and peel the carrots. Place them in a large bowl and toss with 2 tablespoons of the oil and season with salt, black pepper, and cayenne. Spread out in one layer on a baking sheet and roast for 12 minutes, stirring every 5 minutes. Carrots should be tender and slightly colored. Remove from oven and dump them back into bowl. Toss the carrots with the cane syrup and return to the baking sheet. Roast for an additional 5 minutes, and remove from the oven.

To assemble the dish, layer the chèvre spread on a platter and place the carrots on top. Garnish with the pecans, the reserved carrot greens, and the microgreens. Use a clean olive oil mister to mist the salad with the apple cider vinegar and serve. If you don't have a misting bottle, just sprinkle carrots with apple cider vinegar.

BOWL GAMES
THE THINGS *of* LEGEND PRESENTED *in* BOWL FORM

My dad is convinced that my love of things eaten from a bowl (and, more often than not, with a spoon) is some sort of conspiracy or perversion. When at my house these days, a meal doesn't pass that he doesn't insist that, no matter what we are having, he wants to eat off of a plate and with a fork. It is hilarious because his "plate pig-headedness" is due to nothing more than the fact that we eat a lot from bowls in our house out of nothing more than my gluttonous personal preference.

The same reason I like things that come in bowls also happens to be the same reason these items are perfect for tailgate settings: Whatever you are eating gets ladled into a bowl, and all you need is a spoon to eat that well-contained item from the bowl in the palm of your hand. This is the part where I am painfully honest: I don't just love the convenience or economy of this manner of eating. Since I was little, I loved mixing my food together and getting everything in one bite. Like many little ones, my fascination started with mashed potatoes, peas, and meatloaf, the gateway drug to bowl-eating. This combined with the fact that so much of what I grew up eating (gumbo, red beans and rice, étouffée, grillades, etc.) were all dishes more easily eaten from bowls, combined with my gluttonous tendencies, has led to an environment more easily serviced with bowls and spoons.

So, Dad, this is not a conspiracy or perversion. I just like to get the foods to my mouth hole and then stomach as efficiently as possible.

WHITE BEAN *and* CHICKEN CHILI, CORNBREAD CROUTONS

I freely admit it: I was a white chili hater. In my opinion, white chili was pinko, commie bullshit, nonsense. You see, I grew up in south Louisiana. My dad was in the oil and gas business, so we naturally spent a good amount of time with brash Texans, who, as a group, are not known for genteel comportment or bottled opinion. As a result, I grew up with the understanding that chili was made with only beef, unless there was ground game meat that needed to be dispensed with. No matter how gamey that meat might be, enough chili powder, cumin, onions, and garlic could mask any less-than-appealing flavors. In the opinion of everyone around me during those formative years, white chili was some hippie health-food abomination. If beans were used, they were pintos . . . or none at all.

Were it not for my passionate craving for white beans, my narrow-minded opinion may never have been swayed. But fifteen years ago, my bride and I were doing an extensive renovation on our house and had to relocate to a little condominium for the duration of the project. As newlyweds, we decided for Thanksgiving to entertain our whole family in our tiny little phone booth of a living space. We jostled each other around the miniscule galley kitchen and managed to pull off a lavish meal together, which produced far too many leftovers. My dad had brought me several pounds of Camellia brand white beans, and between those and the mountain of leftover turkey, this star was born. I recant everything I once thought about white chili and apologize for the tidal wave of aspersions I once spewed.

Cornbread Croutons

1½ tablespoons bacon fat rendered from 6 to 8 strips of bacon

4 cups cornmeal

1 cup all-purpose flour

2 tablespoons sugar

2 teaspoons baking powder

2 teaspoons baking soda

3 tablespoons black pepper

1½ teaspoons salt

5 eggs

4 cups buttermilk

1 cup sour cream

¾ cup butter, melted

1 teaspoon salt

Chili

½ cup lard or vegetable oil

1 tablespoon cumin seeds

3 cups diced yellow onion

¼ cup plus 2 tablespoons minced garlic

3 jalapeño peppers, seeded and diced

2½ cups chopped Anaheim peppers or other mild chiles

2 tablespoons ground cumin

2 tablespoons ground coriander

1 teaspoon cayenne pepper

2 teaspoons paprika

¼ cup chopped fresh oregano leaves

8 cups chicken stock

3 (14-ounce) cans white beans, drained and rinsed

1 (14-ounce) can hominy, drained and rinsed

Meat of 2 (3-pound) rotisserie chickens, chopped

Grated zest and juice of 4 limes

½ cup masa harina

3 cups thinly sliced corn tortillas

2 bunches fresh cilantro, chopped

Salt and black pepper

Garnishes

3 cups sliced red or green cabbage

2 cups thinly sliced radishes

2 cups sliced avocados

continued

MAKE THE CORNBREAD CROUTONS Preheat the oven to 375°F. Place the bacon fat in a 10-inch cast-iron skillet and put the skillet in the oven until ready to bake.

In a large bowl, whisk together the cornmeal, flour, sugar, baking powder, baking soda, pepper, and salt until well blended. Whisk together the eggs in a medium mixing bowl and add the buttermilk and sour cream, blending well. Stir the wet ingredients into the dry and continue stirring until well combined.

Remove the skillet from the oven. Pour the cornbread batter into the hot skillet and bake for 30 minutes, or until fully set up (a toothpick or cake tester will come out clean). Remove from the oven and cool completely in the pan.

Cut the cornbread into ¾-inch cubes. Place 6 cups in a large mixing bowl and toss with the melted butter and salt. Lay the croutons on a baking sheet in a single layer. Bake for 12 to 15 minutes, or until the croutons are slightly crispy on the outside. Remove from the oven and cool.

MAKE THE CHILI In a large Dutch oven, melt the lard over medium heat. Add the cumin seeds and stir for 30 seconds, or until fragrant. Add the onion, garlic, and jalapeños and sauté until the onion is transparent. Stir in the Anaheim peppers, the cumin, coriander, cayenne, paprika, and fresh oregano and blend well. Stir in the chicken stock and white beans and bring to a boil. Turn down the heat and simmer for 20 minutes, or until the beans are very tender. Mash the beans with a potato masher to release their starches. Add the hominy, chicken, lime zest and juice, and masa and simmer for another 25 minutes. Stir in the tortilla strips and cilantro. Season with salt and black pepper. Garnish with the cabbage, sliced radishes, avocados, and the cornbread croutons.

ROASTED CRAWFISH *and* CRISPY ANDOUILLE MAC *and* CHEESE

The best mac and cheese that has ever freaking existed was the one we made at Crook's Corner in Chapel Hill, North Carolina, in the early '80s. It was layered with sautéed mushrooms and onions and bound with the perfect proportions of béchamel sauce and cheese. The bread crumb topping was loaded with butter. I am not romanticizing; it was that freaking good. This is version also includes crawfish and andouille. Okay, just stop reading this bullshit now and go ahead and make it.

4 tablespoons olive oil

2½ cups thinly sliced andouille sausage

2 cups diced yellow onion

2 tablespoons minced garlic

½ cup diced red bell pepper

½ cup diced green bell pepper

⅓ cup minced celery

1 teaspoon dry mustard

¼ teaspoon cayenne pepper

½ teaspoon thyme

¾ teaspoon oregano

4 tablespoons flour

3½ cups whole milk

1 pound crawfish tails

1 pound elbow macaroni, cooked al dente

3 cups grated sharp cheddar

2 cups grated Gruyère

½ cup grated Parmesan

Zest and juice of 1 lemon

1½ teaspoons salt

2 teaspoons black pepper

1 cup panko bread crumbs

Preheat the oven to 375°F.

In a medium Dutch oven, heat 2 tablespoons of the olive oil over medium heat. Add the andouille and sauté, stirring regularly, until brown and crispy, about 7 minutes. Remove with a slotted spoon and reserve. Add the remaining 2 tablespoons oil to the pan and stir in the onion and garlic. Sauté for 3 to 4 minutes, or until the onion is transparent. Stir in the bell peppers and celery and sauté for another 5 minutes, or until the celery is wilted. Blend in the mustard, cayenne, thyme, and oregano and then sprinkle with flour and blend again. Add milk and stir for 3 to 4 minutes, or until the mixture thickens.

In a medium-size mixing bowl, stir together the sharp cheddar, Gruyère, and Parmesan.

Add 3½ cups of the cheese mixture to the pot and stir until melted and smooth. Add the cooked sausage, crawfish tails, and macaroni and combine fully. Stir in lemon zest and juice, salt, and black pepper and combine well.

In a small bowl, mix the remaining cheeses and bread crumbs. Sprinkle over the top of the macaroni and bake for 30 minutes, until the mac and cheese is golden and bubbly.

PERFECT "10" CHICKEN POT PIE

My wife is a saint; she somehow tolerates my cooking obsessions, bordering on perversions. I will get an idea about some dish and how I want it to taste, look, and feel and then begin the experimentation process, making a total mess as I try to actualize my vision. At this point in my career, lots of this experimentation happens in my home kitchen, and frequently the testing process will involve thirty or more versions of whatever it is I am working on. When we started on donuts, we worked almost daily with different versions of donut dough recipes for over eight months before we were happy. Then we blew it up and started over again for another two months.

A year ago I got a version of chicken pot pie stuck in my head and began working on what I wanted to be the CPP of my childhood memories. I wanted an over-the-top chicken flavor, lots of béchamel and vegetables, and a tasty crust. This is what came out of the mountain of pies that inhabited our refrigerators for several months in the winter of 2018. I cooked, Bess cleaned, and she ate more chicken pot pie than most people will consume in a lifetime—and she managed to do so without choking or stabbing me.

Crust

1½ cups butter

¾ cup lard

5 cups all-purpose flour

2½ teaspoons salt

2 teaspoons sugar

¾ teaspoon cayenne pepper

2 teaspoons apple cider vinegar

¾ cup ice water

1 egg, lightly beaten

Filling

1 (3-pound) chicken, split in half

Salt and black pepper

¼ cup olive oil

1 yellow onion, coarsely chopped, plus 1 cup diced yellow onion

1 carrot, peeled and chopped, plus ½ cup diced carrots

2 celery stalks, coarsely chopped, plus ¾ cup diced celery

3 garlic cloves, smashed

1½ teaspoons black peppercorns

2 bay leaves

1½ cups white wine

1 cup butter

½ cup all-purpose flour

½ cup duck fat or extra-virgin olive oil

1 cup sliced mushrooms

¾ cup English peas

½ cup chopped fresh tarragon

¼ cup fresh thyme leaves

¼ cup chopped fresh rosemary

2 tablespoons red pepper flakes

MAKE THE CRUST Preheat the oven to 350°F.

Cut the butter into small cubes and freeze for 30 minutes. Freeze the lard for 1 hour. Place the flour, salt, sugar, and cayenne in a food processor and process briefly. Break the lard into several pieces, drop it into the flour, and add the butter cubes. Pulse several times until the mixture looks like coarse meal. Transfer to a medium bowl. Stir in the vinegar and half the water with a fork and continue stirring until

continued

the water is absorbed. The dough will start coming together in large chunks. Blend in the rest of the water; the dough should still be chunky. Flour your hands and fold the dough by hand to bring it together into a ball. If the mixture is dry, add a touch more water (1 teaspoon at a time). Turn out the dough onto a floured surface and, working quickly, knead the dough into a smooth ball. This should take about three or four turns of kneading and folding. Flatten into a disk, wrap in plastic wrap, and refrigerate for 1 hour.

Divide the cold dough into four equal pieces (for two tops and two bottoms), and form each one into a ball. Roll out one of the balls into a circle 11 inches in diameter and ¼ inch thick. Place in a deep 9-inch pie pan and prick all over with a fork. Repeat with a second ball of dough, placing it in a second pie pan. Roll out the remaining two balls of dough to ¼ inch thick.

MAKE THE FILLING Pat the chicken dry with paper towels and season liberally with salt and pepper. In a medium stockpot, heat the oil over high heat. One at a time, sear the chicken halves on both sides until golden brown, about 5 to 7 minutes per side.

Add the coarsely chopped onion, coarsely chopped carrot, coarsely chopped celery, the garlic, peppercorns, bay leaves, and 1 cup of the wine to the pot with the chicken. Add water to cover and bring to a boil. Turn down the heat to medium-low and simmer the chicken halves until tender and falling apart, about 45 minutes. Remove from the heat and allow to cool for 15 minutes. Strain the stock and set aside 5 quarts for the recipe. Remove the chicken, and discard the vegetable solids. Pick the chicken meat off the bones and chop coarsely. Set aside.

In a small cast-iron skillet, whisk the butter and flour together over medium heat. This will foam up at first. Once it does so, turn the heat to low and whisk until the roux turns light brown and smells nutty. Remove from the heat and set aside.

In the stockpot, heat the duck fat over medium heat and add the remaining diced onions, celery, and carrots, and the mushrooms. Sauté until tender, about 10 to 12 minutes. Stir in the remaining ½ cup wine, scraping the bottom of the pot to loosen any caramelized bits stuck to the bottom of the pot. Add the chicken and peas into mix and warm through. Add the reserved chicken stock and bring to a simmer. Whisk the warm roux until smooth and slowly blend it into the chicken mix, stirring constantly. As the filling begins to thicken, add the tarragon, thyme, rosemary, and red pepper flakes. Season with salt and black pepper and set aside.

Fill each pie pan with half the filling and cover with a circle of dough. Crimp the edges decoratively and brush the top with the beaten egg. Cut vents into the top of each one. (At this point, the pies can be wrapped and stored in the freezer for up to 2 months. Thaw in the refrigerator for 12 hours before baking.)

Bake the pies for 30 minutes, or until golden brown. Remove from oven and allow to cool for 10 minutes before serving (the inside will be like hot lava when it comes out of the oven).

ITALIAN SAUSAGE *and* TOMATO TABBOULEH

It took going to Israel with my brother Michael Solomonov to first understand how wrong my (and the traditional American) idea of tabbouleh actually was. Like so many other exotic dishes we mimic and eat in the States, until you have had them in their native setting, more often than not, you get a sadly Americanized version of whatever it is you want to dive into. Stateside, we typically steam bulgur and sprinkle it with a little parsley and mint, and then pat ourselves on the back for our "international" cuisine. Tabbouleh actually is quite the opposite: a mountain of parsley with a smattering of bulgur. Seeing this for the first time was confounding, but totally eye-opening.

I have taken a few liberties with this version. While some of the ingredients are untraditional, the ratio of parsley to bulgur is classic. Roman Catholics may wonder why the hell I would take perfectly delicious Italian sausage and pile it into this mess, while Jews and Muslims *might* agree I was a total heretic for putting pork in their tabbouleh. I guess this is where I admit shameless cultural appropriation. The end result, however, is out-freaking-standing. Make it first, judge me later.

This a great make-ahead dish, which will survive sitting at a tailgate buffet extremely well. If you are not crazy about Italian sausage (and if so, we really don't have shit to talk about), feel free to substitute an equal amount of cooked or smoked salmon, rotisserie chicken, spiced ground lamb, or cooked shrimp. Just about anything works to pump this dish up.

2 tablespoons olive oil

1 pound spicy Italian sausage

6 cups diced Roma tomatoes

Salt

5 cups chopped fresh flat-leaf parsley

¾ cup bulgur

2 cups finely diced cucumbers

2 cups chopped fresh mint

1 cup minced green onions, white and light green parts

2 tablespoons extra-virgin olive oil

Grated zest and juice of 1 lemon, plus more juice as needed

Heat the olive oil in a large sauté pan over medium heat. Split open the sausage casings and add the meat to the pan. Cook, stirring constantly, until the sausage is fully cooked and slightly crispy. Remove from the pan and drain on paper towels. Pat the sausage with paper towels to remove as much oil as possible. Set aside.

Toss the tomatoes with 2 teaspoons salt until well combined and place in a sieve with a bowl underneath to catch the tomato water. Allow to sit for 45 minutes

Line a baking sheet with paper towels. Toss the parsley with 1½ teaspoons salt and spread out on the baking sheet. Allow to sit for 30 minutes. Blot the parsley from time to time to absorb the water drawn out by salt.

Take the captured tomato water and add tap water (if needed) to make a total of 1½ cups. Bring to a boil in a small saucepan. Place the bulgur in a medium bowl and pour the boiling tomato water over it. Allow to sit for 45 minutes. Drain and transfer to a large bowl.

Add the sausage, parsley, tomatoes, cucumbers, mint, green onions, extra-virgin olive oil, and the lemon zest and juice. Stir to combine well and allow to sit for 15 minutes. Season with salt and add extra lemon juice if needed.

TURKEY NECK *and* BACON BLACK-EYED PEA GUMBO

At otherwise friendly gatherings in south Louisiana, a howling chorus can erupt over what goes or doesn't go into gumbo. We take food very seriously and personally where I come from. As far as I am concerned, there are classic gumbos (seafood and okra, chicken and andouille) that stand on their own, and their relatively standard ingredients should not be messed with. But it is also true that gumbo was originally a survival dish, and anything could go in for the sake of using the food on hand. So, while some folks would consider it repulsive, I like to make a bean or pea gumbo from time to time.

In all my years, I have seen few gumbos that employ dried beans beyond the occasional south Louisiana red bean gumbo, which made use of the red beans left over from the traditional Monday meal of red beans and rice. In this one, I use black-eyed peas as well as the wildly unsung protein hero, turkey neck. It is fun, unusual, and delicious. Served over crumbled cornbread with a poached egg, it is just stupid good.

Turkey Neck Stock

10 turkey necks

Salt and black pepper

¼ cup olive oil

1 medium yellow onion, chopped

3 celery stalks, chopped

2 medium carrots, chopped

6 garlic cloves

1 jalapeño pepper, seeded and chopped

3 bay leaves

2 teaspoons dried oregano

2 teaspoons black peppercorns

8 sprigs fresh parsley

1 cup white wine

6 quarts water

Black-Eyed Peas

2 cups dried black-eyed peas

¾ cup diced yellow onion

½ cup diced celery

½ cup diced carrot

1½ tablespoons minced garlic

6 cups chicken stock

Gumbo

2 cups chopped bacon

Vegetable oil for the roux

1½ cups all-purpose flour

2½ cups diced yellow onion

1½ cups diced green bell pepper

1½ cups diced celery

¼ cup minced garlic

3 bay leaves

2 tablespoons dried oregano

2 teaspoons dried thyme

1½ teaspoons cayenne pepper

1 teaspoon red pepper flakes

1 tablespoon paprika

2 tablespoons filé powder (see Note on page 126)

Salt and black pepper

Tabasco sauce

Hot cooked rice for serving

Slivered green onions, green part only, for garnish

continued

MAKE THE STOCK Sprinkle the turkey necks with salt and black pepper. Heat the oil in a large stockpot over medium heat until it shimmers. In batches, brown the turkey necks on both sides, removing them from the pot and setting them aside as they finish. Combine the onion, celery, carrots, garlic, and jalapeño in the pot and sauté until lightly colored. Return the necks to the pot and stir in the bay leaves, oregano, peppercorns, parsley, and white wine. Bring to a simmer and add the water. Bring to a boil, turn down the heat to low, and simmer gently, covered, for 1 hour, or until the turkey necks come apart easily.

Remove from the heat, and strain the stock. Set aside 6 quarts for the gumbo. Allow the solids to cool until comfortable to handle. Pick through and discard the vegetables. Pick the meat off the necks and set aside. Discard the bones, unless you'd like to make a necklace, which I am totally behind, by the way.

MAKE THE BLACK-EYED PEAS Combine the black-eyed peas, onion, celery, carrot, garlic, and stock in a large pot and bring to a simmer over medium heat. Turn down the heat to low and simmer, covered, for 25 minutes, or until the peas are completely tender. Remove from the heat, drain, and set aside the peas and vegetables.

MAKE THE GUMBO In a large soup pot, cook the bacon over medium heat until crisp. Remove from the pot, drain on paper towels, and set aside. Pour the bacon fat into a 2-cup measure and add enough vegetable oil to give you 1¼ cups. Return to the soup pot, stir in 1¼ cups of the flour, and blend together well. Turn down the heat to low and cook the roux, stirring constantly, until it turns a deep reddish brown (but not dark brown).

Stir in the onion, bell pepper, celery, and garlic and cook, stirring constantly, until the vegetables are cooked through and lightly colored. Whisk in the reserved 6 quarts of turkey stock, the bay leaves, oregano, thyme, cayenne, red pepper flakes, and paprika. Turn up the heat to medium and bring to a simmer. Return the heat to low and let the gumbo simmer for 30 minutes, skimming off the fat that floats to the top.

Measure the filé powder into a small bowl and pour 1 cup of the gumbo liquid over the filé powder. Stir vigorously. The filé will thicken the liquid immediately. When completely blended, add to the gumbo pot and simmer for an additional 10 minutes. Stir in the black-eyed peas, reserved turkey neck meat, and bacon and simmer on low for 1 hour, stirring regularly.

Season the gumbo with salt, black pepper, and Tabasco. Serve with white rice and slivered green onions.

NOTE

► Filé powder is made from dried ground sassafras leaves. It provides both flavor and a thickening property to your gumbo. If you live outside of the South, it's best to look for this on the internet. No matter what you may read, there is no "substitute" for filé powder. Not all gumbos use filé, so this recipe can be made without it, but the flavor and texture will be a little different.

HOT CHICKEN FRIED RICE

I wrote this recipe for the catering service that does the food for the suites and clubs inside of Vaught-Hemingway Stadium, home of the Ole Miss Rebels. One of the greatest things I get to do every year is work with my buddy Darren Hubbard and his tireless team to feed the sixty or seventy thousand people who fill the stadium on the weekends in the fall.

Darren is as big as a house with a diaphragm the size of a grand piano. He commands attention everywhere he goes, and because his heart is also generously proportioned, he gets a lot of devotion and respect. I am always amazed when I walk into his kitchens; the very same faces are in there every season doing the brutal, thankless job of getting all of those people fed on game days. It says the world about him.

¼ cup lard

¾ cup vegetable oil

¼ cup plus 2 tablespoons cayenne pepper

2 tablespoons chili powder

1 tablespoon hot paprika

1 tablespoon garlic powder

1½ teaspoons onion powder

2½ tablespoons brown sugar

3 cups diced fried chicken tenders (from Popeyes or your favorite chicken shack)

Fried Rice

6 tablespoons clarified butter (see Note on page 43 and recipe on page 238)

4 eggs, well beaten

Salt and black pepper

1 tablespoon sesame oil

2 cups diced yellow onion

1½ cups diced carrot

1 cup fresh or frozen peas

1 serrano pepper, seeded and minced (optional)

2 tablespoons minced garlic

5 cups cold cooked white rice

2 teaspoons oyster sauce

3 tablespoons black sesame seeds

¾ cup sliced green onion

In a small saucepan, melt the lard, add the oil, and heat to 185°F. Remove from the heat and carefully stir in the cayenne, chili powder, paprika, garlic powder, onion powder, and brown sugar. Set aside and allow to steep.

Preheat the oven to 450°F. Place the diced tenders on a baking sheet lined with parchment paper and set aside.

MAKE THE FRIED RICE In a large wok over medium heat, cook 3 tablespoons of the clarified butter until it begins to shimmer. Carefully pour in the eggs and season lightly with salt and black pepper. Scramble the eggs until just done, chop into small bites with a spatula, remove from the wok, and set aside. Add the remaining 3 tablespoons clarified butter and the sesame oil and turn up the heat to high. Stir in the onion and carrot and sauté, stirring constantly, for 2 minutes. Stir in the peas, serrano pepper, and garlic and coat well. Immediately stir in the cold rice. Cook, stirring occasionally, until the rice begins to brown, about 4 minutes. Stir in the reserved scrambled eggs, the oyster sauce, and sesame seeds and remove from the heat.

Place the tenders in the oven and warm for 5 minutes. Remove from the oven and transfer to a large stainless-steel bowl. Spoon 3 tablespoons of the spicy oil over the chicken and toss well. Add more if desired. Sprinkle with ¾ teaspoon salt and toss again. Stir the hot chicken into fried rice, and stir in the green onion. Serve hot.

ROASTED SHRIMP *and* VEGETABLE PASTA SALAD

There is something very 1985 about pasta salad. It was not the "best" time for food in the States. Fortunately, ingredients and techniques have come a long way in the last thirty-five years, so there's opportunity to revisit and reimagine the sins of past dishes. For this one we lightly roast vegetables to mimic a Low Country boil and then infuse oil with Old Bay Seasoning to make a light, creamy vinaigrette. It holds well at room temperature and is nice and filling. Also, the farther in advance it is made, the better the flavors get!

Creamy Old Bay–Lemon Vinaigrette

¾ cup mayonnaise, preferably Duke's

1½ teaspoons Old Bay–infused oil (see Note)

Grated zest and juice of 2 lemons

2 tablespoons minced shallot

2 tablespoons chopped capers

2 tablespoons white wine vinegar

1 tablespoon chopped fresh parsley

Salt and black pepper

Pasta Salad

1 pound extra-large shrimp

2 tablespoons Old Bay Seasoning

¼ cup plus 2 tablespoons olive oil

4 tablespoons extra-virgin olive oil

Salt and black pepper

2 cups diced smoked pork sausage

3 cups peeled and diced russet potatoes (½-inch dice)

2 cups fresh corn kernels

1½ cups diced yellow onion

1½ cups diced zucchini

1½ cups diced yellow squash

2 tablespoons minced garlic

1 pound orecchiette, cooked according to the package directions until al dente

1 cup chopped pimento

½ cup chopped fresh parsley

½ cup chopped green onion

Preheat the oven to 350°F. Line a baking sheet with parchment paper.

MAKE THE VINAIGRETTE In a small bowl, whisk together the mayonnaise, Old Bay oil, lemon zest and juice, shallot, capers, vinegar, and parsley. Season with salt and pepper. Set aside 1 cup for the pasta salad and store in the refrigerator.

MAKE THE PASTA SALAD In a medium bowl, toss the shrimp with 2¼ teaspoons of the Old Bay Seasoning, 2 tablespoons of the olive oil, and 1½ tablespoons of the extra-virgin olive oil. Sprinkle with salt and pepper and stir to combine. Spread out the shrimp in a single layer on the prepared baking sheet and roast for 7 minutes, or until cooked through and firm to the touch. Remove from the baking sheet and transfer to a large bowl. Leave on the oven.

Spread out the sausage on the same baking sheet and roast for 7 minutes, or until lightly browned. Remove from the oven and add to the shrimp. Leave on the oven.

In the bowl in which you seasoned the shrimp, toss the potatoes with 2 tablespoons of the olive oil, 1 tablespoon of the extra-virgin olive oil, and 1½ teaspoons of the Old Bay Seasoning. Sprinkle with salt and pepper and spread out in a single layer on the baking sheet. Roast for 15 minutes, or until the potatoes are lightly colored and cooked through. Add to the shrimp and sausage.

In the same medium bowl, toss together the corn, onion, zucchini, yellow squash, and garlic with the remaining 2 tablespoons of olive oil, 1½ tablespoons of extra-virgin olive oil, and 2¼ teaspoons of Old Bay. Sprinkle with salt and pepper and roast for 8 minutes, or until the vegetables begin to color lightly. Add to the shrimp mix.

Add the pasta, pimento, parsley, and green onion. Add the reserved vinaigrette and stir to combine. Allow to sit for 20 minutes, season with salt and pepper, and serve.

NOTE

▶ To make Old Bay–infused oil, blend 3 tablespoons Old Bay with enough boiling water (about 1½ tablespoons) to make a thick paste. The paste should be slightly looser than wasabi. Add 1½ cups vegetable oil, place a tight lid onto the container, and shake vigorously. Repeat shaking every couple of hours for 2 days. Allow the solids to settle and spoon off the infused oil. This will keep in the refrigerator for up to 6 months.

CILANTRO *and* PEANUT RICE NOODLES

I have zero training in Asian food. To be honest, I cannot even cook a decent basic fried rice. It's humiliating. That said, I understand flavor profiles, so when putting together things that don't take a load of technical skill, I manage to skate by without exposing my ineptitude. These noodles are an excellent example. Short of being able to boil some noodles, this requires no skill whatsoever. The dish has little that can go bad sitting out at room temperature. And you can add chicken, shrimp, sautéed pork, or whatever you like to take it to the next level.

2 (1-pound) packages rice noodles, or 2 pounds soba noodles

3 tablespoons olive oil

1 teaspoon sesame oil

2 teaspoons cumin seeds

¾ cup minced shallot

2 tablespoons minced garlic

2 tablespoons minced ginger

1¼ cups chopped roasted peanuts

1 cup freshly ground peanut butter

1½ cups unsweetened coconut milk

Grated zest and juice of 2 limes

1½ tablespoons sugar, plus more as needed

1 tablespoon sambal (see Note on page 69)

1 teaspoon turmeric

½ teaspoon ground cumin

½ teaspoon cayenne pepper

2 cups chicken stock (or water or vegetable stock for a vegetarian dish)

Salt

1 cup chopped fresh cilantro

¼ cup toasted sesame seeds

Break the noodles in half and cook according to the directions on the package until al dente. Drain but do not rinse. Return to the pot, stir in 2 tablespoons of the olive oil, and set aside.

Heat the remaining tablespoon of olive oil and the sesame oil in a medium saucepan over medium heat. When the oil begins to shimmer, stir in the cumin seeds and cook, stirring, for 10 seconds. Add the shallot, garlic, and ginger and sauté an additional 3 minutes, until the shallot is transparent. Do not burn. Stir in the peanuts and sauté for another minute or so. Whisk in the peanut butter, coconut milk, lime zest and juice, sugar, sambal, turmeric, cumin, cayenne, and chicken stock and bring to a boil. Turn down the heat and simmer for 10 minutes. Season with salt and add more sugar if needed. Stir in the noodles and blend well.

Pour the noodles into a large bowl and garnish with cilantro and sesame seeds. Serve hot or at room temperature.

SPICY FIVE-BEAN SALAD

Bean salad is a relic; I am pretty sure that all the grandmothers who used to make it with any regularity have passed on, leaving this wonderful dish alone to trundle off into obscurity. On first blush, I admit, a bean salad can seem one-dimensional. But depending on the bean types, their provenance, and how they are cooked, the potential depth of earthy flavor is astounding. Add some lentils; some fresh, crispy, aromatic vegetables; and a pithy, acidic vinaigrette; and fleck it with the brightness of fresh herbs, and you have a mellifluous little symphony that is both healthy and filling.

If you are even the slightest bit hesitant, just trust me. This is a winner, and the longer it sits, the better it gets. If you must, you can use a variety of well-rinsed canned beans and get a decent result, but for the best taste, I recommend cooking all the beans and lentils from scratch.

Beans and Lentils

1 cup dried chickpeas

1¾ cups green lentils

1 cup dried white beans

1 cup dried kidney beans

1 cup dried black beans

2½ cups coarsely chopped yellow onion

1¼ cups coarsely chopped celery

1 tablespoon plus 2 teaspoons minced garlic

5 bay leaves

10 cups chicken stock

1 teaspoon ground coriander

1 teaspoon cumin seeds

1 teaspoon red pepper flakes

2 teaspoons grated ginger

1½ teaspoons turmeric

1 tablespoon tomato paste

½ cup cubed smoked ham (½-inch cubes)

2 teaspoons chopped fresh oregano

¼ teaspoon cayenne pepper

2 teaspoons fresh thyme leaves

½ teaspoon paprika

2 teaspoons ground cumin

1 jalapeño pepper, sliced

2 tablespoons fresh lime juice

Sweet and Sour Vinaigrette

Rind of 7 lemons, plus ¼ cup lemon juice, and more as needed

1½ cups sugar

½ cup olive oil

¼ cup extra-virgin olive oil

¼ cup buttermilk

3 tablespoons minced shallot

1 teaspoon minced garlic

2 tablespoons chopped fresh parsley

1 tablespoon chopped fresh rosemary

1 teaspoon salt

1 tablespoon black pepper

1 cup diced sweet onion

1 cup diced avocado

¾ cup diced celery

¾ cup diced cucumber

¾ cup sliced canned hearts of palm

¾ cup diced pimento

½ cup diced yellow bell pepper

½ cup diced green bell pepper

1 thinly sliced serrano pepper

2 tablespoons minced jalapeño pepper

½ cup chopped fresh parsley

SOAK AND COOK THE BEANS AND LENTILS Place the chickpeas, lentils, white beans, kidney beans, and black beans in separate medium bowls and cover with water by 2 inches. Allow to sit, covered, overnight. Drain and put the lentils and each bean in separate medium saucepans or small pots. To each pan add ½ cup of onion, ¼ cup of celery, 1 teaspoon of garlic, 1 bay leaf, and 2 cups of chicken broth.

To the chickpeas, also add the coriander, ½ teaspoon of the cumin seeds, and ½ teaspoon of red pepper flakes. Add water to cover and bring to a simmer over medium heat. Simmer until tender. Drain and set aside until cooled to room temperature.

To the lentils, add the ginger, turmeric, tomato paste, and the remaining ½ teaspoon cumin seeds. Add water to cover and bring to a simmer over medium heat. Simmer until tender. Drain and set aside until cooled to room temperature.

To the white beans, add the ham, oregano, and the remaining ½ teaspoon red pepper flakes. Add water to cover and bring to a simmer over medium heat. Simmer until tender. Drain and set aside until cooled to room temperature.

To the red beans, add the cayenne, thyme, and paprika. Add water to cover and bring to a simmer over medium heat. Simmer until tender. Drain and set aside until cooled to room temperature.

To the black beans, add the cumin, jalapeño, and lime juice. Add water to cover and bring to a simmer over medium heat. Simmer until tender. Drain and set aside until cooled to room temperature.

MAKE THE VINAIGRETTE Chop the lemon rinds coarsely and place them in a medium bowl. Add the sugar and stir to combine well. Cover and let stand at room temperature for several hours, stirring from time to time, until the sugar has completely dissolved. Strain the syrup and discard the rinds.

Measure ½ cup of the lemon syrup, saving the rest for another use. Pour into a mason jar, and add the lemon juice, both olive oils, the buttermilk, shallot, garlic, parsley, rosemary, salt, and black pepper. Shake vigorously and allow to sit for 15 minutes at room temperature. Adjust the salt and lemon juice to suit your taste. Measure 1¼ cups for the bean salad and set aside.

In a large bowl, combine the beans and vinaigrette. Add the onion, avocado, celery, cucumber, hearts of palm, pimento, both bell peppers, the serrano, jalapeño, and parsley and stir. Allow to sit, covered, at room temperature for 30 minutes, stirring every 5 minutes. Adjust the seasoning to suit your taste and serve. Store the bean salad in the refrigerator for up to 5 days. This is actually at it's best after it has had the chance to marinate for 24 hours.

POBLANO PEPPER *and* CARAMELIZED ONION QUESO FUNDIDO

The best queso fundido I ever had was cooked by a Greek man on a Southern barbecue rig on the curb of Bond Street in New York City—the epitome of cultural appropriation. This was also the moment I fell in love with this greasy, cheesy, delicious mess. It is a dish in which you can truly put anything you want: roasted mushrooms, chorizo, carnitas, roasted chicken, shrimp—it will all work. I have intentionally left this version vegetarian-friendly, but do yourself a favor and run with this.

4 poblano peppers

3 tablespoons butter

2 large yellow onions, chopped, plus
3 tablespoons minced

2 tablespoons sugar

1 teaspoon salt

2½ tablespoons chopped fresh oregano

3 cups grated Oaxaca or mozzarella cheese

1 cup Monterey Jack cheese

2 tablespoons cornstarch

2 tablespoons olive oil

1½ teaspoons ground cumin

½ teaspoon cayenne pepper

2 teaspoons minced garlic

Grated zest and juice of 2 limes

2½ tablespoons extra-virgin olive oil

¼ cup chopped fresh cilantro, plus more for garnish

Salt

20 corn tortillas

Position one rack at the bottom of the oven and a second rack at the top and preheat the oven to 375°F.

Roast the poblanos over the open flame of a gas stove burner or wood fire, turning constantly, until charred all over. Place in a bowl and cover with plastic and allow to sweat for 20 minutes. Peel under cool running water, remove the stems, skins, seeds, and interior membranes, and slice very thin. Set aside.

In a medium sauté pan, melt the butter over medium heat. Add chopped onions and sauté, stirring constantly, until the onions wilt. Turn down the heat to low and stir in sugar, salt, and oregano. Continue cooking, stirring constantly, until the onions brown and turn sweet. Remove from the heat and set aside.

Toss the cheeses with the cornstarch and set aside. In a medium cast-iron skillet, heat the olive oil over medium heat. Add half of the sliced poblano peppers and all of the caramelized onions. Sprinkle with the cumin and cayenne and cook, stirring, until the vegetables are warmed completely. Add the cheeses to pan, stir to combine, and immediately place in the oven on the bottom rack. Bake for 15 minutes.

While the queso is cooking, place the remaining sliced poblano in a blender and add the garlic, minced onion, lime zest and juice, extra-virgin olive oil, and cilantro and blend until pureed. Season with salt and set aside.

Adjust the oven to Broil and remove the queso from the oven while the broiler warms.

In a dry skillet over medium heat, warm the tortillas, one at a time, on both sides. Wrap them in a kitchen towel to keep warm.

Place the cast-iron skillet to the top rack of the oven and brown the top of the cheese lightly, about 4 to 6 minutes. Keep a vigilant eye on your queso during this process so the top doesn't burn. Remove from the oven and drizzle the poblano puree over the top. Sprinkle with the cilantro and serve hot with the tortillas. You can transport and hold this in the makeshift Igloo warming box described on page 5.

HAM HOCK—RED BEANS *and* RICE

There is little in this world that I crave like I crave red beans and rice. For those of you who are blithely unaware, red beans are *the* Monday special dish in New Orleans. Traditionally, Monday was wash day, when the week's worth of laundry was done. So a pot of red beans made with Sunday's ham bone was perfect because it could be left simmering on the stove while laundry was tended to.

My friend, raconteur extraordinaire Pableaux Johnson has made a living of taking his red beans on nationwide potluck road shows. After Hurricane Katrina, on Monday nights he hosted a cathartic gathering of souls struggling to get their footing in a city ravaged and unsure. We have held deep debates in the years since over the merits of different seasoning meats for red beans. Pableaux is a firm advocate of andouille, while I espouse the beauty of the smoked ham hock. We have agreed to disagree, knowing the greatest thing is sharing what we love most with our friends.

2 pounds red kidney beans, preferably Camellia

¼ cup plus 1 tablespoon lard

2 large yellow onions, diced

4 celery stalks, diced

3 medium green bell peppers, diced

3 tablespoons minced garlic

6 bay leaves

2 teaspoons dried thyme

1½ tablespoons dried oregano

1½ tablespoons garlic powder

2 teaspoons cayenne pepper

1 tablespoon salt, plus more as needed

2 teaspoons black pepper, plus more as needed

2 tablespoons brown sugar

2 ham hocks

8 cups chicken stock

3 tablespoon hot sauce, preferably Crystal, plus more as needed

4 pounds good-quality andouille, grilled, for serving (see Note)

Sliced green onion, green part only, for garnish

Hot cooked rice for serving

Dump the red beans into a large bowl. Cover with water by 2 inches, cover the bowl with a kitchen towel, and allow to sit in the refrigerator overnight.

In a large pressure cooker or an Instant Pot set to Sauté, melt the lard over medium heat and stir in the onions, celery, bell peppers, and garlic. Sauté until the vegetables are wilted and the onions are translucent. Drain the beans and stir into the pot. Add the bay leaves, thyme, oregano, garlic powder, cayenne, salt, black pepper, and brown sugar and stir to blend well. Bury the ham hocks in the beans and add enough of the chicken stock to cover the beans by ¾ inch. Add the hot sauce and cover the pressure cooker with the lid. As soon as cooker begins to hiss or whistle, turn down the heat to low; alternatively, set the Instant Pot to Pressure Cook. Cook for 30 minutes. Remove from the heat and allow the pressure to release naturally. Season with more salt, black pepper, and hot sauce as needed. Remove the hocks and, when cool enough to handle, pick the meat off the bones, chop, and return it to the beans. Stir to blend in well.

Garnish the beans with sliced green onions and serve with rice and grilled andouille.

NOTE

▶ While andouille sausage is widely available, *good* andouille is not. Most store-bought is as close to authentic as bug spray is to Chanel Nº5. Fortunately for you, two of the best andouille makers (Jacob's and Bailey's—both in LaPlace, Louisiana) will pack and ship to you. Accept no substitutes!

MEDAL-WINNER BLACK BEAN CHILI

I wrote this recipe totally on the fly for a buddy competing in a chili cook-off in Florence, Alabama, right before we opened Big Bad Breakfast there in a beautiful old building on Court Street. We wanted to participate in the cook-off as the new kid in town and help raise money for a local charity. The chili took first place, and the trophy still sits on the bar at BBB, as I write.

Chili just makes folks happy and warms them like little else when it is cold. This is great for a bar setup with lots of add-ins. I have listed a few below for your consideration. I can't guarantee your team will get a trophy with this recipe, but I can promise you'll have happy friends the minute you pull the lid off that chili pot.

Condiments (optional)

Pickled jalapeños

Grated cheddar cheese

Sour cream

Diced onions

Sliced green onions, green part only

Fried tortilla strips

Crushed soda crackers

Crumbled cotija cheese

Sliced avocado

¼ cup lard or olive oil

1½ pounds ground pork

1½ pounds ground beef

Salt and black pepper

2 tablespoons chili powder

4 cups diced yellow onion

3 cups diced yellow bell pepper

¼ cup plus 2 tablespoons minced garlic

2 large jalapeño peppers

5 (15-ounce) cans black beans, drained and rinsed

3 (15-ounce) cans crushed tomatoes

3 (15-ounce) cans diced tomatoes and green chiles, such as Rotel

¾ cup tomato paste

2 (15-ounce) cans roasted corn

1 (15-ounce) can creamed corn

½ cup masa harina (see Note)

¼ cup fresh lime juice

¼ cup plus 1 tablespoon cumin seeds

3 tablespoons hot chili seasoning mix, preferably Wik Fowler's 2-Alarm chili kit or McCormick, plus more as needed

3 tablespoons ground cumin

3 tablespoons dried oregano

1½ tablespoons dried thyme

¼ teaspoon ground cinnamon

3 cups water

In a large Dutch oven or stockpot, melt the lard over medium heat. Add the pork and beef and season with 2¼ teaspoons salt, 1½ tablespoons black pepper, and the chili powder. Cook, stirring constantly and breaking up the meat as much as possible, until the meat is browned and cooked through. Remove with a slotted spoon and set aside. Stir in the onion, bell pepper, garlic, and jalapeños and sauté until the vegetables wilt.

Return the meat to the pot and stir in the black beans, both crushed and diced tomatoes, tomato paste, both roasted and creamed corn, masa harina, lime juice, cumin seeds, chili seasoning mix, cumin oregano, thyme, and cinnamon. Stir in the water and cover. Bring to a simmer and continue simmering for 45 minutes, stirring every 5 minutes. Remove the lid and simmer for an additional 30 to 45 minutes, until the chili reaches the desired consistency. Season with salt, pepper, and chili mix, as needed, and serve with your choice of condiments.

NOTE

▶ You can skip paying $2.25 for a bag of masa, if you must, but it gives good chili an abundance of flavor.

SPICY VEGETARIAN STEWED LENTILS

I was given a dream writing assignment in the summer of 2017. *Afar* magazine sends one writer quarterly to a blind destination somewhere on the globe to spend two weeks learning about the culture and people. My destination was Kuala Lumpur, Malaysia. I planned to write about food, so I traveled the country for two weeks eating in as many places as I possibly could and intending not to eat anywhere twice. But I was captivated by a street stall I discovered under an elevated metro train track early one morning. They were making stuffed roti (a delicious crêpe or flatbread thingy) served with spicy stewed lentils and sweet Malaysian coffee. It was so good that I went back twice more. I would go to the stall at 5:00 a.m., having an early breakfast at the stall so I would not ruin breakfast somewhere else. It's genius, I know.

These lentils are similar to those I enjoyed in Kuala Lumpur and are excellent with some crusty bread or naan. Like so much of the food I had while there, this is spicy with a surprising touch of sweetness. You can knock down the spiciness and punch up the sweetness as much as you like.

6 cups coarsely chopped tomatoes

3 cups coarsely chopped shallot

½ cup coarsely chopped garlic

2 tablespoons olive oil

2 chiles de árbol

¼ cup plus 1 tablespoon mild curry powder

6 cups yellow lentils

3 cups coconut milk

2 tablespoons sambal (see Note on page 69)

1½ tablespoons brown sugar

Grated zest and juice of 4 limes

2 teaspoons salt, plus more as needed

5 cups vegetable stock, plus more as needed

Crusty bread or naan for serving

Combine the tomatoes, shallots, and garlic in a food processor and process until pureed. Set aside. In a medium pan, heat the oil over medium heat until it begins to shimmer and add the chiles de árbol. Fry the chiles for 2 minutes, stirring constantly, and add the pureed tomato mix. Sauté for 3 to 5 minutes, stirring constantly, until the puree is fragrant. Add the curry powder and lentils and stir to combine well. Stir in the coconut milk, sambal, brown sugar, lime zest and juice, salt, and vegetable stock. Bring to a simmer, cover, and turn down the heat to low. Simmer for 20 minutes, or until the lentils are tender. Uncover and add more vegetable stock to reach the desired texture and simmer briefly. Season with salt and serve hot with bread or naan.

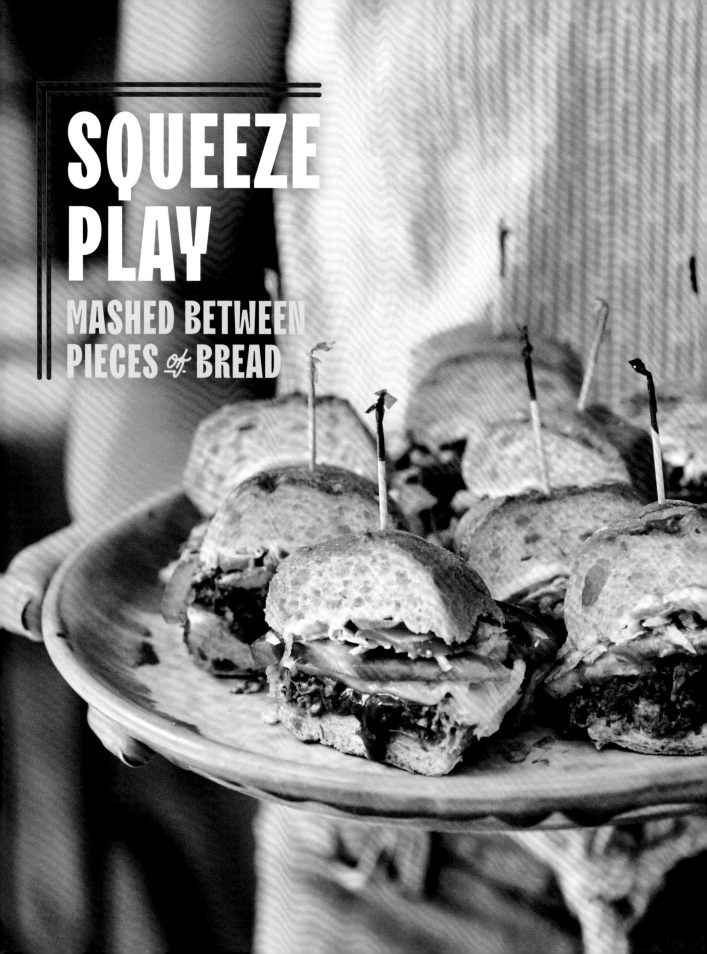

SQUEEZE PLAY

MASHED BETWEEN PIECES *of* BREAD

The sandwich is rarely given its due credit. While I recognize that, in Philly, the cheesesteak is heralded as the gold-standard of sammos, in New Orleans, the po'boy is celebrated ad nauseum, and in the far Northeast they talk lobster roll until they are blue in the face. The sandwich, as an integral part of our national menu, is largely glossed over. It is a truly unfortunate fact. The PB&J is fuel for millions of school kids daily. Bologna sandwiches and ham sandwiches fill the air of summer at swimming holes and playgrounds. As significant a role as the sandwich plays in the pantheon of American food, we just seem to gloss over it in the greater academic analysis. I'm here to do the diligence.

We tend to limit, for the most part, our definition of "sandwich" to protein or vegetable that is slapped between slices of traditional or loaf bread. In reality, however, anything that involves any sort of bread and filling that uses the hand as the delivery vehicle falls into the category, and what's more, they mostly (with proper consideration) make excellent tailgate additions. Burgers, dogs, bao, pao, quesadillas, burritos, wraps, and rolls all make the classification criteria and, as stated, deserve robust attention when creating your tailgate menu.

The sandwich is versatile. It can be dressed up or down. The variations are infinite, and they can easily service the appetites of both the voracious and the finicky. They are filling, and, most importantly, when designed properly, they are the perfect item for a tailgate spread. Here are some of my very favorites.

PORK BELLY STEAMED BUNS

Every few years a dish sets off sparks in the American culinary mind. In the 1980s there was the molten lava cake, in the '90s there was shrimp and grits, and since then we've seen Nashville hot chicken, blackened redfish, avocado toast, and dozens more. Little has had the panache of the bao movement, arguably nudged into the spotlight by Eddie Huang (restaurateur, author, TV sensation, and social media superstar), but sent into the stratosphere at Christina Tosi's original outpost of Milk Bar.

The steamed buns themselves are easy enough to make, but they are a little time-consuming. Frozen buns (available in most Asian specialty stores), if handled properly, do very nicely. While I freely admit that these are never better than immediately after they come out of the steamer, (1) they are still fucking incredible as room-temperature bites, and (2) you can easily set up a bamboo steamer over a pan of water and a portable burner, if you desire to be a tailgate megachamp.

Pork Belly

¼ cup kosher salt

¼ cup brown sugar

3 tablespoons Chinese five-spice powder

1½ tablespoons liquid smoke

1 (3-pound) slab pork belly

2 cups Hoisin Sauce (page 65)

2 cups Mississippi Delta Cucumber and White Onion Salad (page 109)

½ cup chopped fresh cilantro

1 cup thinly sliced green onion, green part only

Steamed Buns

1⅓ cups whole milk

3½ teaspoons active dry yeast

2½ tablespoons sugar

4 cups all-purpose flour

¾ teaspoon salt

1½ teaspoons baking powder

2¼ tablespoons vegetable oil

MAKE THE PORK BELLY In a small bowl, combine the kosher salt, brown sugar, five-spice powder, and liquid smoke. Rub both sides of the pork belly with all of the mix and place the pork belly in a zip-top freezer bag. Seal and refrigerate overnight.

Preheat the oven to 450°F.

Remove the pork from the freezer bag and allow to come to room temperature, about 15 minutes. Heat a large ovenproof skillet over high heat, and sear the pork on both sides. Place the pork, still in the skillet, in the oven for 1 hour. Turn down the oven temperature to 250°F, cover the skillet with aluminum foil, and roast for 1 hour more, or until tender. Remove from the oven and allow to cool to room temperature. Wrap the pork in plastic wrap and refrigerate until cold. Pour the pork juices remaining in the pan into a pitcher or bowl and skim off the fat. Save the fat and discard the juices.

MAKE THE STEAMED BUNS Warm the milk to 95°F in a stainless saucepan and whisk in the yeast and sugar. Allow to stand for 10 minutes. Combine the flour, salt, and baking powder in the bowl of a stand mixer fitted with the dough hook and blend together well. Drizzle in milk-yeast mix. Mix on low speed until the dough comes together. Once it forms a ball, raise the mixer speed to medium and knead for 5 minutes, until the dough is smooth and elastic. Remove from the bowl and form into a smooth ball. Coat lightly with the oil and return to the bowl. Cover with plastic wrap and allow the dough to rise for 1 hour, or until doubled in size.

Remove the dough from the bowl, punch down, and divide into ¼-ounce portions. Roll the portions into balls and flatten slightly. Roll into ovals 3 to 4 inches long and about 2 inches wide, dust lightly with flour, and fold in half crosswise. Set up a bamboo steamer on the stove top. Place the folded ovals of dough on small squares of parchment paper and steam them in batches on their parchment squares for 10 minutes, or until fluffy and firm. Set aside.

When ready to serve, remove the pork from the refrigerator and cut into bite-size chunks. Set aside with the reserved pork fat.

In a large skillet, heat 3 tablespoons of the pork fat over medium heat until it begins to shimmer. Cover the bottom of the skillet with the pork and sear all over. Smear the inside of each bun with hoisin. Add a pinch of cucumber and onion salad, a piece of hot pork, and finish with cilantro and green onion.

MUFFULETTAS

In the pantheon of tasty delights New Orleans is known for, the muffuletta gets little recognition, considering how amazing it is. The love child of Italian immigrant grocery store staples and New Orleans excess, the muffuletta is a tailgater's dream come true.

My favorite one comes from one of the quintessential joints, R&O's, in Bucktown. They serve their muffuletta hot and toasty, unlike the traditional version, which mimics an old-school Italian sandwich and is served at room temperature. When heated, the extra-virgin becomes fragrant, the cheese melts, and the meats crisp around the edges. The bread turns soft, the aroma of the vinegar comes alive, and best of all, the garlic in all the meat and giardiniera wakes up and explodes. For the life of me, I can't understand why you would eat one at room temperature, unless there was a power outage.

MAKE THE OLIVE SALAD Combine both olives, the onion, celery, cauliflower, carrot, pepperoncini, garlic, celery seeds, oregano, red pepper flakes, salt, black pepper, vinegar, and olive oil in a non-reactive bowl and stir to blend thoroughly. Allow to sit at room temperature for 2 hours, stirring well every 15 to 20 minutes. Transfer to a large glass jar. If the olives and vegetables are not covered, add more red wine vinegar and extra-virgin olive oil, in equal parts. Refrigerate at least 8 hours. It starts to get really good on about day three.

MAKE THE SANDWICHES Halve the loaves of bread horizontally, and drizzle each cut side of the tops and bottoms with 1 tablespoon of the extra-virgin olive oil. Spread with equal amounts of the olive salad (between ¼ and ½ cup). On each of the bottoms, layer 4 ounces each of mozzarella, mortadella, salami, provolone, and prosciutto. (It is important to layer in this order). Close up the sandwiches, wrap tightly in plastic wrap, and allow to sit in the refrigerator overnight. (There is nothing perishable, so technically they can sit out on the counter without any problem. These can also be consumed the minute you close them up.)

When ready to serve, preheat the oven to 375°F. Remove the sandwiches from the refrigerator, and when the oven has reached temperature, unwrap the sandwiches. Open them back up, separating the provolone and salami layers, and lay the halves on baking sheets. Bake until the cheese melts and begins to bubble around the edges, about 12 minutes. Remove from the oven, reassemble, and slice into quarters. Serve immediately.

Olive Salad

2 cups chopped pitted green olives

1 cup chopped pitted Kalamata olives

¾ cup diced red onion

½ cup chopped celery

¾ cup chopped cauliflower florets

½ cup chopped baby carrot

½ cup chopped pepperoncini pepper

3 tablespoons minced garlic

1 teaspoon celery seeds

1 tablespoon dried oregano

1 tablespoon red pepper flakes

1 tablespoon salt

2 tablespoons black pepper

¾ cup red wine vinegar

1¼ cups extra-virgin olive oil

Sandwiches

4 (1-pound) loaves seeded Italian bread

½ cup extra-virgin olive oil

1 pound mozzarella cheese, thinly sliced

1 pound mortadella, thinly sliced

1 pound salami, thinly sliced

1 pound provolone cheese, thinly sliced

1 pound prosciutto, thinly sliced

NOTE

▶ To be clear, Cochon Butcher makes a superior version of this sandwich, but ultimately I lean toward the one I grew up with.

BEEF *and* CHEDDAR HOT DOG LINKS

Here's the definition of irony: You have arrived at the most technically challenging recipe in this book and that recipe happens to be for—hot dogs. I am frequently asked one of the most mundane questions there is: "What would you eat as your last meal?" And the look I get when I respond without hesitation, "Hot dogs!" is either puzzlement, amusement, or disappointment. So, I take hot dogs seriously. I love them with a passion, so much so that Morgan Freeman once came to dinner at my house and, much to his delighted amazement, we had chili dogs.

This is a killer recipe, but you must follow it closely to get the best results. It requires a meat grinder. Whether or not you are able to make a perfect emulsion in this process, you will still end up with a delicious hot dog. Brag to your friends. This is shit to be *way* proud of. I mean, they don't know jack about emulsifying protein. Just watch the masses flock when you start talking about the delicate suspension of fat molecules within the structure of protein to give the perfect snap to your dog. Get a stick. You'll be beating them off.

2½ pounds chuck roast, cut into 1-inch cubes

Lamb sausage casings (see Notes on page 148)

2½ tablespoons white vinegar

1 tablespoon salt, plus more as needed

1½ teaspoons paprika

⅛ teaspoon pink salt (see Notes on page 148)

2 teaspoons white pepper, plus more as needed

1½ teaspoons mustard powder

1 teaspoon garlic powder

1 teaspoon onion powder

½ cup ice water

3 cups shredded sharp cheddar cheese

Spread out the beef cubes on a baking sheet in an even layer and place in the freezer. You don't want to freeze the meat, just chill it until the outside is beginning to get crunchy. Place the meat grinder attachment, die, and blade in the freezer as well.

Find the end of the lamb casing and fit it over the nozzle of your faucet. Gently rinse the casings, looking for any leaks. Snip out any portions with holes and discard. Place the rinsed casings in a small bowl and add water to cover and the white vinegar. Soak for 10 minutes.

In a small bowl, blend together the salt, paprika, pink salt, white pepper, mustard powder, garlic powder, and onion powder.

Remove the grinder parts from the freezer and set up the grinder quickly. Nest a medium bowl inside a large bowl filled with ice. Grind the chilled meat into the medium bowl. Stir in the seasonings and 2 tablespoons of the ice water. As you mix, the meat blend should become tacky and begin to stick to the sides of the bowl. As soon as the meat is fully blended, divide into two balls, flatten each slightly, and return them to the freezer.

As soon as the meat is chilled again, take one portion and place it in a food processor. Add 3 tablespoons of the ice water and process for 4 to 5 minutes. Remove the meat and chill. Repeat with the second batch of meat. When the second batch is finished, pinch off a small piece, flatten it slightly, and sauté on both sides until cooked but not browned. Cut in half and squeeze softly between your thumb and forefinger. If it weeps water and looks grainy,

continued

the emulsion is broken. You are not dead in the water, but your hot dogs will not be as smooth as the store-bought ones. Taste the sample for seasoning and adjust as needed.

In a large bowl, blend the two batches of meat together. Adjust the salt and pepper as needed and stir in the cheese. Cover the meat tightly with plastic wrap and refrigerate for at least 2 hours or up to overnight. Place the clean grinder and stuffing tube in the freezer.

Attach the stuffing tube to the grinder, and stuff the lamb casings, twisting off every 7 to 8 inches. Poach the dogs in lightly salted water or cheap beer for 10 minutes or smoke in a smoker.

To serve, grill, sear, or boil the hot dogs, and brace yourself for adulation like you have never imagined.

NOTES

► Lamb casings are about ¾ to 1 inch in diameter and make the perfect casing for a standard dog. They snap nicely when you bite into them, and they are easily edible (unlike most of their artificial counterparts). Lamb casings are available online from www.waltonsinc.com. They are packed in 300-foot packages. Use what you need, vacuum seal the remainder, and freeze for future use.

► Pink salt, also known as Cure No. 1, is a blend of salt and sodium nitrate. The nitrates help preserve the color and longevity of the protein in a cure. Once cooked, the remnants of the nitrates are almost nonexistent. Pink salt is found in the canning section of the grocery store.

BOUDIN-STUFFED KOLACHES, HOMEMADE SPICY YELLOW MUSTARD

The kolache, a Czech (by way of Texas) pastry is one of the best breakfast/brunch/lunch items that most of you never knew existed. Traditionally, the kolache, a yeast dough pastry, was filled with fruit paste or sweetened farmers' cheese in a large indentation made in the top of the pastry (shaped like a bun). They look a little like giant Linzer cookies. As they made their way into immigrant Czech communities in west Texas, the kolache ultimately made friends with German immigrant–made smoked sausage and together ultimately became a regular breakfast item in Texas donut stores and bakeries, frequently featuring the addition of cheese, jalapeño peppers, and more. Today, they resemble little of their Czech ancestors, looking now more like enormous pigs-in-blankets than anything else.

We add boudin for yet another twist, and the yellow mustard recipe is a must. It's super-spicy with a touch of sweet. It is perfect for dipping these little treats in.

Mustard

¾ cup white vinegar

¼ cup white wine

¼ cup peanut oil

1 tablespoon fresh lemon juice

1 cup mustard powder

1 tablespoon sugar

1 tablespoon turmeric

2 teaspoons all-purpose flour

2 teaspoons garlic powder

1½ teaspoons paprika

1 teaspoon salt

1 teaspoon Tabasco sauce

¼ teaspoon cayenne pepper

½ cup water, or as needed

Kolaches

1 cup milk, warmed to 110°F

1 (1¼-ounce) package active dry yeast

¼ cup plus 1 teaspoon sugar

Pinch of ground ginger

¾ cup unsalted butter, melted, plus more for the ball of dough and the bowl

2 eggs, at room temperature, lightly beaten, plus 2 egg yolks

1 teaspoon salt

4 to 4½ cups all-purpose flour

2 cups grated Gruyère cheese

3 cups boudin mix (see Note on page 150)

2 tablespoons water

MAKE THE MUSTARD In a saucepan, combine the vinegar, wine, peanut oil, lemon juice, mustard powder, sugar, turmeric, flour, garlic powder, paprika, salt, and Tabasco and bring to a simmer over medium heat. Turn down the heat to low and cook, stirring, for 3 minutes. Blend in the pan using an immersion blender, or transfer to a blender and blend, adding water as needed to reach the consistency of mustard.

continued

MAKE THE KOLACHES Mix the milk, yeast, 1 teaspoon of the sugar, and the ginger in a small bowl. Set aside for 5 minutes to allow the yeast to fully activate.

In the bowl of a stand mixer fitted with the whisk, whisk together the melted butter, the whole eggs, the remaining ¼ cup sugar, and the salt on medium until well combined. Add 1 cup of the flour and whisk on low until blended.

Add the yeast mixture, whisking just until blended. Remove the whisk attachment and replace it with the dough hook. Knead the dough on low speed, adding 3 cups of the flour. Then add additional flour, 1 tablespoon at a time, just until the dough pulls away from the sides of the bowl. Knead for 3 minutes longer.

Remove the dough from the bowl and form it into a ball. Rub with melted butter and place in a buttered bowl. Cover with a clean kitchen towel and let it rise until doubled, about 1 hour. Punch down the dough and reserve.

Preheat the oven to 425°F. Line two baking sheets with parchment paper.

Punch down the dough and divide it into twelve equal portions. Working one at a time, roll each portion into a 5 by 2½-inch rectangle. Sprinkle 1 tablespoon of the grated cheese down the center, spread ¼ cup of the boudin mix on top, and wrap the dough around the boudin and cheese, pinching to seal the long seam but leaving the ends open. Place the kolaches, seam-side down, on the baking sheets. Cover with plastic wrap and let rise for 45 minutes. Beat the egg yolks with the water and brush the tops of the kolaches with the egg wash. Sprinkle with salt.

Bake the kolaches for 8 to 10 minutes, or until golden. Turn off the oven, open the door, and let rest for 3 minutes more.

Serve hot with copious amounts of yellow mustard.

NOTE

► I recommend ordering boudin mix online from Best Stop in Scott, Louisiana (www.beststopinscott.com/).

BLACK-EYED PEA FALAFEL
and TZATZIKI PITA POCKETS

Falafel never gets its due. I mean it's delicious, it's healthy, and it's freaking fried! Although it's typically made with chickpeas, this version gives it an earthy twist with that Southern staple, black-eyed peas. These crispy gems—tucked inside soft pita bread with some tangy tzatziki—are hard to beat for a tailgate spread.

Tzatziki

2 cups finely diced English cucumber

Salt

2 cups Greek yogurt

Grated zest and juice of 2 lemons

2 tablespoons minced garlic

1½ tablespoons chopped fresh dill

½ teaspoon white pepper

Falafel

4 cups dried black-eyed peas

2 cups diced yellow onion

¼ cup minced garlic

¼ cup all-purpose flour

¾ cup chopped fresh parsley

1 tablespoon black pepper

1 tablespoon salt

2 teaspoons ground coriander

2 teaspoons ground cumin

1½ teaspoons red pepper flakes

1 tablespoon baking powder

Grated zest and juice of 2 lemons

Peanut oil for frying

12 pita breads

4 cups baby arugula

3 cups chopped tomato

3 cups chopped sweet onion

3 cups chopped cucumber

Tabasco sauce

MAKE THE TZATZIKI In a medium bowl, combine the cucumber and 1 teaspoon salt and toss well. Place in a colander over a bowl or in the sink and allow to drain for 30 minutes. Put the cucumber on a length of cheesecloth, gather it up, and squeeze out as much water as possible (this will keep the tzatziki from getting too watery). Transfer the cucumber to a clean bowl and add the yogurt, lemon zest and juice, garlic, and dill. Refrigerate for 1 hour. Season with salt and the white pepper. Store chilled in plastic or glass for up to 3 days.

MAKE THE FALAFEL Put the black-eyed peas in a bowl and cover with water by 2 inches. Cover with a kitchen towel and allow to stand at least 2½ hours but preferably overnight. Drain and place the peas in a food processor. Add the onion and garlic (do this in batches, if need be) and process for about 3 minutes. Add the flour, parsley, black pepper, salt, coriander, cumin, red pepper flakes, baking powder, and lemon zest and juice. Process until the mix is a moist, finely chopped meal. Transfer to a bowl, cover with plastic wrap, and refrigerate for 1 hour.

Preheat the oven to 200°F.

Heat 1½ inches of oil in a large cast-iron skillet over medium heat to 350°F. With a 2-ounce scoop, scoop the falafel mix into balls and flatten slightly. Working in batches, fry the falafel balls until golden on both sides. Drain on paper towels and place on a baking sheet in the oven to keep warm.

Place the pita in a toaster oven on medium heat until warm but not crusty. You can also toast in oven at 350°F for several minutes. Cut a piece off the top of a pita and open the pocket. Slather the inside with several tablespoons of the tzatziki and tuck in 2 or 3 falafel balls. Stuff with arugula, tomato, onion, and cucumber and drizzle with Tabasco. Repeat with the remaining pitas and filling. Wrap falafel pitas in aluminium foil to transport.

NOLA ROAST BEEF PO'BOY BITES

In the summer of 1992, when the original McAlister's store opened in Oxford and Subway was on its explosive rise, I was sitting around, drinking beer with my dear friend and sayer-of-truths, Randy Yates. We were discussing the best spots in New Orleans for individual po'boys. In my hometown, when you went out for a po'boy, your destination was predicated on the type you were hungry for. You went to Parasol's for roast beef, Domilice's for fried shrimp, and Magazine Street Po-boy for hot ham and cheese (and these were just the Uptown selections).

We laughed at the thought that a Subway or McAlister's would dare try to get a foothold in New Orleans. To our thinking, why the fuck would anyone ever go to one of those places when they could eat the best sandwich in the world from a decades-old, family-owned shop?

Well, flash forward twenty-seven years and corporate shitwallas are on every corner, and the local spots are closing up quicker than a screen door when you are loaded with groceries. Well, in response, here's the roast beef recipe we have hacked away at for twenty years. It makes a damn fine po'boy. Do *not* spare the mayonnaise or the Creole mustard. You'll be glad for the few extra calories.

Roast Beef

1 (4-pound) top round roast

25 garlic cloves, plus 4 tablespoons minced garlic

Salt and black pepper

½ cup clarified butter (see Note on page 43 and recipe on page 238)

2 cups diced yellow onion

1½ cups diced celery

1½ cups diced carrot

12 cups chicken stock

3 tablespoons Kitchen Bouquet sauce

5 bay leaves

1 tablespoon Worcestershire sauce

1 tablespoon dried thyme

1½ cups butter

1½ cups all-purpose flour

Sandwiches

3 loaves Leidenheimer French bread, or about 9 feet of the softest baguette available

2 cups mayonnaise, preferably Blue Plate

2 cups Zatarain's Creole mustard

1½ pounds Swiss cheese, thinly sliced

30 slices tomato

9 cups shredded iceberg lettuce

1½ cups dill pickle chips

MAKE THE ROAST BEEF Preheat the oven to 325°F.

Using a thin-bladed knife, pierce slits shaped like plus signs all over the roast, 25 all together, and insert the whole garlic cloves. Season the roast liberally with salt and pepper.

Melt the butter in a large Dutch oven over medium heat and sear the roast on all sides; remove the meat from the pan and set aside.

Add the onion, celery, and carrot (aka the mirepoix) and 1 tablespoon of the minced garlic to the pan and cook, stirring, until tender. Return the roast to the pan. Sprinkle the top with the remaining 3 tablespoons garlic. Fill the pan with enough chicken stock to come three-quarters of the way up the roast. Stir in the Kitchen Bouquet, bay leaves, Worcestershire, and thyme.

continued

NOLA ROAST BEEF PO'BOY BITES, CONTINUED

Roast the beef for 4 hours, or until it is tender and almost falling apart. Remove the roast from the pan and set aside. (Leave the oven on.) Strain the cooking liquid, reserving the veggies and the stock.

In the Dutch oven, melt the butter over medium heat. Whisk in the flour and continue whisking for 10 minutes, or until the roux begins to turn golden brown and smells nutty. Add 8 cups of the reserved stock and bring to a simmer, stirring constantly. As the gravy thickens, continue to add stock until the gravy achieves the desired consistency. Place the reserved vegetables in the bowl of a food processor and puree until smooth. Stir the pureed vegetables into the gravy. Add more stock if the gravy is too thick and season to taste with salt and pepper.

Shred the beef with two forks in a large bowl. Gradually add the gravy to the shredded beef and stir until well coated with the gravy. Reserve extra gravy to moisten the beef after it has had a chance to sit, if needed.

Turn the oven to 400°F.

Slice the bread in half and toast in the oven for 4 to 6 minutes, until lightly toasted. Dress the bottom of the bread with mayonnaise and top with the Creole mustard. Spoon the beef onto the bottom halves and top with sliced cheese. On the tops, layer the lettuce, pickles, and tomatoes and flip the tops over onto the bottoms. Slice into whatever size pieces you like. Eat immediately.

NOTE

➤ **You definitely want to toast the bread at home and assemble these on-site. The gravy will turn the bread to mush if they have to sit more than 30 to 45 minutes.**

SLUGBURGER SLIDERS

Full transparency: No slugs were killed making this recipe.

The slugburger has its origins in the wilds of northeast Mississippi. I am not going to put myself in the middle of the raging debate about whether it originated in Corinth or Baldwin, but the folks from Corinth definitely scream louder when the shoutin' starts.

Russel Smith, one of the finest people I have ever known and my sous chef for years at City Grocery, introduced me to the slugburger about twenty-five years ago. The local slugburger joint, White Trolly in Corinth, sells their slugburger mix by the pound, so Russel would bring some back whenever he went home, and that would be staff meal for a couple days. The slug is a tiny, fried burger patty topped with mustard, pickles, onions, and nothing more. It's one of the few things I have ever experimented with that gain absolutely no benefit from the addition of cheese or bacon. Go figure?

3 tablespoons butter

3 cups diced onion

2½ pounds ground beef

¾ pound ground pork

1½ cups potato flakes

¾ cup all-purpose flour

1 teaspoons Worcestershire sauce

2 teaspoons garlic powder

2 teaspoons onion powder

½ teaspoon cayenne pepper

2 teaspoons salt

1½ tablespoons black pepper

2 teaspoons MSG, such as Accent

1 cup beef tallow (see Note)

2 cups vegetable oil

24 slider buns

1½ cups yellow mustard

2 cups dill pickle chips

In a large skillet, melt the butter over medium heat and stir in the onion. Cook, stirring constantly, until the onion is wilted but not mushy. Remove from the heat and set aside.

In the bowl of a stand mixer fitted with the paddle attachment, beat together the beef, pork, potato flakes, flour, Worcestershire, garlic powder, onion powder, cayenne, salt, black pepper, and MSG until just combined. Refrigerate for 1 hour, then form the meat into 24 flat 2-inch patties.

Preheat the oven to 300°F.

In a large cast-iron skillet over medium heat, melt the tallow with the vegetable oil and heat to 350°F. Fry the patties in batches, turning once, until golden brown, 4 to 5 minutes total for each batch. Drain on paper towels and set aside.

Open the slider buns and brush the inside of each one with a touch of the frying fat. Place on baking sheets and toast in the oven for 3 to 4 minutes. In the meantime, gently rewarm the onions.

Remove the buns from the oven and smear the cut sides of the top and bottom halves with a little yellow mustard. Place a slug patty on each bottom half and top with a spoonful of warm onion and a few pickles. Serve hot. Stacked in roasting pans and covered with foil, these transport nicely and can be held warm in a hot box for a couple of hours.

NOTE

Beef tallow (or rendered beef fat) is available in lots of grocery stores these days. Cooking with it adds an extra beefy kick which bumps up *any* burger and especially a "slug."

BAHARAT-SPICED SLOPPY JOE, APPLE SLAW

I live in a house with two insanely picky eaters: my seven-year-old daughter *and* my wife. It is a totally insulting pain-in-the-ass existence (at times). There are one or two people out there who think I am pretty fucking good at this cooking thing. I mean, shit, the voting public even got drunk enough to give me some sort of medal about a decade ago. But nooo; around my house, most of the time it feels like I can stick that medal right up my ass.

Sloppy Joes are the great equalizer, however. I can completely bring my tiny audience to their knees with a mere mention of Sloppy Joes. Victory is mine.

When I was in Tel Aviv, during the summer of 2015, with my friends Ashley Christensen, Michael Solomonov, and Alon Shaya, we spent a morning at the Carmel Market, one of the most gorgeously aromatic places I have ever been. As I perused the dozens of spice vendors' offerings, I came across baharat for the first time. Exotically spicy and sweet, I immediately imagined how great it would be in ground lamb with cilantro and onion (I was right on with that). So I bought a pint of it and smuggled it home. It quickly made its way into my Sloppy Joe mix, and my game jumped two levels—even in my roommates' estimation.

Enjoy your moment in the sun.

Baharat Seasoning

1 teaspoon black pepper

2 teaspoons ground coriander

1 teaspoon ground cumin

¼ teaspoon ground cloves

1 teaspoon ground allspice

½ teaspoon ground cinnamon

¼ teaspoon ground cardamom

½ teaspoon freshly grated nutmeg

½ teaspoon cayenne pepper

1 tablespoon paprika

Sloppy Joe Mix

¼ cup vegetable oil

2½ cups small diced yellow onion

2 cups diced celery

2 cups diced green bell pepper

¼ cup minced garlic

2 pounds ground chuck or sirloin

2 pounds ground pork

1 tablespoon salt

2 tablespoons black pepper

¼ cup brown sugar

3 cups spicy ketchup, preferably Maggi Hot and Sweet Tomato Chili Sauce

½ cup apple cider vinegar

½ cup all-purpose flour

Apple Slaw

4 cups thinly sliced purple cabbage

4 cups thinly sliced green cabbage

3 cups julienned Honeycrisp apples

2 cups julienned green apples, such as Granny Smith

1½ cups julienned radishes

1 cup thinly sliced sweet onion

1 cup chopped fresh mint

1 cup olive oil

¼ cup extra-virgin olive oil

Grated zest and juice of 4 lemons

⅓ cup white wine vinegar

¼ cup Dijon mustard

3 tablespoons brown sugar

½ teaspoon celery seeds

1½ teaspoons salt

1½ tablespoons black pepper

8 seeded burger buns

continued

MAKE THE BAHARAT In a small bowl, stir together the black pepper, coriander, cumin, cloves, allspice, cinnamon, cardamom, nutmeg, cayenne, and paprika until well blended. If not using immediately, store, covered, in an airtight, opaque container.

MAKE THE SLOPPY JOE MIX In a Dutch oven, heat the oil over medium heat until it begins to shimmer. Add the onion, celery, bell pepper, and garlic and sauté until the vegetables are tender. Stir in the ground beef and pork, and then the salt and black pepper, breaking up the meat with a spoon. Add 2 tablespoons of the baharat and the brown sugar and cook, stirring and breaking up the meat, until it is almost cooked. Pour off most of the liquid in the pan. Add the ketchup and vinegar and bring to a simmer. Turn down the heat, cover, and simmer, stirring frequently, for 5 minutes. Sprinkle the flour over the meat, little at a time, stirring constantly, until all the flour is added. Simmer until the Sloppy Joe mix completely thickens and season with salt and black pepper, if needed.

MAKE THE SLAW In a large bowl, toss together the cabbages, apples, radishes, onion, and mint.

In a medium bowl, whisk together the olive oils, lemon zest and juice, vinegar, Dijon, brown sugar, celery seeds, salt, and black pepper, stirring until the brown sugar and salt have dissolved.

Pour the dressing over the slaw and toss well. Allow it to sit at room temperature for 30 minutes, tossing it every 10 minutes. Taste for seasoning. If not using immediately, store, covered, in the refrigerator in a plastic or glass container for up to 5 days.

SPICY CARNITAS TACOS *with* ROASTED VEGETABLE SALSA

I am not particularly good at reproducing foods I've eaten on my two or three dozen trips to Mexico over the years, but I am not awful at it either, and it doesn't scare me off of trying. This is a wonderfully easy (if a little time-consuming) recipe, which will give you some solid carnitas. The key is that once cooked, you pull and broil the meat a couple of times to create the crunchy bits that are essential to good carnitas.

We had trouble with the photo shoot for this recipe, because everyone kept eating the food—no bullshit.

This recipe is kitchen employee tried and approved.

Carnitas

1 (3-pound) boneless pork butt, cut into large equal-size cubes

1½ tablespoons salt

2 tablespoons black pepper

1 tablespoon ground cumin

1 tablespoon garlic powder

½ teaspoon ground cinnamon

½ cup lard

1½ onions, peeled and quartered

12 garlic cloves

2 limes, quartered

1 orange, quartered

3 bay leaves

½ cup chicken stock

½ to 1 cup olive oil

Roasted Vegetable Salsa

8 Roma tomatoes, seeded

¾ cup coarsely chopped cilantro

½ cup diced yellow onion

2 jalapeño peppers, seeded and diced

Grated zest and juice of 3 limes, plus more as needed

1 teaspoon ground cumin

Salt and black pepper

36 to 40 corn tortillas

2 cups chopped fresh cilantro

3 cups finely diced yellow onion

4 limes, halved, each half cut into 6 wedges

continued

MAKE THE CARNITAS Preheat the oven to 275°F.

Place the pork in a 1-gallon zip-top freezer bag and set aside. Stir together the salt, black pepper, cumin, garlic powder, and cinnamon in a small bowl and sprinkle it over the pork. Seal the bag and mix well, massaging the meat and spices through the bag for several minutes. Refrigerate for at least 2 hours or overnight.

Melt the lard in a large Dutch oven over high heat. When it begins to shimmer, sear the pork cubes in batches, browning them on two or three sides (you just want to give them a little color). Set the browned pork aside.

Turn down the heat to low and return all the pork to the pot, packing it in as tightly as possible. Wedge the pieces of onion and garlic cloves in between the pieces of pork. Squeeze the lime and orange quarters over the meat, and wedge the rinds in, like the onion and garlic. Add the bay leaves, chicken stock, and just enough olive oil to cover the pork. Cover the pot and cook in the oven and cook for 3 hours, or until tender and falling apart.

Remove from the oven and cool for 20 minutes. Pick out the garlic and onion and set aside 1 cup for the salsa. Discard the bay leaves and the lime and orange rinds. Pour the cooking liquid from the pot into a bowl or pitcher. Allow to stand for 10 minutes and then skim off the fat. Return ¾ cup of the cooking liquid to the pot (discarding the rest), drizzling it over the top of the pork. When the pork is cool enough to handle, shred it into medium chunks with two forks or your fingers. Set aside.

MAKE THE ROASTED VEGETABLE SALSA Combine the reserved roasted garlic and onions, the tomatoes, cilantro, diced onion, jalapeños, lime zest and juice, and cumin in a food processor. Pulse several times until the mix reaches the consistency of salsa. Season with salt and black pepper, and add more lime juice to taste, if needed.

When ready to assemble the tacos, preheat the broiler.

Place the pot with the carnitas under the broiler for 5 to 7 minutes, until browned. Remove from the oven, turn over the pork, and brown it again.

In the meantime, heat a large skillet over medium heat. Warm the tortillas, 3 or 4 at a time, browning lightly on each side. Place on a napkin and fold it up to keep them warm. If transporting to site, wrap the napkin in foil to hold the heat.

Remove the pork from the broiler and place in a serving bowl or chafing dish. Serve hot with the chopped cilantro, diced onion, lime quarters, and the salsa. To make the tacos, place 2 tortillas in the palm of your hand (use 2 tortillas per taco, as they may split) and spoon 2 tablespoons of the warm meat in the middle with salsa, onion, cilantro, and a squeeze of lime.

SLOW COOKER MINI PHILLY CHEESESTEAKS

I've made a mission of trying to understand the depth and breadth of the Philly cheesesteak on several trips to the City of Brotherly Love over the last ten years. What I have come away with is that D'Alessandro's is head and shoulders above everything I have ever tried in Philly. They make an, arguably, craft/artisan version of a sandwich that, more often than not, could be better than whatever it is I ate. I recognize that the same thing could be said about po'boys in New Orleans (there is plenty of shit being passed off as "authentic," a particularly abhorrent word when it comes to food). So this is an express train to what I consider the "greatest hits" of the Philly, also known as "what I like best."

In my estimation (and this is where Philly will come down on me hard), mayonnaise is conspicuously absent from the classic cheesesteak equation. I know folks who sneak their own mayonnaise into Geno's sandwiches. To further blaspheme, while some swear by Tony Luke's drippy provolone, I lean toward Cheese Whiz.

All this said, I don't know shit other than what I like. So, to all the purists out there, take this delicious version with a *big* grain of salt. If you can't do that, then kiss my ass.

1 (4- to 5-pound) beef top roast

Salt and black pepper

3 tablespoons olive oil

4 cups beef broth

2 tablespoons Worcestershire

3 tablespoons minced garlic

1 tablespoon Italian seasoning

3 cups sliced yellow onions

2 cups thinly sliced red bell peppers

2 cups thinly sliced green bell peppers

Cheese Sauce

1½ cups shredded mild cheddar cheese

½ cup shredded Havarti cheese

1½ tablespoons cornstarch

2 cups whole milk, plus more a needed

¼ cup cheap beer

1 tablespoon hot sauce, preferably Louisiana or Crystal

Pinch of salt

12 hoagie (aka sub) rolls

3 cups mayonnaise, preferably Blue Plate

Season the roast liberally on one side with salt and black pepper. Heat a large cast-iron skillet over high heat for 3 minutes. Add the oil, carefully place the roast in the pan, seasoned-side down, and sear until well browned. Season the other side, flip, and brown it equally well. Remove from the pan and set aside. Pour 1 cup of the beef broth into the pan and deglaze, scraping the bottom of the pan to loosen all the caramelized bits. Pour this into bottom of a slow cooker.

Whisk together the remaining 3 cups beef broth, the Worcestershire, garlic, Italian seasoning, 2 teaspoons salt, and 2 tablespoons black pepper in a bowl. Place the seared roast in the slow cooker and pour the broth mix over the top. Cover and cook on Low for 8 hours, or High for 4 hours.

If cooking on low, at the 6-hour mark, add the onion and bell peppers, cover, and continue to cook. If cooking on high, add the vegetables on the 3 hour-mark. When the cooking time is up, remove the roast. It should be falling-apart tender. Shred the meat with two forks and set aside. Strain the contents of the slow cooker, reserving the peppers and onion in one bowl and the jus in a separate bowl.

MEANWHILE, MAKE THE CHEESE SAUCE Toss the cheeses and cornstarch together well. In a medium saucepan, bring the milk and beer to a simmer and stir in the cheese mix. Turn down the heat to low and cook, stirring until the cheese melts and the sauce begins to thicken. Add the hot sauce and season with salt. Add more milk, if needed, to thin to the proper consistency.

Split the rolls through the middle and toast them lightly and spread both the tops and bottoms with mayonnaise. On the bottom halves, spoon meat down the center and top with the reserved peppers and onions. Drizzle with a little of the jus and spoon the cheese sauce over the top.

If transporting, pack the cheese sauce, beef, and peppers and onions in separate containers. Bring buns already toasted (unless there is a heat source on-site) and assemble the cheesesteaks when ready to serve.

Call me. I'll be right over.

GRILLED PORTOBELLO *and* PROVOLONE SLIDERS

Twenty-five years ago, as portobello mushrooms burst onto the culinary scene, the battle cry of the vegetarian was, "Oh my *God*, grilled portobellos taste *just* like steak!" Horseshit. They taste as much like fucking steak as my goddamn shoe does.

Fortunately for my blood pressure, that battle cry is nothing but a whimper now in the age of the Impossible Burger, which, contrary to current marketing misdirection/outright lies, does not begin to taste "just like beef."

All of this said (and now that I am more tolerant of definitively inconsiderate vegan nonsense in my old age), a grilled portobello sandwich is more than decent in the right hands. Fortunately for you, those hands are now yours. Enjoy, but don't you dare let me hear you utter "steak" when referring to these, unless it's to say, "These are fine, but steak would be better."

12 large portobello mushrooms, stems removed	1 tablespoon salt
1½ cups red wine	1½ tablespoons black pepper
1 cup extra-virgin olive oil	24 slider buns
½ cup Worcestershire sauce	1½ cups mayonnaise, preferably Duke's
¼ cup soy sauce	1 pound provolone cheese, thinly sliced
2 tablespoons Dijon mustard	4 cups arugula
½ cup minced garlic	2½ tablespoons extra-virgin olive oil
1 tablespoon chopped fresh rosemary	Grated zest and juice of 1 lemon
1½ teaspoons fresh thyme leaves	Salt and black pepper

Using a spoon, carefully scrape out the black gills from the underside of the portobello caps. Set the mushrooms in a shallow casserole or roasting pan, gill-side up. In a medium bowl, whisk together the wine, olive oil, Worcestershire, soy sauce, Dijon, garlic, rosemary, thyme, salt, and pepper. Pour over the mushrooms, cover, and refrigerate for at least 2 hours and preferably overnight.

Prepare a hot charcoal or wood fire. When the coals have burned down, cook the mushrooms on the hottest part of the fire for 3 minutes, brushing regularly with the marinade. Flip and cook for 3 more minutes. Flip back to the first side and cook again for 3 minutes on each side, brushing with the marinade. Remove from the heat and cool briefly. Cut the mushrooms in half on the diagonal, and slice the halves on the diagonal to create as much surface area as possible.

Preheat the broiler. Open the slider buns and toast them lightly.

Spread 1½ teaspoons of mayonnaise on each of the slider tops and bottoms. Spread the sliced portobellos over the bottoms and top each one with a half slice of provolone. Place under the broiler to melt the cheese.

In a medium bowl, toss the arugula with the olive oil and lemon zest and juice, sprinkle with salt and pepper, and toss again. Place a pinch of arugula on each of the tops, and assemble tops and bottoms as soon as they come out of the broiler.

Wrap finished sandwiches in foil and hold warm to transport.

GRILLED CHICKEN CONFIT, BREAD and BUTTER PICKLES, WHITE SAUCE

Big Bob Gibson is responsible for bringing this concoction to the public at his eponymous Q joint in mid-Alabama, but my buddy Pat Martin is the one who pulled the pin on this grenade and blew it up everywhere. He once told me, "Mine's so good I'd eat it out of Nick's belly button." (Nick Pihakis, founder of Jim 'N Nicks BBQ, is my business partner and best friend. He's a hilarious, hairy, and diminutive Greek man who everyone loves but few would envision as a sushi platter.) I am certain white sauce is better on chicken than on Nick's belly button, but I have yet to do true beta testing. These sandwiches, though, are ridiculously good.

8 chicken leg quarters

2 tablespoons salt

1 teaspoon sugar

2 teaspoons dried thyme

2 teaspoons garlic powder

2 teaspoons onion powder

4 cups duck fat (see Note on page 18)

White Sauce

2 cups mayonnaise, preferably Duke's

½ cup apple juice

½ cup apple cider vinegar

¼ cup white vinegar

Grated zest and juice of 1 lemon

1½ tablespoons prepared horseradish

1 tablespoon minced garlic

2¼ teaspoons sugar

1½ teaspoons salt, plus more as needed

1 tablespoon coarsely ground black pepper, plus more as needed

1½ teaspoons onion powder

1½ teaspoons liquid smoke

½ teaspoon Tabasco sauce

16 hamburger buns (white, not whole-grain)

3 cups bread-and-butter pickles

Blend together the salt, sugar, thyme, garlic powder, and onion powder. Wash the chicken and pat it dry. Sprinkle the leg quarters liberally with the mix, cover, and set in the refrigerator overnight.

Preheat the oven to 225°F.

Melt the duck fat. Place the chicken leg quarters in a baking dish, packing them tightly together, and cover with the melted duck fat. Place the pan in the oven and cook 5 hours. Remove from the oven and allow to come to room temperature, then cool completely in the refrigerator overnight. Set aside some of the duck fat for the buns.

MAKE THE WHITE SAUCE Whisk together the mayonnaise, apple juice, both vinegars, lemon zest and juice, horseradish, garlic, sugar, salt, pepper, onion powder, liquid smoke, and Tabasco and refrigerate overnight. Season with more salt and pepper if needed.

Prepare a hot charcoal or wood fire. Remove the chicken legs from refrigerator and place on the hot grill. Mark each side twice with grill marks and cook until warmed through, being careful not to let the meat break up much on the grill. Remove from the fire, pull the meat off the bones, and set aside.

Brush the buns lightly with the reserved duck fat and toast briefly on the grill. Heap the bun bottoms with the chicken, white sauce, and pickles. Close the buns and serve hot.

GRUYÈRE *and* PROSCIUTTO GRILLED CHEESE *with* FIG PRESERVES

I am a one-man crusade against the myth of the bullshit Parisian ham and cheese baguette. Why on God's green earth is this pathetic excuse for a sandwich fetishized? With very few exceptions, the bread is impossibly chewy, the ham mediocre, the cheese flavorless, and the whole thing miserably dry. Sorry to all you misguided Francophiles and your silly-looking berets, but the national French sidewalk sammo sucks.

Here are the same ingredients stacked in a slightly different way, that is perfectly sublime. You can continue eating your crapwich out of spite or the hope you might magically become a little more French, but you're just wrong. If I have offended you, well, so be it. Try my sandwich and then tell me that I'm not right here.

2 loaves crusty country bread, sliced

2 cups butter, melted, plus 1½ cups cold butter

2 cups fig preserves

1 pound prosciutto, thinly sliced

1 pound Gruyère cheese, thinly sliced

Lay out the bread slices and brush one side of each with melted butter. Spread fig preserves on half the slices. (These will the tops.) Lay an equal amount of prosciutto over the remaining bread slices (the bottoms). Lay the cheese evenly over the ham, close the sandwiches, and press them down gently.

Set a large sauté pan over medium heat and melt 2 tablespoons of the cold butter. Place two of the sandwiches in the pan and brown one side, pressing firmly, for 3 to 4 minutes. Flip over and brown the second side for an additional 3 minutes. Repeat until all the sandwiches are browned. Set aside at room temperature.

When ready to serve, preheat the oven to 325°F. Place the sandwiches on a baking sheet and warm them in the oven until the cheese is melted. Remove from the oven, dust with powdered sugar, and serve hot.

To transport, cook the sandwiches and wrap them in foil. At the last minute, dust with powdered sugar.

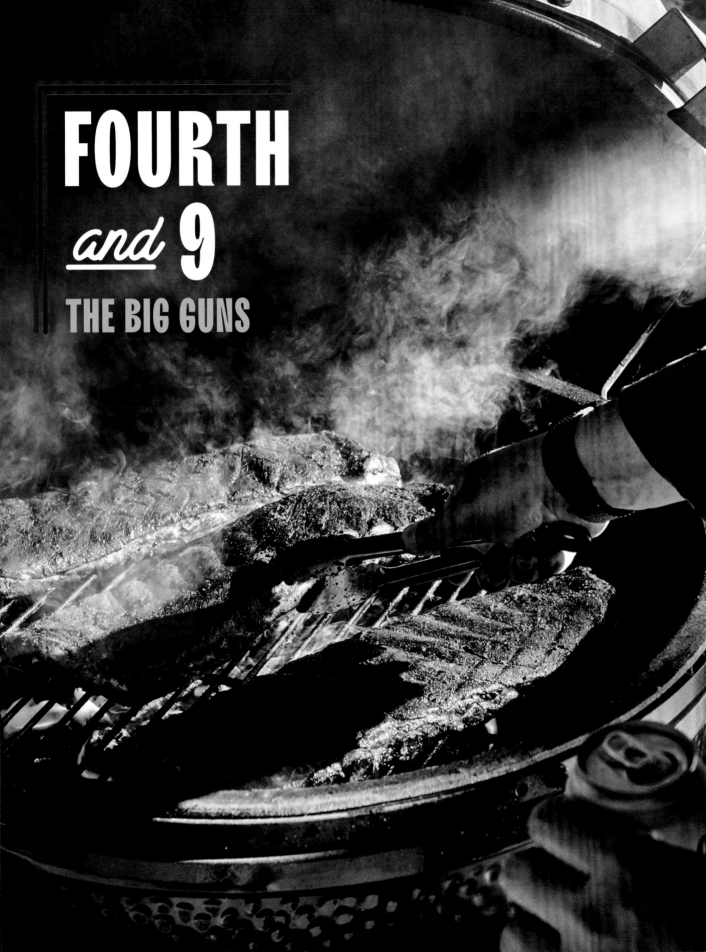

FOURTH
and 9
THE BIG GUNS

The tailgate gathering, on its surface, implies easy pickup food. Folks drift into a tailgate area, are offered a drink, and sink into conversation. Or they drift toward a big screen to watch a rival team or pregame analysis and, at some point, slide over to the food table to, more often than not, grab a wing, a lettuce wrap, a cookie, or a slider. The bold ones will make a plate and graze over it. It is food, for the most part, that teases the appetite and forestalls "actual" eating. It is food meant for grazing.

Enter the Big Guns. Moving into the heartier items in this chapter, your guests have no choice but to make a full plate and have a small (or large) meal. These are dishes of commitment and the sorts of things we ought to be eating during a prolonged period of drinking, hollering, and burning emotional fuel at the same rate as the space shuttle coming off the launch pad.

What's more, committing to a larger-format dish cuts down on labor and the total number of dishes you might otherwise might need on a buffet spread. On more than one occasion, a bowl of chili, étouffée, or gumbo has saved my life in a tailgate/day-drinking situation, when I would have otherwise passed on nibbling on chicken wings. There is no shortage of significance to being able to scoop something simple into a bowl and power it down on the fly when you are preparing for battle. Trust me on this. . . .

ITALIAN SAUSAGE RAGU—STUFFED PEPPERS

Stuffed peppers are another of those yester-world dishes from the 1960s and '70s that have been neglected for reasons I just don't understand. Yes, they are big and clunky and don't make the most elegant presentation, but good God, can they be outstanding in the right hands.

When I was growing up in New Orleans, they were a regular player in my mom's dinner lineup. And whether stuffed with seafood, meat, or vegetables, they were one item we never questioned and just dove into, knowing the treasure inside would be divine.

These are perfect for a tailgate: They're a crowd-pleaser and are arguably as good cold as hot.

¼ cup extra-virgin olive oil

3 pounds Italian sausage, sliced into thin rounds

1 cup thinly sliced yellow onion (root to stem)

3 tablespoons minced garlic

1 cup sliced red bell pepper (root to stem)

1 cup sliced yellow bell pepper (root to stem)

4 cups chopped Roma tomatoes

1 tablespoon red pepper flakes

1 tablespoon dried oregano

Salt and black pepper

¼ cup tomato paste

2 cups red wine

2¼ cups grated Parmesan cheese

1¼ cups roughly chopped fresh basil

12 mixed red, green, and yellow bell peppers, tops cut off and seeds removed

¼ cup olive oil

12 slices provolone cheese

Preheat the oven to 350°F.

In a large Dutch oven, heat the extra-virgin olive oil over medium heat. Brown the sausage in the oil in batches, remove from the pan, and set aside. Add the onion and garlic to pot and sauté until the onion is transparent. Add the bell pepper strips and cook until they begin to wilt. Stir in the tomatoes, red pepper flakes, and oregano and season lightly with salt and black pepper. Cook, stirring continually, until the tomatoes begin to soften. Add the tomato paste and red wine and cook, stirring, until well combined.

Bring to a simmer, turn down the heat to low, and simmer for 30 minutes, stirring every 5 minutes. Return the sausage to the pot and simmer, uncovered, for another 15 minutes. The sauce should have thickened significantly. Stir in 1½ cups of the Parmesan and the basil, remove from the heat, and allow the ragu to cool.

Brush the insides and outsides of the 12 whole bell peppers with olive oil and sprinkle lightly with salt and black pepper. Place on a baking sheet or in a roasting pan and bake for 15 minutes, or until the peppers begin to soften. Remove from the oven and cool.

Spoon the ragu into the peppers and top with the remaining ¾ cup Parmesan cheese. Bake for 25 minutes.

Preheat the broiler.

When ready to transport or serve, place a slice of provolone cheese on top of each pepper and broil for 3 minutes, or until the cheese begins to brown and bubble on top. Remove from the broiler and serve hot or transport in foil.

FOURTH AND 9

GOAT SHEPHERD'S PIE

One of my favorite exchanges ever was with my dear friend and personal hero, Floyd Cardoz, one of the funniest and crustiest chefs I have ever known. Floyd has a heart of gold and cooks some of the finest food I've ever eaten. When I returned from my first trip to India, he lit up like a Christmas tree when I told him about everything I had seen, done, and eaten. During that chat, I expressed one regret.

Me: The one thing I was a little disappointed with, was that we didn't eat more goat while we were there.

Floyd: Did you eat lamb?

Me: Dude, we had all kinds of lamb!

Floyd: Yeah, you ate goat. . . .

Goat meat, not all that long ago, was completely looked down upon by most of the American public. It was seen as substandard peasant food. But in the last decade, it has been celebrated by chefs and introduced in new iterations by recent immigrants. Now it seems almost exotic. About ten years ago, I was directed to a new Charleston, South Carolina, eatery, Two Boroughs Larder (tragically now closed), for a boozy breakfast. Josh Keeler, the chef-owner, was serving a goat pozole with poached farm eggs that morning that is still, to this day, one of the very best dishes I have ever eaten. Josh and goat rocketed to the top of the list of my favorite things.

Goat is not the easiest meat to find. On occasion I run across it at farmers' markets, and it can frequently be found in specialty markets. If it's too much of a stretch, this recipe will work well with beef, pork, chicken, turkey, or lamb. It's great for a buffet because the mashed potato "insulation" will keep the filling hot as hell for a week.

¼ cup olive oil

2 pounds ground goat meat (or any ground meat)

Salt and black pepper

1½ cups diced yellow onion

3 tablespoons minced garlic

2 cups sliced mushrooms

1½ cups diced carrot

1½ cups English (aka shell) peas

1 cup corn kernels

½ cup all-purpose flour

3 cups chicken stock

1½ tablespoons Worcestershire sauce

3 tablespoons chopped fresh rosemary

Mashed Potatoes

5 large russet potatoes, washed and peeled

Salt

½ cup butter, cut into several pieces

½ cup whole milk

½ cup heavy cream

½ cup sour cream

1 tablespoon minced garlic

2 eggs, lightly beaten

¾ cup grated Parmesan cheese

White pepper

Preheat the oven to 400°F.

Heat the oil in a large Dutch oven over medium heat until it begins to shimmer. Add the goat, season with salt and black pepper, and sauté, stirring constantly, until the goat is cooked through. Remove it from the pot with a slotted spoon and set aside. In the same pan, stir in the onion and garlic and sauté until the onion is transparent. Add the mushrooms, carrot, peas, and corn and continue cooking until the mushrooms begin to wilt.

Return the goat to the pot, stir in the flour, and cook, stirring, until well combined. Add the chicken stock, Worcestershire, and rosemary and cook, stirring, until the liquid begins to thicken. Turn down the heat to low, cover, and simmer for 30 minutes. Remove from the heat, season with salt and black pepper, and set aside.

MAKE THE MASHED POTATOES Place the potatoes in a large pot, cover with water, and add 1½ teaspoons of salt. Bring to a boil, turn down the heat to medium, and simmer until the potatoes are tender enough that a knife passes through easily, about 25 minutes. Drain and, while still hot, mash the potatoes by hand (a ricer or food mill will make fluffier potatoes). Add the butter, stirring until melted. Turn down the heat to low and add the milk, cream, sour cream, and garlic, stirring constantly. You want the potatoes to stay warm, but not hot. Stir in the eggs and Parmesan. The potatoes will be a little bit loose. Season to taste with salt and white pepper. Remove from the heat and allow to sit for 15 minutes.

Spoon the goat filling into a large baking dish and spread the potatoes across the top to cover completely. Bake for 30 minutes, or until the top is very lightly browned.

EASY AS PIE OVEN BBQ RIBS

I love smoked ribs, but some folks (1) don't have a super-cool smoking rig, (2) don't have time, (3) aren't as much as of a 'que snob as some of your friends, or (4) just want to do their thing and put their *Braveheart* face paint on and start pounding beers before the game.

So, you wanna make some ribs that will keep most folks happy, though probably not your snotty barbecue critic friends? Head to the store and get to it . . . and get over yourself.

Dry Rub

½ cup brown sugar

½ cup kosher salt

¾ cup smoked paprika

¼ cup mustard powder

¼ cup garlic powder

¼ cup onion powder

½ cup chili powder

1 tablespoon ground cumin

1 tablespoon red pepper flakes

½ teaspoon ground cinnamon

4 full racks St. Louis–cut pork ribs

1 tablespoon liquid smoke

2 cups of your favorite barbecue sauce (optional)

MAKE THE DRY RUB Blend the brown sugar, salt, smoked paprika, mustard powder, garlic powder, onion powder, chili powder, cumin, red pepper flakes, and cinnamon together in a small bowl and set aside.

One at a time, place the rib racks on a cutting board with the concave (bottom) side up. You should see a milky membrane covering the inside of the rib cage. Working carefully and deliberately, dig underneath the membrane with a knife at one corner of the rack and begin pulling it up. The entire membrane usually comes away from the ribs relatively easily. It is slippery, so it is best to grab with a paper napkin or kitchen towel.

Place each rack on a piece of plastic wrap and sprinkle liberally with the dry rub. Drizzle with a few drops of liquid smoke. Wrap the ribs in plastic wrap and then aluminum foil. Refrigerate for at least 4 hours or up to overnight.

Preheat the oven to 225°F.

Place the ribs, wrapped in plastic wrap and foil, on a baking sheet, keeping them in one layer if possible. Cook for 2½ hours. Remove from the oven and allow to cool briefly. (Leave the oven on.) Carefully remove the aluminum foil and plastic wrap. With the ribs still on the baking sheet, cover loosely with foil and return to the oven. Cook for 2 hours more, or until a skewer pushes through the ribs easily.

Thirty minutes before the ribs are supposed to come out of the oven, prepare a hot charcoal or wood fire.

Remove the ribs from the oven and either sprinkle them again with the dry rub or brush with your favorite barbecue sauce, if desired. Place the ribs on the grill and mark each side with grill marks for extra texture and flavor. Remove from the grill, cut between the ribs to separate, and serve immediately.

ROASTED CHICKEN ENCHILADAS

In the spring of 1987, I was living in a farmhouse in the Virginia countryside with my two best friends, down the road from Hampden-Sydney College, where I was failing miserably.

One afternoon I got a craving for Mexican food, and while I was not necessarily an aspiring cook per se, I had begun cooking for my roommates pretty regularly. And I had spent a summer on a tugboat in the Gulf of Mexico as the boat's cook. I had amassed just enough "knowledge" in my lifetime to be confident *and* dangerous. So I trundled off to the store (and remember this is way pre-internet) and bought what I imagined I needed to make enchiladas. (I also bought what I needed to make really strong margaritas, in order to distract my friends from the potentially shitty enchiladas.) The end result was a smashing success—and smashed roommates (there is actually photo evidence of us all on the kitchen floor eating at some point in the evening, and laughing our asses off).

I have been tweaking the recipe ever since. This is perfect when quickly made with store-bought ingredients and divine made with homemade. Leftovers keep beautifully and can be reheated in the microwave in a snap.

Red Enchilada Sauce

¼ cup butter

¼ cup all-purpose flour

2 cups small diced yellow onion

5 cups tomato sauce

3½ tablespoons chili powder

3 tablespoons dried oregano

1 tablespoon ground cumin

3 tablespoons minced garlic

1 tablespoon brown sugar

Green Enchilada Sauce

1 tablespoon olive oil

1 small yellow onion, diced

1 jalapeño pepper, seeded and diced

4 garlic cloves, minced

1 cup vegetable stock

4 (4-ounce) cans diced green chiles

1½ teaspoons ground cumin

1 teaspoon salt

½ teaspoon black pepper

¾ cup minced yellow onion

2 tablespoons minced garlic

Salt and black pepper

1 (3- to 4-pound) roasted chicken, meat removed from bones and shredded

2 to 4 tablespoons vegetable oil

16 (6-inch) corn tortillas

2½ cups shredded sharp cheddar cheese

1 cup shredded Monterey Jack cheese

1 bunch fresh cilantro, coarsely chopped

Olive oil

1 cup salsa

1 cup sour cream

Preheat oven to 425°F.

MAKE THE RED ENCHILADA SAUCE Combine the butter, flour, onion, tomato sauce, chili powder, oregano, cumin, garlic, and brown sugar in a medium saucepan and place over medium heat. Bring to a boil, turn heat to low, and allow to simmer, stirring constantly, for 30 minutes. Remove from the heat and allow to cool.

MAKE THE GREEN ENCHILADA SAUCE Combine the olive oil, onion, jalapeño, garlic, vegetable stock, green chiles, cumin, salt, and black pepper in a medium saucepan and place over medium heat. Bring to a boil, turn heat to low, and allow to simmer, stirring constantly, for 30 minutes. Remove from the heat and allow to cool.

Using cooking spray or olive oil, grease a 9 by 13-inch baking dish. Set aside.

In a medium saucepan, combine the minced onion, garlic, and 1½ cups of the red enchilada sauce. Bring to a boil over medium heat, turn down the heat to low, and simmer for 15 minutes, stirring constantly. Generously sprinkle salt and black pepper over the shredded chicken, combine well, and stir the chicken into the sauce until well combined. Remove from the heat. Allow the sauce to cool while you warm the tortillas.

Heat about ½ teaspoon of the vegetable oil in a large cast-iron skillet and briefly fry the tortillas, in batches, until they are pliable, about 10 to 12 seconds per side, adding more oil as needed. Keep these warm, wrapped in a kitchen towel.

Spoon about ⅓ cup of the chicken mixture along the center of a tortilla. Sprinkle generously with both cheeses and top with a generous pinch of cilantro. Gently, but firmly, roll the tortilla around the filling and place into the baking dish, seam-side down. Repeat with remaining tortillas. Brush the tops of the enchiladas with olive oil and bake, uncovered, in the oven for 15 minutes, or until the tortillas begin to brown on top.

Remove from oven and turn down the oven to 400°F. Pour 1½ cups of the green enchilada sauce over the enchiladas and sprinkle liberally with more cheese. Cover the baking dish loosely with aluminum foil and bake for 20 minutes. Carefully remove the foil and bake for another 5 to 10 minutes, or until the cheese is golden.

Allow the enchiladas to cool for about 10 minutes. Garnish with salsa and sour cream and the remaining cilantro. Serve warm.

SWEET MUSTARD PULLED PORK

This is by no means intended as a substitute for real pit-smoked barbecue. There is none. While the evolution of smokers has made pit smoking more accessible to us mere mortals, the pit masters are still masters for a very good reason. This recipe delivers falling-apart pork, which, when served in a pillowy bun with South Carolina–style mustard barbecue sauce, makes for an altogether delicious sandwich. It will do in a pinch, and it's relatively quick.

Pork

1 (5- to 6-pound) boneless pork butt

3 tablespoons salt

¼ cup black pepper

4 tablespoons Barbecue Spice Rub (page 236)

3 tablespoons olive oil

2 tablespoon liquid smoke

Mustard Barbecue Sauce

4 cups yellow mustard

1½ cups brown sugar

2 tablespoons molasses

¼ cup honey

1 tablespoon Tabasco sauce

1 tablespoon Worcestershire sauce

½ cup strong brewed coffee

⅛ teaspoon ground cinnamon

2 tablespoons liquid smoke

2¼ teaspoons salt, plus more as needed

1½ tablespoons black pepper, plus more as needed

12 buns

MAKE THE PORK Cut the pork butt into four to six large pieces, place in a large bowl, and sprinkle liberally with the salt, pepper, and barbecue spice mix, coating it completely and evenly. Cover with plastic wrap and refrigerate for at least 3 hours or up to overnight.

Season the pork again with salt and pepper and the barbecue spice mix. In a large pressure cooker over medium-high heat or an Instant Pot set to Sauté, heat the oil and brown the pork in batches on all sides. Return all the pork to the pot, cover with water, and add the liquid smoke. Cover the pressure cooker with the lid, and bring the water to a boil. As soon as the cooker begins to hiss or whistle, turn down the heat to low. Alternatively, set the Instant Pot to Pressure Cook and cook the pork for 1 hour. Remove from the heat and allow the pressure to release naturally. Remove the pork from the pot and allow to rest for 5 minutes.

MAKE THE MUSTARD BARBECUE SAUCE Combine the mustard, brown sugar, molasses, honey, Tabasco, Worcestershire, coffee, cinnamon, and liquid smoke in a medium saucepan and bring to a simmer over medium heat. Remove from the heat and allow to cool briefly. Stir in salt and pepper, adding more if needed.

Preheat the broiler to High.

Pull the pork apart with two forks until shredded. Spread out the meat on a large baking sheet. Taste for seasoning and add salt, pepper, and barbecue spice mix as needed. Place under the broiler for 7 to 9 minutes, or until the ends get a little crispy.

Place 1 cup of pork in a bun with 3 to 4 tablespoons of mustard barbecue sauce drizzled on top. Serve hot.

CHICKEN *and* ANDOUILLE JAMBALAYA

Jambalaya is one of those dishes that folks approach with cautious apprehension. Success is entirely predicated on a delicate balance of ingredients, spices, and trust. Beyond that, there really isn't much to it but throwing it together, popping it in the oven, and getting it out on time. The beautiful thing is that you can adapt the recipe to anything you want. Duck, rabbit, alligator, tasso, and even (God forgive me) roasted vegetables all make excellent jambalaya.

The key to this recipe is getting the jambalaya out of the oven just before it finishes cooking so the last of the liquid is absorbed on the stove top. If it cooks too long, it turns into a sticky, starchy mess. Pay attention and give a little love to this dish, and you are officially on your way to becoming a real, live Cajun chef.

Preheat the oven to 325°F.

Pick the meat off the chicken, setting aside the skin. Chop the meat into bite-size pieces and set aside.

In a large Dutch oven, heat the oil over medium heat until it begins to shimmer. Sauté the andouille, stirring frequently, until the sausage is lightly browned. Remove from the pan and set aside.

Add the onion, bell pepper, celery, and garlic to the pan and sauté until the vegetables are tender. Add the tomato paste and stir until well blended. Add the hot sauce, Creole seasoning, black pepper, tomatoes, chicken stock, chicken, andouille, rice, and bay leaves. Stir together briefly and bring to a boil. Cover and cook the jambalaya in the oven for 25 minutes, just before all the liquid is absorbed.

Remove from the oven and stir in the shrimp. Cover and return to the oven for 5 minutes. Taste and season with salt and more black pepper and hot sauce if needed. Garnish with the green onion and serve hot.

1 (3-pound) rotisserie chicken

¼ cup vegetable oil

2 pounds andouille sausage, sliced, or substitute any smoked pork or beef sausage

3 cups diced yellow onion

2 cups green bell pepper

2½ cups chopped celery

¼ cup minced garlic

1½ tablespoons tomato paste

¼ cup hot sauce, preferably Crystal, plus more as needed

3 tablespoons Creole Seasoning (page 236)

1½ tablespoons black pepper, plus more as needed

2 (28-ounce) cans diced or chopped tomatoes

6 cups chicken stock

4 cups long-grain white rice

5 bay leaves

2 pounds extra-large shrimp, preferably Gulf brown shrimp

2 cups chopped green onion

Salt

DUCK *and* TASSO RED BEAN CASSOULET

There is little better than the delicious, earthy silkiness of a perfectly cooked cassoulet. It is the quintessential French fireside dish. I will not lie, it requires dedication and care to get it right. It is a little like cooking risotto in that you have to slowly and meticulously add stock and bread crumbs to the bean base until the beans are perfectly cooked, which can take a solid 2 hours. When the dish is done, however, it is satisfying, stick-to-your-ribs, complex proteins and a punch in the mouth of flavor. Yes, it is an investment in time, but holy hell, it is worth it.

4 cups dried red beans

Duck

1 (5-pound) whole duck

3 tablespoons olive oil

1 yellow onion, chopped

3 celery stalks, chopped

2 carrots, peeled and chopped

12 garlic cloves, halved lengthwise

2 teaspoons black peppercorns

3 bay leaves

10 sprigs fresh parsley

2 tablespoons Creole Seasoning (page 236)

2 lemons, sliced

Bread Crumbs

6 cups bread crumbs

3 cups grated Parmesan cheese

3 tablespoons olive oil

1 tablespoon red pepper flakes

1½ tablespoons salt

1½ tablespoons black pepper

2 cups chopped bacon

2 tablespoons olive oil

2 cups minced shallots

¼ cup minced garlic

½ cup chopped fresh thyme

¼ cup chopped fresh oregano

2 cups diced tasso ham (see Note) or andouille

Cayenne pepper

To soak the beans, place them in a large bowl and cover with water by 3 inches. After 1½ hours, check the beans and add enough water to just cover. Cover the bowl with a kitchen towel and allow to sit for at least 5½ more hours or up to overnight. Alternatively, if you don't have time to soak the beans, place them in a large pot, cover with water by 3 inches, and bring to a boil over medium heat. Immediately remove from the heat, cover the pot, and allow to stand for 30 minutes. Check the water level. If needed, add enough water to just cover the top of the beans. Re-cover the pot and allow it to sit for another 30 minutes, then drain.

MAKE THE DUCK Rinse the duck and wash the giblets in cold water. Heat the oil in a large stockpot over high heat. Sear the duck until golden brown all over. Add the giblets, onion, celery, carrots, garlic, peppercorns, bay leaves, parsley, Creole seasoning, and lemons to the pot and cover completely with water. Bring the water to a boil and turn down the heat to low. Cover and simmer for 1½ hours, or until the duck is falling apart. Remove the duck from the pot, and strain the stock. Set aside 10 cups of the stock. When cool enough to handle, pull the duck meat off the bones and set aside. You should have about 4 cups. Discard the bones.

MAKE THE BREAD CRUMBS Combine the bread crumbs, Parmesan, olive oil, red pepper flakes, salt, and black pepper in a bowl and set aside.

Preheat the oven to 375°F.

In a large Dutch oven, sauté the bacon in olive oil over medium heat for 4 to 5 minutes, or until the bacon colors lightly. Add the shallots, garlic, thyme, and oregano and cook for 5 minutes without browning. Add the drained beans and stir together. Add the duck meat and tasso and stir to combine well. Add 4 cups of the duck stock, or however much it takes to just reach the top of the beans. Sprinkle with 1 cup of the bread crumbs and bake in the oven for 30 minutes. Remove the cassoulet from the oven, again add just enough duck stock to come to the top of the beans, and sprinkle with another 1 cup or so of bread crumbs. Return to the oven for another 30 minutes. Repeat this process two or three more times, until the beans are completely tender. On the last turn, taste for seasoning and add only enough bread crumbs to create a nice brown crust.

NOTE

▶ Tasso ham is a product largely limited to south Louisiana. Though called "ham," it technically is not. It is made from the shoulder roast, or occasionally the cheek, and cured/smoked like traditional hams are. It is used mostly for seasoning and from time to time as an enhancer in salads and sandwiches. It is available widely on the internet. Savoie's is great, but even though at the opposite end of the planet, Zingerman's Roadhouse in Ann Arbor does a nice job, as does Cochon Butcher in New Orleans.

LAMB BIRYANI *and* RAITA

A perfectly cooked biryani is one of the most wonderful things you will ever eat. Perfectly cooked rice and well-seasoned, falling-apart lamb under an immaculately executed pastry dome is a tall order to get to come together all at once. Biryani is the freaking chicken pot pie of India, but better. It may be the consummate comfort food. Should you find yourself in Delhi, try Gulati at the Pandara market. They are known for their butter chicken, but they do an insane biryani.

There is a long list of steps to execute a biryani, but believe me when I tell you it is entirely worth the time and effort that goes into it. This particular recipe breaks the dish into individual components, which makes assembling the dish a little easier. Take a Saturday to do this, and you will thank me, but not as much as your friends will thank you.

3 cups basmati rice

8¼ cups plus 2 tablespoons water

½ cup cold butter, cubed

4 cups thinly sliced yellow onion (root to stem), plus 2 cups diced

½ cup slivered almonds

3 tablespoons minced garlic

3 tablespoons minced ginger

2 tablespoons golden raisins

2½ pounds lamb shoulder meat, cut into ¾- to 1-inch cubes

Salt and black pepper

½ cup olive oil

1¾ cups Greek yogurt

1¾ cups chicken stock

¼ cup coconut milk

1½ teaspoons crumbled saffron threads

2 teaspoons cumin seeds

1½ teaspoons ground coriander

1 teaspoon freshly grated nutmeg

¾ teaspoon cayenne pepper

½ teaspoon ground cardamom

¼ teaspoon ground cinnamon

¼ teaspoon ground cloves

Grated zest and juice of 1 lemon

¼ cup chopped fresh cilantro

1 (12 by 12-inch) frozen pie dough sheet

In a large bowl, cover the rice with 3½ cups of the water and soak for 3 hours.

Melt ¼ cup of the butter in a large Dutch oven over medium heat. Stir in the 4 cups sliced onion and sauté until lightly browned, about 10 minutes. Remove the pan from the heat and, with a slotted spoon, remove and set aside the onion.

Combine the chopped onion, ¼ cup of the slivered almonds, the garlic, ginger, and ¼ cup of the water in a food processor and process until it becomes a smooth a paste. Set aside.

Place the raisins in a small dish, cover with hot water, and set aside.

Season the lamb with salt and black pepper. Return the Dutch oven to high heat and add the olive oil. When it begins to shimmer, brown the lamb cubes in batches, removing them with a slotted spoon as they're cooked and setting them aside in a shallow bowl. Turn down the heat to medium and add the reserved onion paste to the pot. Cook, stirring constantly, until the mix turns a light brown. Stir in the browned meat and any accumulated liquid. Add the yogurt and chicken stock and stir to blend well. Cover the pot, turn down the heat to low, and simmer for 45 minutes.

In a small bowl, warm the coconut milk briefly in the microwave and stir in the saffron threads. Set aside.

Drain the basmati rice. In a large saucepan, bring the remaining 4½ plus 2 tablespoons water to a boil over medium heat. Stir in the rice and simmer for exactly 5 minutes. Drain the rice and rinse in cool water to stop the cooking. Set aside.

To the lamb, add 1 teaspoon black pepper, the cumin seeds, coriander, nutmeg, cayenne, cardamom, cinnamon, and cloves. Stir, cover again, and continue cooking until the meat is tender and easy to pull apart.

Preheat the oven to 350°F.

Spoon the meat and sauce into a large bowl and set aside. Layer half the rice over the bottom of the Dutch oven, spreading it out evenly. Next, spread out the meat evenly over the rice, and dress with the remaining liquid (about 2 cups). Stir the lemon juice and zest into the remaining rice and spread the rice over the top of the meat. Drizzle the saffron-flavored coconut milk over the top of the rice. Crumble the remaining ¼ cup cold butter cubes over the top of the rice and then the browned onion, plumped raisins, the remaining ¼ cup almonds, and the cilantro. Cover the top of the biryani with pie dough and cut several vent holes. Bake for 30 minutes, or the until pie dough is golden brown. Remove and serve hot.

TURKEY À LA KING *with* BUTTERMILK BISCUITS

Turkey à la king (TALK) saw its heyday at that saddest time in American cookery, the mid-1960s through the '70s. And unfortunately, lazy versions of the dish dominated the landscape. Taken seriously, TALK is sublime and unctuous and one of my favorite things to surprise folks with. This works great for a tailgate because the sauce holds its temperature and consistency well, and the biscuits, if held even a little warm, still put out a killer dish.

Turkey

2 (2-pound) boneless turkey breasts

Salt and black pepper

3 tablespoons extra-virgin olive oil

8 cups chicken stock

4 cups white wine

2 lemons, sliced

6 garlic cloves, halved

4 shallots, sliced

4 bay leaves

6 sprigs fresh thyme

1 tablespoon black peppercorns

Sauce

4 tablespoons butter

2 cups diced yellow onion

1½ cups diced celery

3 tablespoons minced garlic

1½ pounds mushrooms

Salt and black pepper

2½ cups sliced sugar snap pea pods, or 1¾ cups English (aka shell) peas

¼ cup plus 2 tablespoons all-purpose flour

6 egg yolks

1¼ cups heavy cream

¾ cup chopped pimentos

¼ cup plus 1 tablespoon chopped fresh rosemary

Grated zest and juice of 2 lemons

½ cup dry sherry

12 large Biscuits (page 9) cut into 2½- or 3-inch biscuits

½ cup chopped fresh parsley for garnish

¾ cup chopped green onions for garnish

COOK THE TURKEY Season the turkey breasts generously with salt and pepper. In a large Dutch oven, heat the oil over high heat and sear the turkey breasts on each side for 3 to 4 minutes until browned. Remove from the heat. Remove the turkey from the pot and set aside, leaving the cooking oil in the pot.

In a stockpot, stir together the chicken stock, wine, lemons, garlic, shallots, bay leaves, thyme, and peppercorns. Add the turkey breasts and bring to a boil. Turn down the heat and simmer for 12 to 15 minutes, or until the breasts are firm when poked with a finger. Remove the turkey from the pot. When cool enough to handle, dice the meat and set aside. Strain the cooking liquid, discarding the solids, and set aside.

MAKE THE SAUCE In the Dutch oven, rewarm the remaining oil over medium heat and add the butter, stirring until it melts. Stir in the onion, celery, and garlic and sauté until tender, about 5 minutes. Stir in the mushrooms and season lightly with salt and pepper. Sauté until wilted, then add the peas. Stir briefly and sprinkle in the flour. Stir to combine well and sauté for 5 minutes, stirring constantly. Add 6 cups of the reserved turkey cooking liquid and stir until the sauce begins to thicken. In a medium bowl, whisk together the egg yolks and cream. Whisk 2 cups of the sauce from the pot into the egg mix, and then stir the egg mix into the Dutch oven. Stir in the pimentos, rosemary, lemon zest and juice and season with salt and pepper. Add the diced turkey and return to a simmer. Finally, stir in the sherry and season again with salt and pepper.

To serve, split the biscuits and ladle the sauce over the biscuit halves. Garnish with parsley and green onions.

THE 19TH HOLE
SWEET THINGS *worth* WAITING FOR

Desserts and sweets are the unsung heroes of the tailgate table. Often taken for granted and frequently overlooked, these little gems can be pure gold amid the ocean of savory offerings. More than that, if you are dragging and exhausted or pulling a difficult little one along on a marathon day of athletic supportsmanship, a gooey brownie or good chocolate chip cookie can turn the tide. If one or two of these offerings end up in your pocket/purse for consumption later, don't feel alone. On a particularly rainy day in the Grove, my daughter and I made a stop by the chancellor's sky box during the game to say hello. His box is always stocked with plates of perfectly decorated, individually packaged cookies that Mamie loves. While I had a couple of conversations, my daughter wandered off and back a couple of times, but we made our exit rather quickly. When we arrived back at home, cold and wet, Mamie went straight to her room, while I made a drink and tuned into the last quarter of the game. Shortly thereafter I went to check on her (she was conducting herself more quietly than normal). When I walked into her room she was dumping packages full of crushed cookies from her rain boot and pouring them on a plate, preparing for a little cookie feast. All is fair in love and baked goods, I suppose, but more importantly I can now say I have eaten cookies from my daughter's rain boot.

SISTER'S CHOCOLATE CHIP COOKIES

My great-grandmother was an amazing cook by all measures and accounts. Both my mother and grandmother spent time in her kitchen before getting married. When I first was old enough to be aware of her, she must have been in her seventies. Even then, her days were spent in the kitchen frying chicken, making meatloaf, or baking squash casserole. But the thing I remember most clearly is the smell and taste of her chocolate chip cookies. They rose enough to encase a chewy center, but the outside bled out to a razor sharp, crispy, almost burned blade of an edge. They were perfect.

"Sister," as she was known, passed in the mid-1970s, when I was eleven. Her recipe, for all I knew, went along with her. For most of my life, I have chased it and come up short. It wasn't until I stumbled on some little notations in her copy of *The Joy of Cooking* that I unlocked her secret. Her choice of part lard and part butter, combined with baking at a slightly higher temperature, are the keys.

2¾ cups all-purpose flour

¾ teaspoon salt

¾ teaspoon baking soda

1 cup unsalted butter, at room temperature

2 tablespoons lard

¾ cup granulated sugar

1¼ cups brown sugar

2 eggs

2 teaspoons vanilla extract

2 cups semisweet chocolate chips

1 cup chopped pecan pieces, toasted (see Note; optional)

Preheat the oven to 375°F.

In a medium bowl, sift together the flour, salt, and baking soda and set aside. In a stand mixer fitted with the paddle attachment, cream the butter with the lard on medium setting. Beat in the granulated sugar and brown sugar and cream again until smooth. Add the eggs, one at a time, and blend well. Add the vanilla.

Add the sifted dry ingredients to the mixer, ½ cup at a time, beating until well combined. Stir in the chips and pecans (if using), blend well, and refrigerate the dough for 15 minutes.

Scoop out the dough in heaping tablespoon–size balls onto a parchment-lined baking sheet, about 1½ inches apart. Bake for 8 minutes, or until golden brown. Remove from the oven and cool on a rack.

NOTE

► To toast the pecans, preheat the oven to 375°F. Line a baking sheet with parchment paper and spread out the nuts. Toast for 8 to 10 minutes, or until fragrant.

MISSISSIPPI MUD BROWNIES

Our old pastry chef, Austin Agent, and I were once invited to cook for an event at which each chef was to create a dish representative of his or her home state. We decided we would do a Delta tamale, which has its roots firmly in the Mississippi Delta and tells a very interesting tale about the socioeconomics of the state. Unfortunately, this did not fit the campy theme of the event, and the organizer insisted we do a Mississippi mud pie instead.

Thing is, Mississippi mud pie doesn't have a goddamn thing to do with Mississippi. In the quarter of a century I have lived in Mississippi and deeply studied the state's foodways, I have never heard of it served on a menu in any restaurant or in anyone's home. It simply doesn't exist in the state for which it is named. No amount of explaining could make that intellectual midget understand, so we politely declined when he insisted we prepare the mud pie or nothing.

In experimenting, however, we came up with a couple of decent combinations of the ingredients this farcical dish employs, and, to be fair, it isn't a bad list of ingredients to try and stack. This brownie version makes for a killer tailgate offering, especially for kids (and some grown-up kids as well). These are *not* diabetic friendly.

Brownies

2 cups all-purpose flour

3 cups cocoa powder

3 cups unsalted butter

2 cups finely chopped semisweet or bittersweet chocolate

6 eggs

4½ cups granulated sugar

½ cup brown sugar

1 tablespoon kosher salt

1½ tablespoons vanilla extract

Pecan "Mousse"

3½ cups toasted pecans

1½ pounds cream cheese, at room temperature

3 cups powdered sugar

1½ cups heavy cream

2 tablespoons vanilla extract

¼ teaspoon salt

Whipped Cream

2½ cups heavy cream

4 tablespoons powdered sugar

1½ teaspoons vanilla

¾ cup Caramel Sauce (page 237)

¾ cup grated semisweet or bittersweet chocolate

1 cup chopped toasted pecans

continued

MAKE THE BROWNIES Preheat the oven to 350°F. Grease two 9 by 13-inch pans with butter, or nonstick cooking spray if you prefer.

Whisk together the flour and cocoa powder in a bowl and set aside. In the top of a double boiler, melt the butter and chocolate, stirring constantly to blend. Remove from the heat and allow to cool for 5 minutes.

Meanwhile, in the bowl of a stand mixer fitted with a whisk, mix together the eggs, granulated sugar, brown sugar, salt, and vanilla on low speed until well combined. Increase the speed to medium and beat for 3 minutes, then increase the speed to high and beat for an additional 5 minutes, until light yellow.

Turn down the mixer speed to low and whisk in the melted chocolate. Slowly add the flour mix, ½ cup at a time, blending well after each addition. Divide and spread the batter evenly in each pan and bake for 25 minutes, or until completely set in the middle. Remove from the oven and allow to cool completely.

MAKE THE MOUSSE Place the pecans in food processor and process until they become almost a paste. Set aside.

In the clean bowl of a stand mixer fitted with the paddle attachment, beat the cream cheese until smooth. Slowly add the powdered sugar until well incorporated. Beat in the cream, vanilla, and salt and continue beating until smooth. Spread the mousse over the top of the cooled brownies and place in the refrigerator to set up.

MAKE THE WHIPPED CREAM In the clean bowl of a stand mixer fitted with the whisk attachment, combine the cream, powdered sugar, and vanilla. Turn the mixer on low and whisk for 3 minutes, until the cream begins to thicken. Slowly turn the speed up as the cream thickens, so as not to sling cream all over the room, and whisk until cream is thick and holds stiff peaks.

Remove the pans from the refrigerator, and spread the tops evenly with the whipped cream. Drizzle with caramel and sprinkle with chocolate shavings and pecans.

BLUEBERRY *and* CINNAMON HAND PIES

New Orleans is *not* a hand pie town. This may not seem like news to most. Hell, I am not sure how many folks are familiar with the term "hand pie" in New Orleans, even though my hometown housed the last outpost of an early twentieth-century bakery chain called the Hubig Pie Company, whose signature item was a glazed hand pie with a variety of fillings made from the freshest ingredients. At one point, Hubig's had as many as nine storefront bakeries across the South. The not-so-great Depression forced all of the stores but the one in New Orleans into receivership. And, until a fire destroyed the bakery in New Orleans in 2012, their pies were delivered to gas stations, po'boy shops, and so on, in beer-flat-style boxes across the city. They were considered as proprietary a part of the culinary landscape as gumbo, po'boys, or Dixie beer.

The first morning the bakery came back on line after Hurricane Katrina, I was at a gas station when the delivery man came in and dropped off his flat of pies. I was so happy, I started crying like a baby and bought the entire flat to give out to everyone I saw. I recounted the story in an interview I did shortly after, in which I said I would have paid $50,000 for a Hubig's pie at that moment. Several days after that interview released, I got a box of a dozen pies from the owner of the bakery—and an invoice for $600,000.

The company is currently building a new facility. Cross your fingers; they are supposed to come back on line just about the time this book is released. Good chance you will find me somewhere in the city, blubbering over that flat of pies, once they get back up and running.

Pie Dough

3 cups all-purpose flour

¼ cup sugar

2 tablespoons baking powder

1½ teaspoons salt

1 cup shortening

½ to ⅔ cup whole milk

Filling

1 cup sugar

¼ cup cornstarch

4 cups fresh blueberries (individually quick frozen, if you must)

Grated zest and juice of 2 lemons

½ cup sugar

1½ teaspoons ground cinnamon

5 egg yolks, for brushing pastry

MAKE THE DOUGH Combine the flour, sugar, baking powder, and salt in a food processor and pulse several times to combine. Add the shortening and pulse again several times until the mixture resembles a coarse meal. Pour the mix into a medium bowl and add the milk, 1 tablespoon at a time, mixing with a fork until the dough is moistened and comes together. Gather into a ball and turn out onto a floured work surface. Knead and fold a few times, just until the dough begins to look uniform and smooth. Form into a large ball, press down into a disk, and wrap in plastic wrap. Refrigerate for 30 minutes.

MAKE THE FILLING Stir together the sugar and cornstarch in a small bowl. Place the blueberries and lemon zest and juice in a medium saucepan over medium heat. Pour the sugar mix over the blueberries and turn down the heat to low. Cook, stirring continuously while the berries release their juices, the sugar dissolves, and the mixture thickens significantly. Remove from the heat and cool.

continued

Preheat the oven to 350°F.

Remove the dough from the refrigerator and cut it into 4 equal-size pieces. On a lightly floured work surface, roll each piece of dough into a ¼-inch-thick round about 12 to 14 inches in diameter. Cut a total of twelve 6-inch squares, rerolling the scrap dough. If necessary, gather all the scraps of dough and reroll. Place 3 table-spoons of pie filling on each square. Fold each square in half and seal the edges by brushing them with water and pressing with the tines of a fork. Combine the sugar and cinnamon in a bowl. Beat the egg yolks in another bowl. Cut vents in the tops of the pies, brush with the egg, and coat with cinnamon sugar. Bake for 15 min-utes, or until golden brown. Cool on a rack and store sealed in plastic. These will keep up to 3 days.

AUSTIN'S MUDDY BUDDY MIX

Austin Agent, our pastry chef of about four years, is one of the most talented team members we have had in our thirty-year history. He is smart, visionary, humble, funny as shit, loyal, and as hardworking as anyone you will ever meet. Sadly for us, he has followed a super-smart young lady out into the wilds of Nevada so she might pursue her career dream of robbing the earth of precious metals.

When Austin first took the pastry chef job with us, we sat down and talked for a couple of hours about where he would find his richest path to creative success. We talked about the importance of mining the deepest childhood and adolescent food passions of our lives and sharing those stories with our guests through food. It may sound a little hyperbullshit on first blush, but Austin totally got it and, from the beginning, created food that carried you to a different place and time. He dug up things long forgotten or otherwise eschewed as too pedestrian for serious consideration. This is one of those things. Muddy Buddies (or puppy chow) is stuff for a sandwich bag in a first-grader's lunch box. But Austin can turn chicken shit into chicken salad.

5 cups Corn Chex cereal

5 cups Rice Chex cereal

1 cup finely-chopped high-quality semisweet chocolate, such as Olive and Sinclair, Valrhona, or Callebaut

¼ cup unsalted butter

2 teaspoons coconut oil

½ cup freshly ground natural peanut butter

¼ teaspoon salt

2 teaspoons vanilla extract

2 cups powdered sugar

Combine the cereals in a large bowl and set aside. In the top of a double boiler, melt the chocolate, butter, and coconut oil over low heat, stirring until smooth. Remove the top of the double boiler and stir in the peanut butter. If the mixture thickens, reassemble the double boiler and warm until the mixture reaches a pourable consistency. Stir in the salt and vanilla and combine well. Pour over the cereal and stir gently until the cereal is fully coated.

Pour the powdered sugar into a 2-gallon zip-top freezer bag and add the cereal. Zip it shut and toss until the cereal is fully coated. Store in an airtight container in the refrigerator for several weeks.

TRIPLE CHOCOLATE/CHERRY LAYER CAKE

My business partner Stefano Capomazza is one of my favorite people on the planet. It's true, and his wife, Toni, is totally my partner in crime. Years ago, while she was pregnant (she did that a lot), we had an impassioned conversation about chocolate cake and the depths of her pregnancy cravings. It was clear in that instant that someone needed to get that woman the chocolatiest cake that had ever been made, and it seemed I was the guy who needed to do it.

Here's the rub: I fucking suck at baking. I was, however, dead set on getting that enormously pregnant woman exactly what she needed. As an unapologetic devotee of boxed cake mixes, I headed to the store, determined to make my friend the best cake she had ever had. Apparently I did, because six years later, I am still making that cake regularly on demand (though I am sure not regularly enough). FYI: If you feel the need to call in your first insulin prescription, it's totally understandable. It doesn't mean you are a sissy.

This recipe is a cross between that cake and my dad's favorite cake in the world, which was the Black Forest gâteau served at the Carlton Tower Hotel, in London. So, I mean, who doesn't like a boozy combination of chocolate and cherries? Strap it on; this is a total chocolate bomb.

Cake

Melted butter instead of the oil called for in the package directions

¼ cup all-purpose flour

1 (15-ounce) box of your favorite fudgy chocolate cake mix

¼ cup sugar

¼ cup cocoa powder

½ teaspoon salt

Eggs called for in the package directions, plus 2 yolks

Milk instead of the water called for in the package directions

2 teaspoons vanilla extract

½ cup semisweet chocolate chips

Filling

2½ cups whipping cream

2 teaspoons vanilla extract

¼ cup powdered sugar

1 (14-ounce) jar maraschino cherries, preferably Luxardo, drained and syrup reserved

2 tablespoons kirsch (see Note on page 200)

Icing

4½ cups powdered sugar

1 cup cocoa powder

¾ cup unsalted butter, at room temperature

⅓ cup whole milk

½ cup heavy cream

¼ teaspoon salt

2 teaspoons vanilla extract

¾ cup grated semisweet or bittersweet chocolate

MAKE THE CAKE Preheat the oven to 350°F. Grease 3 (9-inch) nonstick cake pans with butter, dust with flour, and set aside.

In a large bowl, stir together the cake mix, sugar, flour, cocoa powder, and salt and set aside. In another bowl, mix together the eggs and egg yolks, melted butter, milk, and vanilla. Add the wet mix to the dry ingredients and stir to combine thoroughly. Add the chocolate chips and stir again. Divide the batter evenly among the three pans, place them on the middle rack of the oven, and cook according to directions on the box.

continued

Remove from the oven and cool in the pans on cooling racks for 10 minutes. Remove from the pans to finish cooling completely on the racks.

MAKE THE FILLING In the bowl of a stand mixer fitted with the whisk attachment or in a large bowl with a hand mixer, whip the cream to soft peaks at medium speed. Add the vanilla and powdered sugar and whip to stiff peaks. Chop the maraschino cherries coarsely and fold into the cream. Refrigerate until serving.

In a glass measuring cup, stir together the reserved maraschino cherry syrup and kirsch. Set aside.

MAKE THE ICING Whisk together the powdered sugar and cocoa powder in a medium bowl and set aside. In the bowl of a stand mixer fitted with the paddle attachment, cream the butter at medium speed. Add the sugar and cocoa, ½ cup at a time, beating after each addition until combined. Slowly add the milk and then the cream, a few tablespoons at a time, until the icing is creamy, smooth, and spreadable. Add the salt and vanilla, increase the mixer speed to high, and beat for 3 minutes. Set aside.

Drizzle the maraschino and kirsch syrup over the cake layers evenly and allow it to soak in. On top of one of the layers, evenly spread half of the cream filling. Place a second layer on top of the first and spread with the remaining filling. Place the third layer on top and ice the entire cake with the chocolate icing. Sprinkle the top with grated chocolate.

NOTE

▶ You have this barely touched bottle of kirsch. I recommend looking up cheese fondue recipes and cubing some crusty bread; otherwise this bottle will do nothing but work its way to the back of your liquor cabinet and live there until you are buried.

SNICKERDOODLE WHOOPIE PIES

I'd be a liar if I told you I knew anything about the origin of the whoopie pie. I've never been crazy about any version I have ever had, and only the most annoying cooking show personalities seem to champion this forgettable food stuff.

So, why would I enter into this loathsome octagon of culinary mediocrity? Well, that's because nobody loves a challenge as much as I do. The entire MO behind Snackbar (our concept that was awarded a Beard medal in 2019) was to re-envision British pub food, the category in the culinary universe that set the gold standard for dreary. So, taking on something stacked with chocolate and marshmallows seemed like a short putt.

These are solid and simple to make. My daughter, Mamie, loves them, so not only do I love a challenge, I am also not above pandering to an audience.

Snickerdoodles

2¾ cups all-purpose flour

2 teaspoons cream of tartar

1 teaspoon baking soda

¼ teaspoon salt

1 cup unsalted butter, at room temperature

1½ cups plus 2 tablespoons sugar

2 eggs

2 teaspoons ground cinnamon

Filling

1 cup unsalted butter, at room temperature

4 cups marshmallow cream

2½ cups powdered sugar

¼ cup cocoa powder

2½ teaspoons vanilla extract

¼ teaspoon salt

2 pounds good-quality semisweet chocolate

Preheat the oven to 350°F.

MAKE THE SNICKERDOODLES Combine the flour, cream of tartar, baking soda, and salt in a bowl. In the bowl of a stand mixer fitted with the paddle attachment, cream the butter and 1½ cups of the sugar until light and fluffy. Add the eggs, one at a time, beating until well combined.

Add the dry ingredients to the butter-sugar mixture and mix until combined.

Blend together the remaining 2 tablespoons sugar and the cinnamon in a separate bowl. Form the dough into small walnut-size balls, roll them in the cinnamon sugar, and bake 8 to 10 minutes, until golden brown. Cool on a rack.

MAKE THE FILLING Cream the butter in a stand mixer fitted with the paddle attachment at medium speed until smooth. Beat in the marshmallow cream, powdered sugar, cocoa powder, vanilla, and salt. Turn up the mixer speed to medium and beat until well blended.

continued

Spread 2½ tablespoons of the filling across the bottom of a warm cookie and top with a second one. Place on a cooling rack set over a baking sheet. Repeat with the remaining cookies and filling.

To temper the chocolate, break it into small pieces and place two-thirds in the top of a double boiler, preferably a dry glass bowl (heat-proof glass will maintain the temperature of the chocolate best). Melt the chocolate, stirring constantly. When completely melted, immediately remove the top of the double boiler and wipe its bottom of excess moisture. Add the remaining third of the chocolate, stirring until melted. If the chocolate will not melt, reassemble the double boiler and warm slightly (chocolate should never exceed 120°F).

Remove from the heat and stir constantly until it cools to about 82°F. Reassemble the double boiler and rewarm, stirring, until the chocolate reaches 90°F. Remove from the heat. Spread ½ teaspoon onto parchment paper or wax paper. The chocolate should appear uniform and glossy.

Spoon 1½ teaspoons of the tempered chocolate on top of each whoopie pie and allow it to set up. If the chocolate falls below 85°F before you're done, return to the double boiler and rewarm it to 90°F. When the whoopie pies are completely cooled, store in an airtight container in the refrigerator for up to 4 days.

"ELVIS" PEANUT BRITTLE *and* PEANUT BUTTER–BANANA PUDDING

Little known fact: In the state of Mississippi, businesses are required by statute to "reference or memorialize Elvis Presley in order to continually cement the legacy of Elvis's birthplace, Tupelo, Mississippi, so that the heathen hoard from Memphis cannot undermine Mississippi's true and rightful place in the history of rock 'n' roll." (See Note below.)

Our continued participation in the state's edict comes in the form of rehashing different versions of the Elvis sandwich. Though the exact concoction is hotly contested and recipes vary, the Mississippi DEA (Department of Elvis Affairs), which oversees all matters Elvis, seems to be satisfied with any food tributes that have at least peanut butter and banana at their core.

This version goes a step further and combines those two things with the Mississippi official state dessert, banana pudding, for a unique twist, guaranteed to satisfy folks of all ages. Trust me.

NOTE

► By "fact," I mean total bullshit. I made all of this up. I may have had too much sugar today.

Peanut Butter Mousse

1½ pounds cream cheese, at room temperature

2¼ cups powdered sugar

1¼ cups crunchy peanut butter

½ cup half-and-half

½ cup chopped roasted peanuts

2 cups heavy cream

1 tablespoon vanilla extract

Vanilla Pudding

5 cups whole milk

1¼ cups granulated sugar

¼ cup plus 2½ tablespoons cornstarch

¼ teaspoon salt

6 egg yolks, lightly beaten

1 tablespoon plus 1 teaspoon vanilla extract

Whipped Cream

2 cups heavy cream

¼ cup plus 1 tablespoon powdered sugar

2 teaspoons vanilla extract

1 (16-ounce) package Nutter Butter cookies, chopped

¾ cup crushed peanut brittle

MAKE THE PEANUT BUTTER MOUSSE In the bowl of a stand mixer fitted with the paddle attachment, beat the cream cheese with 1¾ cups of the powdered sugar until smooth. Add the peanut butter and mix until well combined. Add the half-and-half and chopped roasted peanuts and mix again until well combined. Transfer the mousse to another large bowl, wash and dry the mixer bowl, and fit the mixer with the whisk attachment. (Alternatively, use another mixing bowl and a hand mixer.) Whip the cream, vanilla, and the remaining ½ cup of powdered sugar to stiff peaks. Fold into peanut butter mix, cover with plastic wrap, and refrigerate while making the pudding.

continued

MAKE THE VANILLA PUDDING Warm 4 cups of the milk in a medium saucepan over medium heat until bubbles appear around the edges of the pan. Remove from the heat.

Whisk together the granulated sugar, cornstarch, and salt in a medium bowl. Add the egg yolks and the remaining 1 cup of milk, whisking until well combined. Stir the yolk mixture into the scalded milk and return to medium heat. Bring to a simmer, stirring constantly, then turn down the heat to low. Cook, stirring, until the mixture reaches a pudding consistency. Remove from the heat and stir in the vanilla. Transfer to a bowl, cover with plastic wrap, and refrigerate.

MAKE THE WHIPPED CREAM In a clean bowl, whip the cream and powdered sugar to soft peaks. Add the vanilla and whip to stiff peaks. Set aside.

In trifle dish or a deep glass bowl, spread a third of the Nutter Butter cookies. Spread the vanilla pudding on top and then sprinkle with another third of the Nutter Butter cookies. Spread the peanut mousse on top and then the last third of the Nutter Butters. Just before serving, top with the whipped cream and sprinkle with crushed peanut brittle.

BUTTERMILK CHESS PIE BITES

I aspire to be like my friends Lisa Donovan, Ashley Christensen, Kelly Fields, Angie Mosier, Joli Nichols, and my wife, Bess (among others). While they are all insanely talented, they also happen to be amazing humans. What defines all of them, whether culinarily or philosophically, is their embrace of minimalism. Political issues are deeply complex at times, but if we can submit ourselves to the simple minimalist reality that we just need to respect, accept, and celebrate individual liberty, life would be much easier and enjoyable. This recipe is about minimalism. With roughly a dozen pedestrian ingredients, you get a result that is simple perfection.

Here's to you incredible women and all my friends who have enriched my life and inspire me every day. The world is a better place for all of you.

(Jesus, that was unnecessarily, deep—it's just a goddamn cookbook, Currence. Maybe lay off that seventh cup of coffee.)

Preheat the oven to 375°F.

MAKE THE CRUST Place the toasted and cooled pecans in a food processor and pulse until the pecans turn into a fine meal (stop before they become a paste). Add the flour, brown sugar, salt, and frozen butter and pulse again until the butter is fully incorporated. Pour the mix into a buttered 9 by 13-inch baking dish and press down to distribute the shortbread crust evenly across the bottom of the dish. Bake for 15 minutes, or until the edges brown slightly. Remove and allow to cool.

MAKE THE FILLING In a large bowl, whisk together the brown sugar, granulated sugar, cornmeal, and salt. Whisk in the melted butter, buttermilk, eggs and egg yolks, vanilla, almond extract, and lemon juice. Stir to combine well and pour over the cooled crust. Bake for 25 minutes, or until the top is golden brown and crusty. Remove from the oven and cool completely in the pan. Dust liberally with powdered sugar, cut into 1½ by 1½-inch squares, and serve.

Crust

1 cup pecan pieces, toasted (see Note on page 190)

1¾ cups all-purpose flour

¾ cup brown sugar

½ teaspoon salt

1 cup unsalted butter, cubed and frozen for at least 1 hour prior to use

Filling

1½ cups brown sugar

1 cup granulated sugar

2 tablespoons cornmeal

¼ teaspoon salt

1 cup unsalted butter, melted

1 cup buttermilk

2 whole eggs plus 4 egg yolks

2 teaspoons vanilla extract

½ teaspoon almond extract

1 teaspoon fresh lemon juice

Powdered sugar for garnish

SWEET POTATO–PECAN CAKES *with* MARSHMALLOW CREAM–RUM SYRUP

As prolific as sweet potatoes are and as deeply intertwined in the culinary cannon of the South, I don't think we eat enough of them. They are highly versatile and good for you, but you just don't see them on the table enough outside of Thanksgiving and Christmas.

This recipe takes the most traditional flavor pairings and twists them into a killer alternative to carrot cake (like anyone needs an alternative to carrot cake, but here it is anyway).

Rum Syrup

4 cups granulated sugar

3 cups rum

2 cups water

3 tablespoons vanilla extract

Sweet Potato Cakes

1 cup unsalted butter

6½ cups all-purpose flour

1½ tablespoons baking powder

2 teaspoons salt

2 teaspoons ground cinnamon

¾ teaspoon freshly grated nutmeg

1 cup shortening

2½ cups granulated sugar

2½ cups brown sugar

4¼ cups cooked and pureed sweet potatoes (see Note on page 210)

8 eggs

1 tablespoon vanilla extract

Marshmallow Cream

¼ cup water

2¼ cups granulated sugar

2¼ cups corn syrup

9 egg whites

2 teaspoons cream of tartar

¼ cup powdered sugar

1 tablespoon vanilla extract

MAKE THE RUM SYRUP Combine the granulated sugar, rum, water, and vanilla in a medium saucepan and bring to a simmer over medium heat. Cook, stirring, until the mixture is clear. Remove from the heat and allow to cool.

MAKE THE SWEET POTATO CAKES Preheat the oven to 350°F. Grease two 9 by 13-inch baking pans with butter and sprinkle with flour. Set aside.

Whisk together the flour, baking powder, salt, cinnamon, and nutmeg in a bowl and blend well. Set aside.

In a stand mixer fitted with the paddle attachment, cream the butter and shortening at medium speed and add the granulated sugar, brown sugar, and sweet potatoes. Beat until light and creamy. Add the eggs, one at a time, beating well before adding the next one. Add the vanilla and then the flour mix, 1 cup at a time, mixing well.

Divide the batter between the two baking pans and bake for 30 minutes, or until fully set in the center. Remove from the oven and allow to cool for 5 minutes in the pans. Turn out onto cooling racks and cool.

Drizzle each sheet cake with the rum syrup (half on each) and set aside.

MAKE THE MARSHMALLOW CREAM Stir together the water, granulated sugar, and corn syrup in a small saucepan and place over medium heat. Swirl, do not stir, until the syrup reaches 240°F.

continued

While the syrup is heating, place the egg whites and cream of tartar in the bowl of a stand mixer fitted with a whisk, add the powdered sugar, and whip to soft peaks. Blend in the vanilla. Lower the mixer speed to medium and slowly drizzle in the hot syrup. Return the mixer speed to high and beat until the marshmallow cream is stiff. (The whites may deflate at first, but they will stiffen back up with beating.)

Cut 12 (3-inch) circles from each rectangular cake. Spread the marshmallow cream on half of them and stack a second cake on each. Spread the marshmallow cream on top and brown with a kitchen torch.

NOTE

► For the pureed sweet potatoes, peel 4 medium sweet potatoes and place them in a large saucepan. Cover with cool water and add 1½ tablespoons of salt. Turn the heat to medium and bring to a boil. Boil for 25 minutes, or until a knife passes through the flesh easily. Remove the potatoes from the water and allow to cool for 5 minutes. Press through a ricer or food mill or, alternatively, beat in a stand mixer with the paddle attachment on medium speed until smooth.

CAYENNE-SPICED PRALINES

I had a moment early in the days at City Grocery when I was challenged to make a praline with a tip of the hat to Texas. Why, I am completely unable to remember. What I do remember, though, was the terror that struck me.

As a kid I had watched women in the French Quarter, in period dress, churn out hundreds of these magical, sugary confections with their copper pots, thermometers, marble slabs, and laboratory-like setups. As a young chef, it never occurred to me that I should hold a recipe to this curiously New Orleanian specialty in my quiver, but one of early Southern Foodways Alliance symposiums called for a sweet bite at the end of a NOLA-inspired lunch. So, we went to work and developed this recipe, which we still use constantly around the restaurants. Get a candy thermometer, follow the recipe, and you'll be a master praline maker in no time.

3 cups granulated sugar

3 cups brown sugar

½ cup water

3 tablespoons unsalted butter

2 tablespoons vanilla extract

2¼ cups heavy cream

Pinch of salt

¾ teaspoon cayenne pepper

¾ teaspoon ground cinnamon

½ teaspoon chili powder

¼ teaspoon ground cloves

4 cups whole pecans, toasted (see Note on page 190) and coarsely chopped

Prepare a clean nonstick surface for the pralines or cover one with wax paper.

In a large saucepan, combine the granulated sugar, brown sugar, and water. Bring to a simmer over medium heat, swirling constantly. *Do not stir with a spoon.* Clip a candy thermometer to the side of the pan and cook to 247°F. Whisk in the butter, vanilla, cream, and salt and continue whisking until creamy and smooth. Add the cayenne, cinnamon, chili powder, and cloves, stirring until well combined. Add the toasted pecans and remove from heat. Scoop the mixture out onto the prepared nonstick surface, about 1½ tablespoons at a time, and cool completely. Store in an airtight container at room temperature for up to 1 week.

THE FREAKING REFS!!!

THEY WILL DRIVE YOU *to* DRINK

I say a little prayer before the first drink of the day or evening, hoping I will never lose the privilege of alcohol. You see, to drink is a privilege, not a right, and it is more easily lost than I ever imagined.

It's something I take seriously, but let's be honest: Adding a couple of drinks to most gatherings makes them more fun. It makes the already enjoyable ones more so and the more challenging ones less so. It sure as hell makes a sporting event more vivid and pushes us to cheer harder and louder for the teams we love. If you have never been inside the Superdome for a Saints game, well, I feel sorry for you. Your life is sadly incomplete (you can fix that). If you have been in there, imagine the volume level if drinks were not part of the experience. I am guessing it would be a decibel or twenty quieter. The same is probably true at a game of the team you love.

Like the other recipes in this book, most of these are batched for ease of execution. Most will require you do little more than ice, pour, and garnish. That said, there are a couple of blender drinks for those hot days and because, well, blender drinks are amazing when done right.

Props to the amazingly talented Ivy McLellan and Taylor Mauer, who head our cocktail programs, for helping me craft most of these drink recipes, not to mention all of the day-to-day work they do for our places. Thanks, guys.

THE FLORA-DIDDY

In spite of her dedication to the nation of cheating thugs from north Alabama, Meighan Coley, our operations director of Big Bad Breakfast, is one of the finest and hardest-working people I have ever known. She started with us as the manager of our store next to Rosemary Beach (on the Florida Panhandle) and just got everything we were about from the minute she came on board. Among the myriad responsibilities that come along with keeping a busy seasonal restaurant on an even keel, Meighan always pushed the envelope to deliver more than folks already expected from us.

Her bar program was part of the operation that always shined. In that store we offer poolside service for guests of the development in which we are located, so outstanding drinks are a must. Her drink list has become the gold standard for the brand, and several of her stalwart cocktails are served at all of our stores.

This is not her Bloody Mary recipe (those remain top secret for the moment), but instead, one I created in her image. I like to imagine she would want it on her home menu because it corrals the flavors she finds appealing and the invitation to day-drink I know she loves, especially on Saturdays when her beloved Turds take the field.

1 (7-ounce) can chipotle peppers, with adobo sauce

1 cup chopped cucumber

1 cup fresh cilantro leaves

¾ cup diced yellow onion

1½ tablespoons minced garlic

½ medium jalapeño pepper, seeded and chopped

2 tablespoons prepared horseradish

½ cup water

1 (48-ounce) can V8 juice

2 cups orange juice

½ cup plus 2 tablespoons fresh lime juice

2 teaspoons Tabasco sauce

2 teaspoons Tajin snack seasoning

1 tablespoon black pepper

½ teaspoon celery seeds, crushed

Vodka, preferably Cathead, for serving

In a blender, combine the chipotle peppers and their sauce, cucumber, cilantro, onion, garlic, jalapeño, horseradish, and water and puree until the mixture is a smooth paste. Transfer to a pitcher and add the V8 juice, orange juice, and lime juice, stirring to combine well.

In a small shallow dish or plate, pour the Tabasco in a narrow line. In another small shallow dish, mix together the Tajin, black pepper, and celery seed. Roll half the rim of each glass in the Tabasco and then roll it in the spice mix.

Serve in a tall glass filled with ice, and add an irresponsibly large amount of vodka (I usually pour about 1 part mix to 1 part vodka) for maximum volume in the stadium. Temper the quantity of vodka slightly if watching live tennis. Trust me, you *will* get your ass thrown out of a tennis arena; more on that another time.

PLANTER'S PUNCH "PUNCH"

The key to tailgating is convenience and aerodynamics (compact, organized, and built for least resistance). There are so many moving parts, and entertaining for a group requires a lot of work and hands, so anything you can do to cut down on what needs to happen when guests arrive, the better. Punch checks all those boxes. It is batched, poured in a bowl, and garnished with something pretty. Or put it in a jug to simply pour over ice and you are ready to go. What's more, in the right hands, punch is a lethal uptown express train to really good times. Just ask my friends Stefano and Toni, who claim my punch is responsible for two of their children.

Like many of the traditional tropical rum drinks of my youth (such as the hurricane, zombie, and mai tai), there is little consensus on the origin of planter's punch. This is our tailgate version; it will definitely warm up those pipes.

½ cup sugar

25 fresh mint leaves, torn, plus 24 to 30 mint sprigs for garnish

5 orange wheels, plus 10 to 12 more for garnish

5 lime wheels, plus 10 to 12 wedges for garnish

28 ounces gold rum

2 cups orange juice

1½ cups pomegranate juice

½ cup fresh lime juice

2 teaspoons Angostura bitters

Crushed ice for serving

20 ounces Champagne or sparkling wine

In a large bowl, muddle the sugar, mint, orange, and lime. Add the rum and stir until the sugar is completely dissolved. Cover the bowl with plastic wrap and refrigerate overnight.

Strain the rum mix, transfer to a punch bowl, and add the orange juice, pomegranate juice, lime juice, and Angostura bitters. Serve each drink in a tall glass filled with crushed ice, and float Champagne on top. Garnish with mint, orange, and lime.

PICKLED PEACH *and* ORANGE SANGRIA BLANCA

When I was sixteen and my brother was fourteen, my mom and dad planned a trip to Pamplona, Spain, for the Festival of San Fermín. I had read just enough Hemingway and knew just enough about what went on there for me to be a fucking testosterone-fueled powder keg when turned loose. My parents were already in Spain before we left, so my brother and I made the international trek from New Orleans to Miami to London to Madrid and, finally, Pamplona all by ourselves. It was amazing.

When we arrived, wound tight as clock springs, we exploded into Pamplona. My brother and I ran all over town, exploring every nook and cranny, running with the bulls, meeting other kids, and desperately searching for girls and trouble. We found both late on our second night. As the nightly fireworks dimmed, we met a group of Spanish girls our age and they took us off to a street dance, where ceramic vessels of a deliciously sweet fruit-and-wine concoction appeared on just about every horizontal space. We drank and danced and laughed and drank some more until time no longer existed. The morning light, thankfully, found us in our completely destroyed hotel room, with headaches we both swore we'd never repeat, and that magic sangria eternally etched in our minds.

Sangria is a great way to give a boost to otherwise crappy wine. It's a nice afternoon drink, but trust me, this will hit you just like a sledgehammer. Just ask my baby brother, Richard; it turned that rhythmless, dance-averse machine into freaking Travolta in a matter of minutes. This version is a little more refined, but equally lethal if not respected. Start the preparation 1 week before serving. This recipe yields more infused bourbon than you will need for the sangria, but you will thank me for having extra on hand for sipping over ice.

Peach-Infused Bourbon

1 (750 ml) bottle bourbon, preferably Maker's Mark

2 ripe peaches, peeled, pitted, and sliced

2 teaspoons red pepper flakes

2 teaspoons black peppercorns

3 cinnamon sticks

10 whole cloves

Pickled Peaches

12 ripe peaches

3 cups granulated sugar

¾ cup brown sugar

2½ cups white vinegar

1½ cups Champagne vinegar

2½ cups water

1 tablespoon mustard seeds

2 bay leaves

2 bay leaves

Sangria

3 cups Peach-Infused Bourbon

1½ cups brandy

6 ounces dry curaçao

¾ cup fresh lemon juice

1½ cups orange juice

3 (750 ml) bottles white wine, preferably Albariño

5 oranges, sliced

5 limes, sliced

continued

MAKE THE INFUSED BOURBON Divide the bourbon and the peaches between two quart-size jars. Screw on the lids and shake for 10 seconds. Refrigerate for 1 week before using. The bourbon will keep for up to 6 months in the refrigerator.

MAKE THE PICKLED PEACHES Prepare an ice bath by filling a large bowl with ice and water, and set aside. Cut an X in the bottom of each peach and set aside. Bring a large saucepan of water to a boil and, working 4 peaches at a time, dunk the peaches in the boiling water for 30 seconds, remove, and immediately place them in the ice bath. Once cooled, pull the skins off, remove the pit, and slice the peach flesh. Set aside in a large plastic container.

Combine the granulated sugar, brown sugar, both vinegars, the water, mustard seeds, bay leaves, red pepper flakes, peppercorns, cinnamon sticks, and cloves in a saucepan and bring to a boil. Pour the liquid over the peaches and allow to cool. Cover the container and refrigerate for 2 to 3 days before using. The longer these sit, the better they become. They keep at least 6 months refrigerated, as long as they are covered in pickling liquid.

MAKE THE SANGRIA In a large glass or ceramic container, combine the infused bourbon, the brandy, curaçao, lemon juice, orange juice, wine, and 3 tablespoons of the peach pickling liquid. Add the orange and lime slices and 5 cups of the pickled peaches and allow this to sit overnight, refrigerated. To serve, pour over ice in whatever the hell kind of glass you like.

PALOMA FIZZ

The paloma has seen a rise in popularity in the past few years as a result of the ongoing national cocktail obsession and culinary fascination with all things bitter. Bitter isn't something I normally traffic in. It has just never been my thing. In the early 1970s, when grapefruit first saw an explosion in popularity and nutritionists wrote extensively on its healthful properties, my mom became an immediate proponent. But no matter how she tried to disguise it, I just could not stand the bitterness.

At fifty-five, I have matured (if only slightly). And while I still don't sit down to breakfast and devour a grapefruit, I do find it surprisingly nice with tequila. Okay, so I'd drink tequila mixed with turpentine—whatever, grapefruit and tequila are still delicious. This is the love child of the paloma and the Ramos gin fizz. It takes a dedicated bartender to make them and keep up, but they are well worth the investment in labor.

1 egg white

1 cup of ice

2 ounces of your favorite tequila (mezcal is too smoky)

1 tablespoon fresh lime juice

¼ cup ruby red grapefruit juice, plus grapefruit peel for garnish

1½ tablespoons pure agave syrup

Remove the spring from a Hawthorne strainer and place it in a cocktail shaker with the egg white. "Dry shake" the egg white for 20 seconds. Remove the spring from the shaker and add the ice, tequila, lime juice, grapefruit juice, and agave. Shake vigorously for 20 seconds more. Double strain (strain twice) into a large old-fashioned glass over ice and garnish with grapefruit peel.

SPROCKET (SPRITZER *with a* ROCKET AFTERBURNER)

A couple of decades ago, my beautiful and brilliant bride (a notorious lightweight, who loves to drink and laugh) decided on the first hot day of late spring that perhaps a wine spritzer should be her drink of choice for the season. It made perfect sense, except for the fact that we were, at that point, still too close to the days of Bartles and Jaymes, Zima, and a number of other shameless attempts corporate liquor companies had employed to get their watered-down hooch (aka coolers) into the mouths of a huge segment of the population.

Being the snotty, arrogant shit-bird that I am, I decided that a simple wine spritzer was *beneath* what we did at the City Grocery bar. So we set to creating one that would satisfy Bess. This isn't your average wine spritzer (or cooler) in concept or alcohol content. Fair warning: These will move the floor underneath you if you aren't careful. They are, however, delicious and nothing short of perfect on a warm afternoon outdoors.

Raspberry-Rosemary Shrub

2 cups fresh raspberries

2 cups sugar

3 tablespoons fresh rosemary leaves, chopped

Grated zest and pulp of 1 lemon (not the white pith)

2 cups apple cider vinegar

Sprocket

1 (750 ml) bottle medium- to full-bodied red wine

10 ounces vodka

8 ounces shrub

Good-quality mineral water for serving

Raspberries for garnish

Rosemary sprigs for garnish (small tops only)

MAKE THE SHRUB Combine the raspberries, sugar, rosemary, and lemon zest and pulp in a medium glass bowl and muddle to break up raspberries and lemon pith. Cover and place in the refrigerator for 3 days (stir once a day, or more). Remove from refrigerator, add ½ cup water and pour the mix into a small saucepan. Turn the heat on low and stir until the sugar *just* dissolves. This should be warm like bath water—if it gets too hot it will cook the citrus and rosemary oils. Remove from heat and cool to room temperature. Stir in the vinegar, cover, and allow to stand in the refrigerator for another 2 days. Strain and use as needed. Store, chilled, for up to 3 months.

MAKE THE SPROCKETS Combine the red wine, vodka, and 8 ounces of the shrub in a large pitcher and mix well. Fill tall glasses with ice and fill halfway (or slightly more) with wine and vodka mix. Top with mineral water and garnish with raspberries and rosemary leaves.

THE FREAKING REFS!!!

JULEP SPRITZ

I've been knocked on my ass on more than one occasion with the mint julep. Being that it is bourbon, mint, and sugar, and that my self-control over at least two of these ingredients is not one of my greatest strengths, that isn't hard to imagine, I am sure. I sleep comfortably at night, however, telling myself that I am not alone. Juleps are an awesome combination, so I set my designs on keeping them enjoyable but a little less lethal. Please meet the Julep Spritz: all the flavor, half the booze. (See Note.)

This is not to say that drinking to the point of making somewhat poor decisions is *always* a bad idea. At the Kentucky Derby in 2019, after several hundred dollars' worth of Woodford juleps, my buddy Kelly dropped a few bucks on the 300-to-1 long shot, who ended up winning and making him one wonderfully intoxicated, rich, equine savant. It was beautiful. These do, however, take some danger out of the game of daytime bourbon drinking.

4 fresh mint leaves, plus a mint sprig for garnish

1 lemon wheel

1 teaspoon sugar

2 ounces bourbon, preferably Buffalo Trace

1 tablespoon spicy ginger beer, preferably Reed's

Splash of soda water

Crushed ice

Lemon wedge for garnish

Muddle the mint leaves and lemon wheel with the sugar in a mixing glass. Add the bourbon, ginger beer, and soda and stir gently to combine and dissolve the sugar. Double strain over crushed ice into a large old-fashioned glass and garnish with the mint sprig and lemon wedge.

NOTE

▶ It's half the booze if you follow the recipe. If you go nuts, these will surely have the normal effect of putting you on your fanny.

DON SHULA

We opened City Grocery in the spring of 1992, on the same day, I am pretty certain, that the last Waring bar blender in the country was retired from service. Gone was the obnoxious whir and rock concert–decibel screaming that emanated from them as they frappéed their sugary, fruity concoctions. There was peace in the countryside. We would drink unfrozen cocktails sans cochlear molestation for the next couple of decades.

When we opened an outpost of Big Bad Breakfast on the Florida Panhandle in 2017, it occurred to me that while cocktails had been experiencing a massive resurgence for the better part of a decade, few folks were revisiting frozen drinks. In retrospect, for all of the foibles of the bar blender, there was potential gold in what they could turn out. A summer of experiments resulted in many revelations, which led to a couple of years of fine-tuning. That work will manifest itself, eventually, in a rum bar on the Square, in Oxford, in the near future.

Carrying a blender out to a tailgate is a small commitment when you see the adulation it can inspire, especially on a hot day. This recipe is a combination of flavors that seem unusual but work together beautifully.

½ cup bay leaves, crumbled

Boiling water

2 cups cracked ice

6 ounces dry gin

1 cup fresh orange juice

3 satsumas (tangerines or tangelos will do)

2 ounces Grand Marnier

Place the bay leaves in a spice grinder and grind to a fine powder. Transfer to a cup and stir in enough boiling water to make a loose paste. Allow to sit for 1 hour.

Combine the ice, gin, orange juice, satsumas, and ½ teaspoon of the bay paste in a blender and blend on high until smooth. Pour into 2 large stadium cups and float Grand Marnier on top.

FROZEN PINEAPPLE, LIME, _and_ PEPPER VINEGAR MARGARITAS

During my high school and college years, my dad and a group of friends organized an annual father-and-son dove hunting trip in northern Mexico, right before we all went back to school. Little that happened down there would have been considered moral, decent, legal, or wise stateside. One of the highlights of those hot-as-all-dog-shit August trips was that our outfitter would set up a bar and generator and make insanely lethal frozen margaritas, which flowed continuously. Yes, I hear you thinking how wonderfully inappropriate and irresponsible that sounds, but we are all still alive, and we all have insane stories to tell for the rest of our lives. The drinks were perfect, and while I have tried, I have never duplicated those simple, perfectly balanced concoctions.

A better margarita is constantly on my mind, and legitimizing a frozen version of it is a fascination bordering on perverted obsession. This one arguably pushes the envelope of the definition of a margarita, but since we have tequila and lime in the recipe, I stand firmly behind the name. It is slightly unusual, but trust me, worth sourcing the ingredients and making a blender full or two. Also, call an Uber and take an aspirin (or six) before the nap that will surely follow. Just sayin'.

3 cups ice

1½ cups fresh pineapple chunks, frozen, plus 4 fresh pineapple wedges, for garnish

Grated zest and juice of 2 limes, plus 4 lime wedges for garnish

10 ounces tequila blanco

1 tablespoon hot pepper vinegar, preferably Texas Pete or Louisiana

4 ounces tepache (see Note)

2 tablespoons agave syrup

Combine the ice, pineapple chunks, lime zest and juice, tequila, vinegar, tepache, and agave in a blender and blend on high until completely smooth. Pour into old-fashioned glasses (or Styrofoam cups—sorry, I make no excuses for my love of Styrofoam), Garnish with the pineapple and lime wedges.

NOTE

▶ Tepache is fermented pineapple juice with natural yeasts on the peel and rind that provide the catalyst. It is usually sweetened slightly with brown sugar and has a low alcohol content. It is a street drink in Mexico, available commercially in the United States.

CHAI-SPICED NOG

Kyani and Company, one of the great Parsi restaurants in Mumbai, does a crazy delicious Irani chai, a spiced hot tea, which I crave regularly. On a trip my dear friend Vishwesh Bhatt took me on in 2016, we stopped in for breakfast, and it was so good that I pestered him until he agreed to take me back. Being the total reprobate that I am, my mind went immediately to how good the tea would be with booze. And that's how a warm, intoxicating breakfast drink was born. It has the spice of Irani chai and the kick and creaminess of eggnog. Thank me later.

2 cups whole milk

2 cups water

½ cup black tea leaves

2 whole star anise, crushed

1 large cinnamon stick, crushed

2 green cardamom pods, crushed

6 whole cloves

1 teaspoon black peppercorns, crushed

½ teaspoon ground allspice

6 eggs, separated

¾ cup powdered sugar

4 cups heavy cream

24 ounces bourbon, preferably Maker's Mark

1 tablespoon vanilla extract

Freshly grated nutmeg for garnish

Bring the milk and water to a gentle boil in a saucepan and add the black tea, star anise, cinnamon, cardamom, cloves, peppercorns, and allspice. Simmer for 10 minutes, remove from the heat, and allow to sit for 20 minutes.

In the meantime, in a large bowl, whisk together the egg yolks and powdered sugar until smooth and pale yellow. Whisk in the cream, cover with plastic wrap, and refrigerate.

In the bowl of a stand mixer fitted with the whisk attachment, whisk the egg whites to stiff peaks and set aside.

Once the tea has steeped, strain it into a large bowl. Stir in the egg yolk–cream mix and fold in the egg whites until well combined. Whisk in the bourbon and vanilla. Cover with plastic wrap and refrigerate for at least 2 hours. When ready to serve, whisk the egg whites back in (they will separate). Serve straight up with a sprinkle of nutmeg.

FROZEN HARVEY WALLBANGER

I am convinced that the Harvey Wallbanger, born in the early 1970s, was invented by restaurant operators to help them move inventory of the omnipresent, phallic bottle of Galliano, since nobody drinks that shit. That said, it could just as easily have been the invention of distributors trying to knock the dust off of those idle bottles. Whatever the case, in order to find out how long this stuff sits around, we date bottles both when they are opened and when they are finished. I don't think we've ever had one for less than ten years.

All that said, a dressed-up version of the Harvey Wallbanger is altogether delightful. It's an easy premix, so it is perfect for doling out at tailgates. This one has all the appeal of a screwdriver with the sophistication of a craft cocktail and the effervescence of a mimosa. What's not to like?

1 (750 ml bottle) vodka, preferably Cathead

4½ cups fresh orange juice

6 ounces Galliano liqueur

¼ cup plus 2 tablespoon orange flower water

¼ cup juice from Luxardo maraschino cherries, plus Luxardo cherries for garnish

1½ cups sparkling wine

Orange wheels for garnish

In a large pitcher or container, stir together the vodka, orange juice, Galliano, orange flower water, and cherry juice. Pour over ice into tall glasses and float the sparkling wine on top. Garnish with orange wheels and cherries.

FRENCH 150

My wife, Bess, and her band of merry reprobate friends make these in bulk and travel everywhere with them, whether it is legal or not. The drinks are the kissing cousin of a French 75, but the volume of them consumed in my general vicinity has led to the name French 150. Though Bess refuses to listen to me, the 75 was originally poured in a Collins glass instead of her ubiquitous, constantly spilling coupe glass.

These are bright, bubbly, and as dangerous as swimming with sharks in a T-bone steak bathing suit. Go ahead and make a batch and waddle around in the sun. You'll have plenty of time later for making "good decisions." Just remember to write a friend's phone number on your forearm, in case you wander off with strangers. Trust me—this happens. Just ask Bess. I found her giving an oak tree directions to the football stadium once.

1 (750 ml) bottle gin, preferably Hendrick's

1 tablespoon bitters

2 ounces St-Germain liqueur

½ cup Simple Syrup (page 237)

¼ cup juice from Luxardo maraschino cherries, plus Luxardo cherries for garnish

7 ounces fresh lemon juice

Sparkling wine (preferably sparkling rosé) for serving

Lemon peel for garnish

In a large pitcher or container, combine the gin, bitters, St-Germain, simple syrup, cherry juice, and lemon juice and stir to blend well. Fill each glass with ice and fill two-thirds full with the gin mix. Float sparkling wine on top and garnish with lemon peel and a cherry.

PUNCH-DRUNK PUNCH

There is a club in New Orleans I stop in from time to time that makes one of the most outstanding drinks I have ever had. It's both wonderfully simple and crowd-pleasing. There is little in this world that I love more than sitting around at the bar and sipping a couple of these before moving on to a cup of turtle soup and a nice piece of sautéed trout. It stuck me several years ago, though, that these would be an excellent addition to our tailgate party, so I broke them out, and hell if I wasn't right. On that particular day, I can report that several of us may not have made it all the way to our seats, choosing to remain and "guard" our tailgate spread and pull for the Rebels from the comfort of the Grove.

¼ cup plus 3 tablespoons sugar

Grated zest of 4 lemons plus 1 cup fresh lemon juice

¾ cup Luxardo maraschino cherries plus ¾ cup of their juice

¼ cup orange flower water

1 (750 ml) bottle bourbon, preferably Old Grandad

Soda water or sparkling wine for serving

Lemon peel for garnish

In a bowl, muddle the sugar, lemon zest, and cherries for several minutes. Add the lemon juice and stir until the sugar is completely dissolved. Strain the syrup into a large pitcher or container, pressing on the solids to extract more syrup. Stir in the orange flower water, bourbon, and cherry juice. Fill tall glasses with ice and fill three-quarters full with the punch base. Float soda or sparkling wine on top and garnish with cherries and lemon peel.

NOTE

► This punch is Wright Thompson–approved after thorough testing.

MOTHERS' RUIN PUNCH

This particular punch came into being at some point during my young derelict life. While I freely admit that the final recipe was not formulated during my college years, I assure you that its caveman cousin originated in those days. We frequently had "parents' booze" left over at our house near campus after grown-ups visited on parents' weekends or homecoming. And seeing as I was raised right and never wanted to let anything to go to waste, occasionally a perfectly good escapist libation would come from my well-intentioned recycling.

1 (750 ml) bottle dry gin

2 cups fresh grapefruit juice

¾ cup Simple Syrup (page 237)

6 ounces Chambord liqueur

½ cup fresh lemon juice

15 sprigs fresh thyme

24 ounces Champagne or sparkling wine

Fresh blueberries for garnish

Fresh blackberries for garnish

In a large pitcher or container, stir together the gin, grapefruit juice, simple syrup, Chambord, and lemon juice. Gently rub the thyme sprigs between your palms and drop them into the punch base. Cover and refrigerate for 2 hours. Fill short glasses with ice and fill three-quarters full with the punch base. Float sparkling wine on top and garnish with fresh blueberries and blackberries.

OLE MARGE

Sometimes you just need a little extra help getting behind your team when they really need you (well, I do at least). Tequila works, if you haven't heard. It also fires you up to jump the wall after a big win and tear down the goalposts. That's when the authorities threaten to put folks in jail (or so I have read). It can also help you fight your way out of an opposing team's stadium, when you have had a big win on the road, if your friend is prone to running his mouth (but I certainly wouldn't know anything about that). Whatever the case may be, Mexico is responsible for providing us with needed bravado straight from a bottle. God bless them for that and for so many other things.

This honors the original margarita: no frills, no nonsense, just one 100 percent straight lung fuel. Stir it up and go yell your chubby little heart out.

1 (750 ml) bottle good-quality tequila reposado

1¾ cups fresh lime juice

8 ounces Cointreau

¾ cup Lime Simple Syrup (see page 237)

2 cups soda water

2 limes, thinly sliced

In a large (¾- to 1-gallon) pitcher, combine tequila, lime juice, Cointreau, and lime simple syrup. Stir together well.

When ready to serve, fill glasses with ice and pour the tequila mixture over. Add a healthy splash of soda water (about 1½ ounces) and stir. Garnish with lime and serve.

MAYBELLE PUNCH

Maybelle Carter was one of the most beautiful voices in the world, and she inspired thousands more. Similarly, this concoction can bring forth the songbird in you. This punch is full of earthy flavors, which will free and soothe you. This is a good drink for the cool days of fall and one that might just get you behind your team a little louder.

½ cup sugar

Grated zest and pulp of 2 oranges (discard the bitter white pith)

½ cup Luxardo maraschino cherries, plus ¼ cup of their juice, and more cherries for garnish

1 (1½-inch) piece ginger, peeled and sliced

12 fresh mint leaves

8 ounces gold rum

1 (750 ml) bottle Cognac or brandy

1 cup fresh lemon juice

3 tablespoons molasses

Ginger beer for serving

Orange peel for garnish

In a large bowl, muddle the sugar, orange zest and pulp, cherries, ginger, and mint until a thick syrup forms. Add the rum and stir until the sugar is completely dissolved. Strain the syrup into a large pitcher or container, pressing on the solids to extract more syrup. Add the Cognac, lemon juice, molasses, and cherry juice, stirring to blend well.

Shake the base with ice, in batches of four (8 to 10 ounces at a time). Serve in short glasses. Float ginger beer on top and garnish with orange peel and cherries.

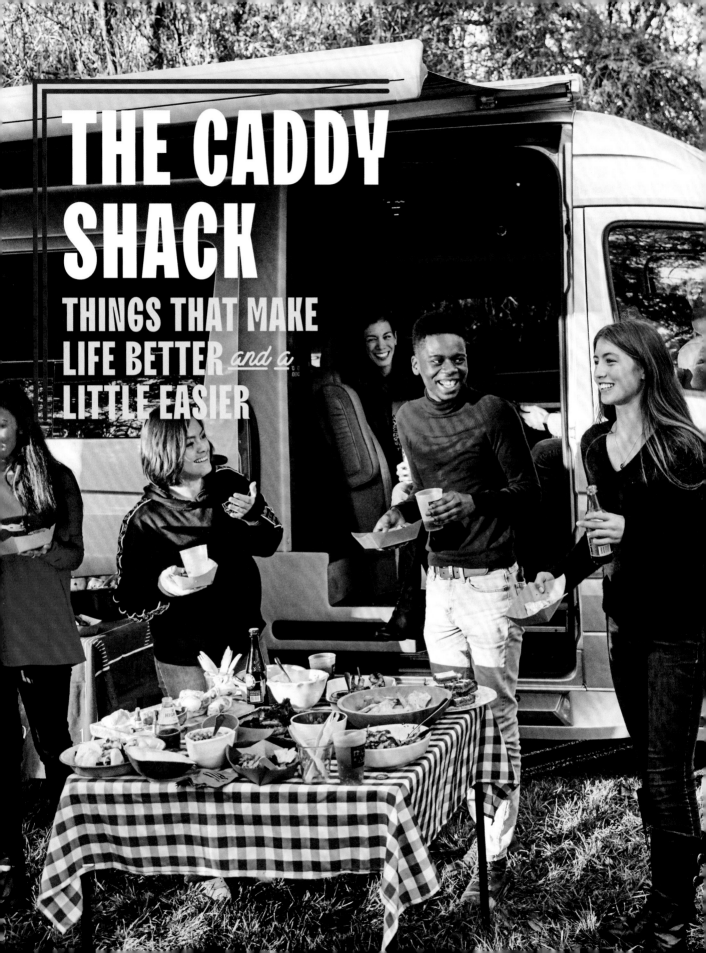

THE CADDY SHACK

THINGS THAT MAKE LIFE BETTER *and a* LITTLE EASIER

Like the caddy shack itself, these little gems are the key to building a "good score" on your tailgate game. While a number of these things can be bought at the store or even glossed over, with the minimal time invested in putting them together yourself, you will totally elevate your final product. These are, like a caddy's help, keys to greater success. Dive in and remember, *always* listen to the caddy's advice.

CREOLE SEASONING

½ cup paprika

6 tablespoons salt

6 tablespoons
garlic powder

3 tablespoons
black pepper

3 tablespoons
onion powder

3 tablespoons
cayenne pepper

3 tablespoons
dried oregano

3 tablespoons
dried thyme

1 tablespoon
dried basil

3 tablespoons fennel
seed, crushed roughly

2 tablespoons red
pepper flakes

Combine all the ingredients and blend together well. Store in an airtight container at room temperature.

BARBECUE SPICE RUB

6 tablespoons paprika

6 tablespoons
garlic powder

6 tablespoons
onion powder

6 tablespoons
black pepper

2 tablespoons
mustard powder

1 tablespoon
chili powder

2 tablespoons
dried thyme

2 tablespoons
dried oregano

1½ teaspoons cumin
seeds, toasted
and crushed

1½ tablespoons
red pepper flakes

1 teaspoon
ground cinnamon

3 tablespoons
ground coffee

1 tablespoon
cayenne pepper

1½ teaspoons
celery seeds

¾ cup kosher salt

4 tablespoons
granulated sugar

½ cup brown sugar

Combine all the ingredients and blend together well. Store in an airtight container at room temperature.

CARAMEL SAUCE

1¼ cups sugar

¼ cup water

¾ cup plus 2 tablespoons heavy cream, warmed for 40 seconds in the microwave

3½ tablespoons butter, sliced thin, at room temperature

¾ teaspoon vanilla extract

¼ teaspoon salt

Combine the sugar and water in a clean, dry stainless-steel pan and heat over medium flame, stirring constantly, until the syrup begins to boil. At this point, do *not* stir, but only swirl the pan to keep the syrup moving. Affix a candy thermometer to the side of the pan and swirl until the thermometer begins to climb above 220°F. Turn the heat to low and continue swirling until the temperature reaches 340°F. Carefully swirl in the cream. Be careful: This will release steam immediately. Begin stirring with a wooden or metal spoon and then stir in the butter and vanilla. Once fully combined, stir in the salt. Store chilled in plastic for up to 2 months.

SIMPLE SYRUP

1 cup sugar

¾ cup plus 2 tablespoons water

Place water and sugar in a small saucepan and set it on the stove over medium heat. Swirl until the sugar dissolves, remove from the heat, and allow it to cool to room temperature. Store chilled for up to 1 month.

LIME SIMPLE SYRUP

Simple Syrup (recipe above)

Peel of 2 limes

Make the simple syrup as described, but as soon as the syrup comes off the stove, stir in the lime peel and allow it to cool to room temperature. Place in the refrigerator and steep for 24 hours before using. Keep, refrigerated, for up to 3 weeks.

CLARIFIED BUTTER

Clarified butter, or ghee, is widely available in grocery stores alongside shortening and cooking oils. It's a simple process to make it yourself. Butter is comprised of three components: butterfat, water, and milk solids. In making clarified butter, you want to separate the butterfat from the two other components, which means slowly simmering the butter until the solids fall out and the water evaporates. Once clarified, you can use the butter to cook at a much higher temperature without the food and butter scorching, turning black, and tasting bitter.

1 pound unsalted butter

Melt the butter in a small saucepan over medium heat. Once the butter is melted, immediately turn down the heat as low as it will go and swirl the pan slowly. Continue swirling for 10 to 15 minutes, until the butter looks clear and steam stops coming off the top when the bubbles pop. Do not overcook and burn the milk solids that sink to the bottom (this will burn the butter and make it bitter tasting). If the solids brown lightly and the butter gets a beautiful nutty aroma, you are in good shape and have made brown butter. Remove the pan from the heat to cool for 10 minutes, then ladle the clarified butter off, leaving the white (or lightly browned) milk solids behind. Discard the milk solids and use the clarified butter to create food that will make you prettier and smarter. Clarified butter will keep in an airtight container for 2 weeks in the fridge.

BAY OIL

½ cup hand-crushed bay leaves

Boiling water

1½ cups vegetable oil or other neutral oil

Place the crushed bay leaves in a spice grinder and blend into a fine powder. Place this in a 2-cup plastic container with a lid and stir in enough boiling water to turn the powdered bay leaves into a paste (slightly looser than wasabi). Pour the oil over the paste and seal. Shake the container vigorously and allow to sit for at least 24 hours, and preferably 3 days. Shake the container to mix every time you think about it. Ladle the bay oil into a glass jar. Store the oil, covered, in the refrigerator for up to 3 months.

ABOUT THE AUTHOR

John is chef and owner of the City Grocery Restaurant Group and Big Bad Breakfast in Oxford, Mississippi. He is the author of *Pickles, Pigs & Whiskey* and *Big Bad Breakfast*, but he feels your life is oddly incomplete without *this* tome. He really just wants to help you be a better person. John lives in Oxford, Mississippi, with his beautiful wife, Bess, and his constantly back hand-springing daughter, Mamie. He is an advocate for civil justice and childhood well-being. He'd love to play tennis whenever you are free (and play tennis way better than he does) and to let you buy him a drink.

Ed Anderson

ACKNOWLEDGMENTS

My teams at the Main Event, City Grocery, Snackbar, and Boure work around the clock during football season to take care of the legion of fans that come to Oxford to pull for their respective teams. Thank all of you guys for your tireless dedication to our culture and mission. I could not be more proud of everything you all do.

To my amazing roommates, Bess and Mamie. Without your constant assignment of chores, interruptions, and a continuous rumble in our house that I can only imagine approaches the sound a division of approaching Panzers made during WWII, there is no way this book would have gotten as far behind deadline as it was. You're astounding. I love you both.

Meghan Anderson, you are a force of nature. Thank you. This train grinds to a halt without you.

My editors Kelly Snowden and Kim Keller, who put up with me dragging ass on deadlines and helped make this book as good as it can possibly be. Sorry . . . and thanks. Thanks also to my designer, Betsy Stromberg, and production manager, Jane Chinn.

David Black, you are a gem. Your work goes entirely uncredited. I have never known anyone more loyal to his friends. I could not be more grateful to be among a group of folks you call "friends."

Lane Wurster and our graphic design team at the Splinter Group in Chapel Hill, North Carolina. You guys are amazing, especially in what you do on the 24-second timelines we frequently provide you with. You are a joy to work with.

Drew, Pam, Ben, and the rest of our team at Evins P.R., you guys never cease to amaze me. Your work is entirely uncredited, but totally invaluable.

To all my friends at Lodge Cast Iron, Butter Pat, Cowboy Cauldrons, Kudu Grills, Green Egg, Yeti, etc., for making products that make tailgate cooking the joy it is.

And to the Rebel Nation for creating the greatest tailgating tradition in college football, seven glorious Saturdays every fall. Hotty Toddy!!

Finally, to my beloved New Orleans Saints, who have taken a city that had no idea how to tailgate ten years ago and inspired us to figure it out and put on pregame tests that stand shoulder to shoulder with any other fan base and to rise above most. *Who dat!?*

INDEX

All rights reserved.
Published in the United States by Ten Speed Press,
an imprint of Random House, a division of Penguin
Random House LLC, New York.
www.tenspeed.com

Ten Speed Press and the Ten Speed Press colophon are
registered trademarks of Penguin Random House LLC.

Library of Congress Cataloging-in-Publication Data
is on file with the publisher.

Hardcover ISBN: 978-1-9848-5652-4
eBook ISBN: 978-1-9848-5653-1

Printed in China

Foam finger graphic by Mike Flippo/Shutterstock.com

Design by Betsy Stromberg
Food and prop styling by John Currence

10 9 8 7 6 5 4 3 2 1

First Edition

TOUCHDOWN! V-I-C-T-O-R-Y!
SCORE! FIGHT! RAH RAH RAH!
HUSTLE! WIN! GOAL! DEFENSE!
WE'RE NUMBER ONE! GO TEAM!
TOUCHDOWN! V-I-C-T-O-R-Y!
SCORE! FIGHT! RAH RAH RAH!
HUSTLE! WIN! GOAL! DEFENSE!
WE'RE NUMBER ONE! GO TEAM!
TOUCHDOWN! V-I-C-T-O-R-Y!
SCORE! FIGHT! RAH RAH RAH!
HUSTLE! WIN! GOAL! DEFENSE!
WE'RE NUMBER ONE! GO TEAM!